The First World War and the International Economy

The First World War and the International Economy

Edited by

Chris Wrigley

Professor of Modern British History, University of Nottingham, UK

Edward Elgar
Cheltenham, UK • Northampton, MA, USA

Published by
Edward Elgar Publishing Limited
Glensanda House
Montpellier Parade
Cheltenham
Glos GL50 1UA
UK

Edward Elgar Publishing, Inc.
136 West Street
Suite 202
Northampton
Massachusetts 01060
USA

A catalogue record for this book
is available from the British Library

Library of Congress Cataloguing in Publication Data
The First World War and the international economy / edited by Chris Wrigley.
Includes bibliographical references and index.
1. World War, 1914–1918—Economic aspects I. Wrigley, Chris.

D635 .F57 2000
940.3'1—dc21

00–033170

ISBN 1 85898 675 3

Typeset by Manton Typesetters, Louth, Lincolnshire, UK.
Printed and bound in Great Britain by Biddles Ltd, *www.biddles.co.uk*.

Contents

Figures

Tables

Contributors

Kenneth D. Brown has been Professor of Economic and Social History at The Queen's University of Belfast since 1988 and Dean of the Faculty of Legal, Social and Educational Sciences since 1997. His published work ranges over labour, business, religious and biographical themes, including, most recently, a study of the British toy industry since 1700 (1995) and a comparative economic and social history of Britain and Japan since 1900 (1998).

Peter Fearon is Professor of Modern Economic and Social History and currently Pro-Vice-Chancellor at the University of Leicester. His publications include *War, Prosperity and Depression: The US Economy 1917–1945* (Philip Allen, Deddington, 1987) and numerous articles on the economic history of twentieth-century America. He is currently working on the impact of the Great Depression and New Deal on the state of Kansas.

Alan Fowler teaches economic and social history at the Manchester Metropolitan University and is the author of a number of studies on the history of the British cotton industry including, *The Barefoot Aristocrats: A History of the Amalgamated Association of Operative Cotton Spinners* (with Terry Wyke) and *Mirth in the Mill: The Gradely World of Sam Filton* (with Terry Wyke).

Andrew Marrison is Senior Lecturer in Economic History at the University of Manchester. In addition to nineteenth- and twentieth-century trade and trade policy, his research interests include the economic performance of the British cotton industry and business government relations. He is author of *British Business and Protection, 1903–1932* (Clarendon Press, Oxford, 1996) and editor of *Free Trade and Its Reception, 1815–1960* (Routledge, London, 1998).

Terence C. Mills is Professor of Economics and Head of the Department of Economics at Loughborough University. He formally held professorial appointments at City University Business School and the University of Hull. His publications include *Time Series Techniques for Economists* and *The Econometric Modelling of Financial Time Series* (both published by Cambridge University Press, Cambridge), and *Economic Forecasting* (Edward Elgar, Cheltenham) as well as over 100 articles in journals and edited volumes.

Sarah Palmer is Professor of Maritime History and Director of the Greenwich Maritime Institute, University of Greenwich. An economic historian, she was previously head of the Department of History, Queen Mary and Westfield College, University of London. Her publications include *Shipping, Politics and the Repeal of the Navigation Laws* (Manchester University Press, 1990).

Hans-Joachim Voth is Assistant Professor of Economics, Universitat Pompeu Fabra, Barcelona and Associate Director of the Centre for History and Economics, King's College, Cambridge. Prior to his appointment in Barcelona, he was Visiting Assistant Professor at the Economics Department, Stanford University, a Senior Associate Consultant at McKinsey & Co., Inc., and a Research Fellow at Clare College, Cambridge. He has written on inter-war Germany and on Britain during the Industrial Revolution. His publications include *Time and Work in England, 1760–1830* (forthcoming), 'Did High Wages Bring Down the Weimar Republic?', *Journal of Economic History*, 1995, 'Time-use in Eighteenth Century London', *Journal of Economic History*, 1998, and 'Did Smallpox Reduce Heights?' (with T. Leunig), *Economic History Review*, 1996.

Chris Wrigley is Professor of Modern British History and Head of the School of History and Art History at Nottingham University. His books include *David Lloyd George and the Labour Movement* (1976), *Lloyd George and the Challenge of Labour* (1990), *Arthur Henderson* (1990), and a three-volume *History of British Industrial Relations* (1982–96, ed.). He was President of the Historical Association 1996–9.

1. The War and the international economy

Chris Wrigley

Jane Austen began *Pride and Prejudice* (1813) with words which were to become famous: 'It is a truth universally acknowledged, that a single man in possession of a good fortune must be in want of a wife.' The certainty of this comment is brought to mind by statements made in the best textbooks when dealing with the impact of the First World War on the international economy. William Ashworth commented, 'After 1914, there still was an international economy, but it was somewhat different from what had been built before, and in a real sense the First World War divided one economic era from another'. A.G. Kenwood and A.L. Lougheed in their well-received introductory textbook observed, 'The international economy which had grown up during the nineteenth century came to an end with the outbreak of war in 1914' and 'World War I affected the whole structure of the international economy'. James Foreman-Peck gave the verdict, 'International economic relations were thoroughly disrupted by the war because of the central importance of Europe in trade before 1914'.[1]

While some writers are less emphatic about the sharpness of the 1914 divide, no-one is likely seriously to question the view that the First World War changed the international economy substantially. The First World War was a massive man-made catastrophe. It was like a severe earthquake, its epicentre in Europe, with massive deaths and destruction, its disturbance reverberating far. The loss of life was well over 20 million when the deaths due to abnormal levels of diseases such as influenza and typhus as well as those in Russia caused by military intervention, civil war, famine and disease are added to military casualties.[2] The First World War's greatest and most direct impact, therefore, was on the 'centre' (as opposed to any 'periphery') of the international economy.

Yet the war itself slips out of sight in some international economic histories. There is a great ending in 1914, or, indeed, with statistics for 1913, and a fresh beginning with 1919 or 1920. In this book the contributors have been mindful of the war years themselves as part of the broad picture of the development of the international economy.

The First World War casts a long shadow over the inter-war years. As well as the immediate post-war economic adjustments and the lengthier readjustment of currencies during the 1920s, the First World War has been seen as a substantial contributor to the world economic crisis of the early 1930s. The war weakened several stabilizing features of the pre-1914 international economic scene. Examples of this include sterling and its ability to be used to rescue other currencies under pressure, central European banking and also the balance between supply and demand in international markets, following the expansion of output of some primary and manufactured goods during the war and its immediate aftermath.

The First World War's impact on longer-term trends in economic growth was substantial, though less so than the Second World War. As one would expect, given the varying degrees of involvement by countries, the impact differed from country to country; a point made in this volume by Terence Mills in the second introductory chapter.

THE WAR AND MANUFACTURING PRODUCTION

The nature, the scale and the length of the war in Europe ensured that the belligerents had to make very substantial adjustments to their economies. With very considerable drops in available male labour and massive increases in demand for war goods and services governments soon found it essential to intervene in economies and establish priorities. Scarcities led to tough choices. High among the belligerents' economic priorities were manpower for the armed forces, the production of munitions, the supply of food and fuel, sufficient transport to meet new patterns of need, and the maintenance of some exports to help finance imports.

Such priorities required substantial switches of industrial resources. Most notable of all was a swing to engineering, with the size of workforces rising even where there was a drop in the overall size of the industrial labour force. Lloyd George put the importance of engineering succinctly, 'This is an engineers' war, and it will be won or lost according to the efforts of the engineers'.[3] In the United Kingdom the numbers in civil employment fell from 19,440,000 to 17,060,000, 1914–18, while the numbers employed in the metal trades rose by 34 per cent from 1,804,000 (9.4 per cent of whom were female) to 2,418,000 (24.6 per cent female), July 1914–July 1918. In Germany the number of workers in industrial enterprises with ten or more employees fell from 7,387,000 to 6,787,000 (with the latter figure including a 46 per cent increase in female workers), 1913–18, while in the same period those employed in war industries (metals, chemicals, petroleum and electricals) rose by 44 per cent from 2,116,000 to 3,050,000. In Russia the estimated industrial workforce rose from 3,114,945 to 3,338,580, 1913 to the start of 1917, with the number of metal workers increasing in the same period by 93 per cent from 150,942 to 291,356. Petrograd was the major industrial centre, with the labour force in metallurgical enterprises growing by 135 per cent in these years, and constituting an estimated 60.5 per cent (up from 41.5 per cent) of the city's workforce. In Italy the industrial expansion was concentrated in the northern cities, with huge expansions of such firms as Fiat, Breda and Pirelli; for instance, Fiat's workforce expanded from 4,300 to 40,000, 1914–18, and its capital increased from 25 to 125 million lire.[4]

However, elsewhere war production was severely disrupted by invasion and military action. France suffered the loss of much industrial production in the north and north-east. Heavy industry was most affected, with areas which in 1913 had produced 64 per cent of France's pig iron, 58 per cent of her steel and 40 per cent of her coal being occupied. Belgium suffered even more, with half her steel mills destroyed, three-quarters of her railway rolling stock ruined and much labour conscripted for work in Germany or volunteered often under duress.[5]

The economies of the Central Powers were constrained by the Allied blockade. German imports fell to 55 per cent of the 1913 level in 1915, rose a little to 59 per cent in 1916, then levelled out at 39 per cent in 1917 and 1918. However, exports fell even further: to 25 per cent of the 1913 level in 1915, 29 per cent in 1916, 20 per cent in 1917 and 28 per cent in 1918; consequently, former export capacity was available for war work. Where Germany could not secure its needs from neutrals, it either took from countries it invaded (notably Belgium, Romania, the Ukraine), used fewer supplies more efficiently, turned to alternatives (such as preparing synthetic ammonia from nitrogen in the air, to replace Chilean nitrates) or went without. The Allied blockade, supported by the US export embargoes from June 1917, increasingly squeezed the European neutrals, who made good profits early in the war but were unable later to benefit from the high wartime demand in the international economy.[6]

The United States gained directly, with the war boosting her already huge manufacturing sector. The impact of the First World War on the US manufacturing industry is analysed by Peter Fearon in Chapter 3. He argues for caution lest one overstate the impact of the war – factory output having risen at a faster rate in 1904–9, and not much more slowly in 1899–1904. He also argues, as others have done for other aspects of the war, that it encouraged the spread of known processes rather than directly introducing innovations. However, many industries which had been boosted by the war could switch afterwards to consumer goods, the US acquiring new export markets and ending with a much expanded merchant fleet, while her European rivals were weakened, at least for a time.

Japan also prospered greatly during the First World War. Her armed forces were only involved in battles at the German naval base at Tsing-tao, September–November 1914. Unlike the United States, which benefited greatly from supplying the Allies, Japan did well from 1915 by supplying Asian countries needs which could no longer be met by European suppliers and also by import substitution (producing for her own economy goods previously imported). During the First World War Japan's balance of trade turned firmly into surplus. Kenneth Brown analyses the impact of the war on Japan in Chapter 5. He also warns against exaggerating the impact of the war. After it, the Japanese economy did not escape the 1921–2 recession, with factory employment and outputs of iron, cotton and coal all temporarily declining in the early 1920s.

Other areas of the world also experienced a period when their usual European supplies of manufactured goods were not available. The First World War (like the Second World War) disrupted the relationship between the European industrialized 'centre' of the international economy and the various underdeveloped 'periphery' areas. Subsequently, there has been some debate among historians as to how important the First World War was, with the need for import substitution for many countries, in stimulating industrial development. Those who see the basic relationship between the industrialized countries and the underdeveloped as one of dependency, an exploiter and exploited relationship, have been likely to see the First World War as a highly important break in the exploitation. Others, sometimes called diffusionists, have argued that economic development comes about through internal changes which are likely to be stimulated by interaction with the international economy.[7]

Some of the older writing about South America and the two world wars suggested that they were decisive in boosting South American industry. A.G. Frank, the leading 'dependency' writer, for instance, stated, 'It is clearly established and generally recognised that the most important recent industrial development … has taken place precisely during the periods of the two world wars', adding, 'Thanks to the consequent weakening of trade and investment ties the satellites initiated marked autonomous industrialisation and growth'.[8]

More recent writing, while agreeing that the First World War caused major economic disruption to South American economies, has suggested that the impact of the war in encouraging industrial growth through its 'adverse shock' has been much exaggerated.[9] The predominant emphasis recently has been on downplaying industrial changes in the First World War (other than to stress the war's disruptive effects). It is now believed that industrial development was more robust between 1895 and the 1913–23 recession than used to be suggested. The loss of German and British imports was less substantial than was once thought, given that before 1914 the US was already dominating many markets, with Britain only exceeding the US in supplying imports in Argentina, Brazil, Chile and Uruguay. After imports from Europe were cut off by the war, the US was able to meet a large part of the requirements of the

South American countries, at least in the latter part of the war, so the picture is very much one of short-term disruption with a return to pre-war patterns in the 1920s.[10]

Nevertheless, the war created major hindrances to industrial development. Writing of Peru in 1920, L.S. Rowe made observations which apply more widely: 'It is [the] complete dependence on the foreign market combined with the fact that all the important national enterprises are dependent on foreign capital that gave to the European war such a disastrous influence on Peru's foreign trade and upon her domestic financial and commercial conditions'.[11] The early part of the war in particular saw a severe fall both in exports and inflows of capital. Exports were hit by shipping shortages, Allied blockade cutting off central European customers and demand for a few commodities, most notably coffee, being drastically cut as they were categorized as non-essentials in war. Domestic demand then dropped. In 1914–15 some sectors of South American economies were very seriously hit, most notably Chilean nitrates.

Even though the various economies benefited from higher export prices as the war went on, there was little 'adverse shock' stimulus of industry. This was so even in Argentina which suffered the greatest cut-off in trade, as Britain's most important South American trading partner. Probably the industries which grew most were textiles and footwear, which drew on local materials. The most marked increases in investment in these industries occurred in Brazil and Columbia in 1919–20, when coffee export prices had recovered. Hence, to those highly sceptical of the notion of the First World War boosting industrial development, such as Rory Miller, Bill Albert and Warren Dean, the question is whether or not industry would have developed faster in South America had the First World War not occurred. Warren Dean, in his study of industrialization in São Paulo, suggested that the annual average growth rates in cotton textiles fell from 15.5 to 8.9 per cent and in footwear from 12.7 to 6.8 per cent in 1915–20 compared with 1904–14.[12]

The First World War generally had a disruptive impact on sub-Saharan Africa. In the case of South Africa, often cited as one of the best examples of industry developing through First World War import substitution, some recent scholarship has been cautious lest such benefits are overstated. John Iliffe has observed, 'The protective stimulus given to manufactures by the war has been exaggerated'. Again, revisionism has suggested, as Iliffe has commented, 'a more gradual process', with a steady development of food processing and other consumer industries as well as the growth of heavier industries linked to the needs of the goldmines and a rail network.[13] West Africa and other parts of Africa, like South America, were hit by shortage of shipping and the Allied blockade closing central European markets. Shortages of shipping space did encourage agricultural processing in the exporting countries, with Senegal's groundnut crushing industry beginning during the war. For West Africa, the problems were mostly agrarian and there was a boom in demand at the end of the war.[14]

In the case of India, firmly under British control, economically as well as politically, the war seriously weakened British domination of India's textile market and boosted the already growing Indian textile industry. Alan Fowler provides details of the wartime decline in the volume of British cotton entering the Indian market in Chapter 4. Lancashire cotton textiles is deservedly the best-known example of a major export industry whose decline was accelerated by the impact of the First World War.

The war and the post-war boom (1919–20) brought about excess capacity in many war-related industries. This was notably so in iron and steel, engineering, shipbuilding and coal. These years (1914–20) had also stimulated great expansions of primary production, especially food. In the case of wheat there was a dramatic drop in prices, in the UK slumping at the start of 1921 from £4.32p a quarter to £2.45p a quarter, and falling further thereafter. Over-production and falling prices for exports were followed by some producers exporting more in an attempt to maintain their incomes. A League of Nations' analysis of 1928 noted of the 1920s that 'in every country for which there is evidence, and in almost every year, the prices of partly manufactured goods tend to be above those of raw materials and those of finished goods above those of semi-manufactured goods'. Faced with the adverse terms of trade, by the late 1920s primary producers imported fewer industrial goods.[15]

THE WAR AND FOOD AND FUELS

Food and fuel were high in the list of critical needs for belligerent nations. The key importance of food in the outcome of the war has been stressed by Lloyd George in his *War Memoirs* and by recent historians, notably Avner Offer. Lloyd George delivered the verdict:

> The food question ultimately decided the issue of this war. It was directly responsible for the downfall of Russia, finally it was the element that led to the collapse of Austria and Germany. Indirectly it was responsible for bringing America into the war, since Germany's indiscriminate submarine warfare was her answer to our blockade.[16]

The war of production required much power, which in this period meant coal and, increasingly, oil. Lloyd George was also characteristically colourful and cogent on the importance of coal:

> In peace and in war King Coal is the paramount Lord of Industry. It enters into every article of consumption and of utility. It is our real international coinage ... It not merely fetches and carries for us; it makes the material and the machinery which it transports. It bends, it moulds, it fills the weapons of war.[17]

During the First World War the supply of food was seriously disrupted for all the main European belligerent nations. Britain's food imports were markedly reduced, as shipping space became scarcer and as much space had to be allocated to the needs of her Allies. In 1917 the tonnage of the UK's food imports had fallen to 75 per cent of the pre-war level, and in 1916 to 65 per cent. However, with the Corn Production Act 1917, domestic output was much intensified. This was marked by a switch in production away from livestock and dairy produce to higher nutritional value grain and potatoes, with their output in 1918 being 40 per cent higher than the average of the pre-war decade. Further gains were made by extracting a higher volume of wheat grain for flour and mixing it with other cereals or potatoes, so providing more bread.[18] In spite of U-boat operations, which were especially effective from 1916, providing food for the civilian population was less of a problem for Britain than for the continental European countries.

There agricultural production was hit by direct war damage as well as by shortages of labour, machinery and fertilizers. In the cases of the Central Powers, food supplies were much restricted by the increasingly effective Allied blockade and (in the latter part of the war) by the US trade embargo. In France, domestic wheat production in 1917 was 40 per cent lower than the pre-war level, while at the same time in Italy grain production was 30 per cent lower. Both countries depended on large imported supplies of food via the inter-Allied shipping and import policy, and in both countries bread was rationed before the end of the war. In Russia, the pre-war granary of Europe, there was a withholding of supplies, as the peasants found the agricultural–industrial terms of exchange moved markedly against them, and there was a serious incapacity of the Russian transport network to distribute sufficient supplies to the industrial cities.[19]

Allied economic warfare was aimed at undermining Germany through cutting off her food and raw materials supplies. British naval supremacy rapidly ended the Central Power's 15 per cent share of world shipping. With the blockade, Germany's imports dropped in value (in gold marks) to 39 per cent of the 1913 level (which, with depreciation of gold, may have pulled import levels down to 20 per cent of the 1913 level).[20] German agricultural output also dropped, with recent estimates suggesting that between 1914 and 1918 output of rye declined by 36 per cent and potatoes by 46 per cent. The German population ate not only substantially less food but also poorer quality. However, Avner Offer has argued that, while they suffered weight loss and were often cold and hungry, they did not starve. However, the decline in supplies undercut morale and faith in the effectiveness of the state.[21] Austria suffered more than Hungary, as very little (in 1916 less than 5 per cent of the 1913 level) Hungarian grain was taken to Austria.[22]

The disruption of much European food production led to greater demand for imports and price rises. Although British food imports fell from the 1913 level of 18.3 million tons to 11.9 million in 1918, there was greater demand from France, which by the end of 1917 was importing some 7.7 million tons of food, and Italy, which by mid-1918 was importing at least 4 million tons of food. Because of the crucial importance of shipping space the Allies chose to concentrate their purchases on the shorter North Atlantic routes. Exports of wheat from the United States and Canada which had averaged 6.4 million tons in the five pre-war years, rose to 9.8, 15.7, 16.6, 12.9 and 11.1 million in 1914, 1915, 1916, 1917 and 1918, respectively. In Canada, for example, there was a rapid expansion of the cultivated prairie acreage from 1915 until 1921, with average prairie farm investment in housing, other buildings, farm machinery and trucks being 78 per cent higher in 1916–20 than 1911–15 and 65 per cent higher than 1921–5 (after which investment rose higher than in 1916–20). The more distant suppliers of the southern hemisphere – Argentina, Uruguay, South Africa, Australia and New Zealand – saw exports of grain fall below the average level of the pre-war five years of 7.5 million tons, other than in 1916 when there were bad grain harvests internationally. The exports were 6.5, 7.3, 7.7, 4.1 and 5.8 million tons in 1914, 1915, 1916, 1917 and 1918, respectively. Yet as the price of exported wheat rose (90 per cent in the first three years of the war), Argentina experienced increased value from a smaller exported volume.[23] The wartime conditions, along with the post-war boom, created strong incentives for expanded production of foodstuffs for the international economy.

The war also accelerated import substitution of some agricultural products. In the case of Mediterranean fruits, US output had been fostered before the war by tariffs and by 1910 the US was producing about 30 per cent of the world's citrus fruit. In the case of figs US production also grew behind tariffs, but imports still rose until the First World War disrupted the trade. This, according to Morilla Critz, Olmstead and Rhode, 'created a window of opportunity for American growers', with a subsequent tenfold increase in acreage devoted to figs, 1916–28.[24]

As with food, there were substantial drops in supplies of coal for those countries which depended heavily on imports. Italy, for example, experienced a 49 per cent drop in coal imports in 1917 from the average volume imported in the five pre-war years (with a lesser 41 per cent drop in 1918). France, which had exported an average of 1,502,000 metric tons in the five pre-war years, now faced with the loss of many northern pits, reduced exports to an average of 119,000 metric tons (8 per cent) during 1915–17. French imports ran in 1915,

1916 and 1917 at 92, 96 and 81 per cent of the average volume of the five pre-war years. The UK, the Allies' main supplier, maintained coal exports to her Allies (at more favourable prices than to neutrals) as a priority, but the overall export levels 1915–18 were well below the very high levels of the pre-1914 years (but higher than the 1890s); running in 1915, 1916, 1917 and 1918 at 66, 59, 53 and 48 per cent respectively of the average of the five pre-war years.[25] As manpower for the armed forces and other priorities impinged on coal production and as shipping problems increased in the latter part of the war, exports to neutrals were squeezed. French and Italian markets had taken 30 per cent of British coal shipments in 1913; by 1916 they took 60 per cent.[26]

The war also accelerated industrialized countries' interest in securing access to oil supplies. Though the overall trade in oil remained small, it was nevertheless judged to be vital in war. In 1913 64 per cent of crude oil was produced in the United States, with Russia producing 16 per cent, Mexico 7 per cent, Romania 4 per cent, Dutch East Indies 3 per cent and Burma and Poland 2 per cent each. The war accentuated the British navy's concern to secure ample supplies of oil for fuel as well as emphasizing the need for toluol-rich oils for manufacturing explosives (trinitrotoluene, TNT). This need was so great that in January 1915, in spite of Dutch neutrality, Shell's whole toluol refinery in Rotterdam was dismantled and shipped to England, being reassembled at Portishead and resuming production within nine weeks. Even before the war, in June 1914, the British government bought a majority of the shares in the Anglo-Persian Oil Company, justifying the move on the grounds of needing to help secure adequate supplies for the navy. This it failed to do, the amount the area supplied remaining small. In the Far East the Burma Oil Company met the Royal Navy's needs there.

Generally, however, the wartime shortages of oil caused much concern. They encouraged Britain to seek a major interest in Mesopotamian oil after the war. By then oil was deemed to be a key wartime commodity; Lord Curzon being widely reported when he gave the view in November 1918 that 'the Allied cause floated to victory upon a wave of oil'. It was also increasingly apparent that it was becoming the key fuel for merchant shipping as well as for naval vessels. Whereas in 1914 only 3.4 per cent of world tonnage used oil, by 1922 26.1 per cent used it and the percentage had risen to 41.1 per cent by 1930.[27]

There were many primary products other than food, coal and oil for which wartime demand was great. These included various metals, chemicals and timber. The Central Powers secured some of their needs through trade with neutral states as well as by conquest. However, a major lesson of the First World War was the extent to which industrialized states could be self-sufficient if public policy prioritized achieving this. Thereafter there was a closer connection between war and autarky.

THE WAR, TRADE AND TARIFFS

The war had an adverse effect on the rate of growth of the volume of world trade. It had encouraged the continuing spread of industrialization, with those who had produced more for their own requirements, when supplies from Europe were cut off, continuing to do so in the post-war period. After 1918 Britain, for example, found that she had lost some of her pre-war cotton textile markets as had Germany for her dyestuffs. Export markets were also adversely affected by the revolutions and boundary settlements of 1917–20 and also by the raising of tariffs.

The rate of growth of world trade was substantially slower during and after the First World War than it was both before the First World War and after the Second World War. In 1913–37 world trade grew in volume at an average rate of 3 per cent per decade compared with 34 per cent per decade in 1881–1913 and 94 per cent in 1953–63. The period after the First World War saw not only a reduction in Europe's share of world trade but also a decline in importance of intra-European trade. As the terms of trade moved in favour of Europe, the European share of the value of world trade fell less than the

Table 1.1 Percentage distribution of world trade by value, 1913–26

	Imports			Exports			Total		
	1913	1924	1926	1913	1924	1926	1913	1924	1926
Europe[1]	61.6	55.5	51.7	55.2	45.2	43.9	58.5	50.4	47.9
North America	12.4	15.7	17.6	15.8	20.6	20.5	14.0	18.1	19.0
Caribbean	1.9	2.3	2.2	2.4	3.5	3.0	2.1	2.9	2.6
South America	5.7	4.9	5.3	6.7	6.6	6.4	6.2	5.7	5.8
Africa	4.0	4.0	4.4	4.5	4.4	4.3	4.3	4.2	4.4
Asia	11.9	14.5	15.6	12.7	16.5	18.7	12.3	15.5	17.1
Oceania	2.5	3.1	3.2	2.7	3.2	3.3	2.6	3.2	3.2
Total	100	100	100	100	100	100	100	100	100

Note: [1]The Europe figure excludes the Netherlands because of the incomparability of 1913 and post-war statistics. Were the post-war Netherlands figures added, Europe's percentage of imports in 1924 and 1926 would be 56.9 and 512; exports 46.5 and 45.2; totals 51.8 and 49.3. The figures for Europe, excluding Russia/Soviet Union (and the Netherlands) are for imports: 1913, 58.0; 1924, 54.7; and 1926, 50.6; exports are 51.0, 44.2 and 42.7; and totals 54.6, 49.5 and 46.7.

Source: League of Nations, Economic and Financial Section, *Memorandum on Production and Trade, 1913 and 1923–6*, Geneva, 1928, p. 51.

volume.[28] Table 1.1 reports League of Nations' estimates of the distribution of world merchandise trade by continental groups based on recorded values. Table 1.2 provides Angus Maddison's estimates of the volume of merchandise exports for eight countries for 1913–29.

Such figures as those in Table 1.1 bring out well that Europe was the main loser in terms of *shares* of world trade. Its own share (including Russia/Soviet Union) was 18 per cent smaller than in 1913 (or, excluding Russia/Soviet Union, 14 per cent smaller than its 1913 share). The main gainers were North America and Asia (their 1926 figures being 36 and 39 per cent greater than their 1913 shares). In terms of *value*, between 1913 and 1925, European exports rose by 48 per cent, while the combined average value of exports from the United States, Canada, Argentina, Malaya, New Zealand, China and Japan increased by 104 per cent, thus displaying (as a League of Nations' memorandum put it) 'a tendency towards a shift of the world's centre of activity from Europe and the Atlantic to America, Japan and the Pacific Ocean'.[29] Table 1.2 displays the changes in *volume* of exports, the Maddison estimates again highlighting the performances of Japan, Canada and the United States, but also showing good performances by France and Italy by the mid-1920s.

The war adversely affected trade in several ways in addition to its direct disruption in 1914–18. The peace treaties signed with the Central Powers in 1919–20 led to major boundary changes and new tariff barriers. The lands of the Habsburg Monarchy had formed something of a *zollverein*, a favourable trade zone to its members. The peace settlements with Austria and Hungary dismembered the old empire, creating in its place six small states, vehemently nationalist in their outlook and protective in their economic policies. There was soon a multiplicity of variations in their economies. For example, there were rapid increases in the notes in circulation in some of these countries. Between the ends of 1920 and 1921 the percentage increases in currency circulation were Czechoslovakia 07.4, Romania 31.2, the Serb Croat Slovene State 40.2, Hungary 76.0, Poland 365.0 and Austria 468.1.[30] There were also substantial boundary changes affecting Germany, Russia, Bulgaria and Turkey. In a Europe of 38 independent nations, not the 26 of 1914, there were many more obstacles to trade: separate currencies, tariffs (for protection or revenue) and economic policies. The adverse effects of these changes have been well summarized by Feinstein, Temin and Tonilo as 'a cause of widespread resource misallocation, resulting in lower output and higher prices, particularly in central and Eastern Europe'.[31]

The peace settlement with Germany also imposed an unrealistically high level of reparations. In 1921 the Reparations Commission (set up under the Treaty of Versailles, 1919) assessed the amount that Germany should pay the Allies at £6,600 million. After the collapse of the German currency in 1923,

Table 1.2 Volume of merchandise exports 1913–29 (1913 = 100)

	1914	1915	1916	1917	1918	1919	1920	1921	1922	1923	1924	1925	1926	1927	1928	1929
Australia	91.2	80.7	86.1	84.5	79.9	92.4	93.2	101.5	106.8	88.3	85.8	98.5	104.5	101.1	105.5	107.2
Canada	100.3	139.6	188.5	213.5	154.8	139.1	118.5	110.5	143.0	175.4	174.1	192.5	194.0	193.4	221.1	193.2
France	71.3	43.0	45.0	36.0	28.0	45.0	86.0	83.0	86.0	103.0	119.0	124.0	134.0	146.0	148.0	147.0
Germany	(80.0)	(50.0)	(20.0)	(20.0)	(15.0)	17.0	36.7	44.4	61.3	52.9	50.8	65.3	72.4	73.1	82.5	91.8
Italy	88.3	89.2	78.9	42.5	48.9	75.1	105.5	70.7	80.8	93.7	117.3	127.4	122.6	116.1	117.9	122.7
Japan	98.1	130.1	164.5	194.6	211.5	168.3	145.0	128.3	137.6	117.6	153.4	183.6	196.2	218.5	234.6	257.9
UK	80.4	56.8	57.4	44.6	37.7	54.7	70.7	49.3	68.0	74.7	76.0	74.7	66.7	77.3	80.0	81.3
USA	86.6	135.7	163.3	142.2	119.7	146.6	141.8	113.4	106.8	108.2	121.0	128.0	137.3	147.8	153.6	158.2

Source: Table F3 in Angus Maddison, *Dynamic Forces in Capitalist Development: A Long-run Comparative View*, Oxford, 1991, pp. 308–23 (at pp. 316 and 318). The German figures for 1914–18 are Maddison's estimates.

Germany's ability to pay (but far less than was envisaged in 1921) was facilitated by a £40 million international loan under the Dawes Plan, thereby only succeeding in creating a new debt to pay off an earlier one. Reparations, and the wider issues of war guilt and territorial losses, played major parts in German instability, both economically and politically.[32]

Reparations combined with the controversies over settling inter-Allied war debts did much to create uncertainty and volatility in international economic relations immediately after the war. The scale of the debt is displayed in Table 1.3. It took until early 1926 for the various Allied countries to negotiate war debt settlements with the United States. In the United States private banking interests co-operated with the government in floating new loans to debtor countries on the condition of satisfactory arrangements to settle the war debts. This was good business for the US as the war loans had been fixed at low interest rates while the post-war rates were high. Italy, for instance, agreed to pay $25 million of war debts to the US over five years while borrowing $100 million. However, the US's major interest was trade, as stated in January 1926 by Andrew Mellon, Secretary of the Treasury. In order to secure European reconstruction, he observed the various countries needed to balance their budgets and have realistic schedules for repaying debts ('We have learned the folly of imposing indefinite and impossible terms from the experiment with Germany before the Dawes Plan'). In addition:

Table 1.3 Inter-Allied government debts at the time of the Armistice, 11 November 1918 (in $ millions)

	Creditors			
Debtors	USA	Great Britain	France	Total
Great Britain	3,696	–	–	3,696
France	1,970	1,683	–	3,653
Russia	188	2,472	955	3,615
Italy	1,031	1,855	75	2,961
Belgium	172	434	535	1,141
Others	21	570	672	1,263
Total	7,078	7,014	2,237	16,329

Note: The other debtors included Serbia, Romania, Greece and some British Dominions. There were minor creditors as well as the USA, Great Britain and France.

Source: G. Hardach, *The First World War*, 1977, p. 148, which was based on H.G. Moulton and L. Pasvolsky, *War Debts and World Prosperity*, Washington, DC, 1932, p. 426.

> ... America with its excess of capital seeking profitable investment, must aid by making private loans to Europe for productive purposes. Only from these private loans during the past year have the countries abroad been able to pay for our wheat and cotton. It is these new loans which make our exports possible... [The] settlements are made in the real interest of those American producers who must have a foreign market to pay ... The entire foreign debt is not worth as much to the American people in dollars and cents as a prosperous Europe as a customer.[33]

In the short run, European trade was boosted by US private loans, but for longer-term recovery. European countries needed to earn trade surpluses rather than secure credit. European (and other) countries were faced with high US tariffs, in spite of the US being eager to export substantially to Europe and to recover war debts and reparations from European nations. The complexities of international commercial policies during and after the First World War are analysed by Andrew Marrison in Chapter 6.

THE WAR AND FINANCE

The outbreak of war in the summer of 1914 was a severe shock to finance. Lloyd George, then UK Chancellor of the Exchequer, wrote later, 'I ... did my best to steady its nerve, for I knew how much depended on restoring its confidence; ... money was a frightened and trembling thing'.[34] All countries very soon stopped or restricted the conversion of their currencies to gold, thereby effectively suspending the gold standard. Convertibility was ended in Russia, Germany and France in July–August 1914 and was severely restricted in Britain then and in the United States in 1917. Russia and Germany prohibited the export of gold in 1914, France restricted such exports in 1914 before prohibiting them in July 1915, while Britain and America (the latter from September 1917) made it very difficult to export gold (with Britain imposing a temporary ban after the war, in April 1919).[35]

The war ended the City of London's international pre-eminence, with New York eclipsing it. Both the Stock Exchange and the acceptance business of the acceptance houses, the great merchant banks and the joint stock banks were heavily dependent on their foreign clients making regular, prompt payments. Overall, in the case of the acceptance business, there was estimated to be some £350 million in outstanding bills of exchange, about two-thirds of which were debts payable by foreigners in London. In 1914 the seven biggest merchant banks alone had £69 million of liabilities on acceptances. Even with massive government intervention, the house of N.M. Rothschild and Sons, for instance, lost nearly £1.5 million in 1914, some 23 per cent of its capital. As E.V. Morgan commented, 'It was the breakdown in the mechanism of international payments that was the cause of the crisis of 1914'.[36]

The British and many other governments exercised moratoria on payment on bills of exchange. In Britain a one-month moratorium was introduced by royal proclamation on 7 August 1914, regularized the next day by an Act rushed through Parliament (which gave powers to extend the moratorium up to six months by further royal proclamations). The rights of holders of bills were safeguarded by the Bills of Exchange Act of 18 September 1914 and debtors who were unable to pay because of the war were helped by the Courts (Emergency Powers) Act of 31 August 1914, which gave courts discretion to delay action on bankruptcies arising from pre-war contracts until six months after the war (or until determined by an Order in Council). In Britain the moratorium on bills was extended until 19 October and the moratorium on general debts until 4 November 1914. Overall, 1914 showed how effective government intervention could be in a major financial crisis. The hub of the crisis was in London because Britain was the main international creditor, with many of those owing money reliant on further loans from London to repay existing ones. There were various forms of moratoria in France, Russia and Belgium as well as Italy, Denmark, Sweden, Switzerland, Bulgaria, Romania, Portugal, Argentina, Peru and Egypt. The United States was also adversely affected by the foreign exchange crisis, being hit by the temporary collapse of cotton exports and by £80 million of £100 million in notes due in the autumn of 1914 being held in Britain and France. After the transfer out of £104 million in gold, the beginning of Allied war purchases and greater cotton exports, the exchange rate of the dollar recovered.[37]

While there were such movements of gold between Allies, notably between Britain and the United States, and also between combatants and neutrals, most trade surpluses were financed by bilateral credit. Indeed, from the outbreak of war the belligerents and most neutrals untied their currencies from gold. From then, as Gustav Cassel commented, 'the various currencies had in the main to be regarded as free paper currencies, and consequently as currencies which were not limited to any metal, and therefore not in any relation to one another'. A point well reiterated by Gerd Hardach that despite a 'carefully maintained façade, there was, in effect, no gold standard during the Great War'.[38]

The break with the restraint of gold facilitated the massive state spending on the war. In all countries taxation paid for only a part, sometimes a small part, of war expenditure, while borrowing in one form or another covered more of the costs. For example, in the case of Britain, in 1915–16 revenue only covered just 21.6 per cent of expenditure, while in 1916–17 and 1917–18 it covered 26.1 and 26.2 per cent respectively.[39] States directly or indirectly printed paper money as well as issuing war bonds. Table 1.4 illustrates one aspect of this, detailing the numbers of notes circulating in several countries between the end of 1913 and the end of 1921. It is notable that for most

Table 1.4 Numbers of notes in circulation at the end of years, 1913–21 (in millions)

	1913	1915	1917	1918	1919	1920	1921
Belgium (franc)	1067	1320	1268	3210	4786	6260	6290
France (franc)	5714	13310	22337	31055	37275	37902	36487
Italy (lira)	2782	5050	10265	14087	18815	22277	21754
UK (pound)	34.6	144.9	266.0	399.2	449.0	486.4	438.4
Portugal (milreis)	87	115	193	274	371	611	723
Spain (peseta)	1931	2100	2799	3334	3867	4326	4244
Switzerland (franc)	314	502	710	996	1046	1039	1015
Denmark (krone)	152	220	338	450	489	557	471
Norway (krone)	108	162	326	436	454	492	419
Sweden (krona	234	328	573	814	748	760	628
Finland (markka)	113	232	764	1156	1124	1341	1356
Netherlands (guilder)	313	582	917	1138	1074	1123	1046
Germany (mark)	2902	8360	18246	33069	50064	81387	122497
Bulgaria (lev)	189	370	834	1493	2299	2858	3354
USA (dollar)	2575	3061	3854	4720	4787	5112	4351
Canada (dollar)	134	130	191	232	254	268	212
Australia (pound)	10.3	36.9	42.0	43.3	53.7	57.3	51.5[1]
Argentina (peso)	823	988	1013	1155	1177	1363	1363
Brazil (milreis)	897	1077	1484	1700	1748	1848	2086
Chile (dollar papel)	186	178	186	228	251	303	331[2]
Japan (yen)	426	430	851	1236	1700	1639	1764
India (rupee)	573	582	1026	1431	1789	1585	1625[3]

Notes:
1 End of September 1921.
2 End of August 1921.
3 End of March 1921.

Source: League of Nations, *Memorandum on Currency 1913–1921*, Geneva, 1922, pp. 43–7 and 54–75.

European countries the greatest wartime increases in note circulation came in the latter part of the war, with the highest rates being in the final year. Apart from Germany, Bulgaria, Belgium, Portugal and Finland, the numbers of notes circulating fell in 1921, after the end of the post-war boom, with the reduction in the quantity of notes issued being much smaller than the fall in prices in each country.[40]

The post-war boom, coming after a brief interlude after the Armistice of 11 November 1918, was brought about by further exceptional demand. There was a need to replace wartime losses and damage: merchant shipping, railway equipment, industrial machinery, buildings and roads. There was a need to restock industry and to replace capital equipment worn out by wartime over-use. For several belligerents there was a major need to import substantial quantities of food. There was much pent-up consumer demand, hitherto frustrated by restrictions on spending and by the lack of available consumer goods. There was also much government expenditure, including on housing and welfare. For countries not devastated by war there were major export opportunities to supply others' former customers and the war-damaged countries. This boom, facilitated by the further increases in the notes and coins circulating, was marked by considerable inflation.

After the greatest war the world had known, democratic governments felt that they had little choice but to meet such economic needs and also provide the lands fit for heroes that had been promised repeatedly to their people while they suffered scarcities yet fought on. Knut Borchardt has written of Germany, 'In the wild political turbulence, with revolutionary threats from the left and threats of *putsches* from the right, a policy of balancing the budget threatened the existence of the state'.[41]

For most countries there was a six-year period after July 1914 of rising prices. There are major problems in presenting comparable price data for a large range of countries, such figures being (as a 1922 League of Nations' memorandum put it) 'at best ... very rough indications of the general trend of relative price movements', 'none of the wholesale price indices are exactly comparable and only a part of the commodities covered by them enter into international trade'.[42] Table 1.5 presents League of Nations' international data on wholesale prices, with 1913 as the base year.

There was a very marked fall in prices in most countries in 1920 and 1921. The fall began in Japan, then occurred in the United States before taking place in Europe. By mid-1920 Japanese prices fell to 86 per cent of their end of 1919 level, while at the end of 1920 British prices fell to 88 per cent of their end of 1919 level. Japanese prices reached their lowest point in April 1921 (at 59 per cent of their high point of March 1920), while British prices only reached their lowest point in April 1922 (at 51 per cent of their high point a year earlier).[43] By 1920–22 many of the exceptional demands behind the 1919–20 boom had been met. Moreover, higher prices curbed consumer and industrial demand.

Those countries which secured the greatest price reductions were also those which followed the toughest deflationary policies. Public policy in these countries was increasingly more responsive to the concerns of the propertied classes as the 1918–19 fears of revolution subsided. Financial orthodoxy and a 'return to 1914', especially in terms of returning to gold at the old parities played their part in determining the severity of the downturn. In the case of the US fears of big outflows of gold helped to encourage higher interest rates in 1920. The US also adversely affected European economic growth by curtailing imports and loans.[44] Britain, Sweden and Japan also

Table 1.5 Wholesale prices, 1914–21 (1913 = 100)

	1914	1915	1916	1917	1918	1919	1920	1921
France	102.2	140.0	188.6	262.0	339.8	356.9	510.3	345.6
Italy[1]	95.1	132.7	201.2	298.8	409.1	364.4	624.4	577.5
UK[2]	98.7	123.1	160.5	204.1	224.9	235.1	283.2	181.0
Spain	101	119	139	160	204	195	222	190
Netherlands	105.3	144.7	221.9	286.0	392.1	297.4	280.7	180.7
Denmark[3]	112	143	189	250	304	326	390	–
Norway[4]	115	159	233	341	345	322	377	269
Sweden[5]	116	145	185	244	339	330	347	211
Germany	106	142	153	179	217	415	1486	1911
Australia	105.6	147.4	138.2	152.8	177.8	188.9	227.9	176.0
Canada	100.4	109.2	134.3	174.9	205.4	216.4	249.7	181.7
New Zealand	104.4	123.0	133.7	150.7	175.3	177.7	211.7	205.1
USA[6]	96.7	107.0	128.4	170.0	203.2	202.7	197.2	123.4
Peru[7]	105	125	160	195	217	227	238	–
Japan[8]	95.5	96.7	117.2	148.6	195.9	239.5	258.1	200.5
India[9]	100	112	125	142	178	200	209	183
South Africa	96.6	107.0	122.6	140.7	153.1	164.8	223.3	160.4

Notes:

1 The Italian index was revised from 1920.

2 The UK figures are those of the *Economist*. Board of Trade figures give 1920 at 313.9 and 1921 at 202.2 (1913 = 100). For more detailed UK figures, see A.C. Pigou, *Aspects of British Economic History 1918–1925*, 1947, p. 234. For the UK working-class cost of living indices, 1915–38, see B.R. Mitchell, *British Historical Statistics*, Cambridge, 1988, p. 739.

3 Alternative Danish figures (*Finanstidende*) give 1921 at 178 (with 1920 at 341).

4 The Norwegian figures are from *Revue Okonomisk*.

5 The Swedish figures are from *Svensk-handelstidning*.

6 The US figures are from *Bradstreet*. The Federal Reserve Board figures give 1919 at 206, 1920 at 233 and 1921 at 145 (1913 = 100).

7 The Peru 1921 figures would be in the region of 220.

8 The Japanese figures are from the Bank of Japan.

9 The India index has 1914 = 100.

Source: League of Nations, *Memorandum on Currency 1913–21*, Geneva, 1922, pp. 104–9 and 115. (The figures are official, other than where stated in the notes above.)

operated deflationary policies and were among the countries which were successful in controlling inflation in the 1920s.

In other countries, notably Belgium, France, Italy and Finland, inflation resumed after 1921–2. In these countries, in spite of a general commitment to return to gold at pre-war parities, governments maintained high levels of public spending. The Belgian government, anticipating the arrival of reparations payments from Germany, financed substantial reconstruction; the non-arrival of German payments undermined confidence in the Belgian franc, the Belgian public debt rising from its pre-war 4.5 milliard francs to 29.5 in 1920, 40 in 1923 and 46 in 1925, with the debt charges in 1926 amounting to 51 per cent of the budget. The French government experienced great difficulties in financing a large internal floating debt. During the war only 15 per cent of expenditure was covered by taxation (roughly half that covered by taxes in the UK). When investors became nervous about the franc and declined to renew short-term treasury bills, the government borrowed from the Bank of France (its debt increasing from 34,186 million francs in July 1914 to 322,819 million francs at the end of 1925. The franc was stabilized by the Poincaré government's stern measures, which included higher taxation, cuts in public expenditure and the refunding of much of the floating debt.) In Italy the public debt soared from 15.7 milliard lire to 112 at the end of 1921. Mussolini's industrial expansion plans entailed a substantial expansion of credit and it was not until 1925–6 that the Italian government reached agreement with the United States and Britain on schedules of repayments of war debts. From August 1926 there was a policy of deflation, which was followed by a fall in wholesale prices (from an index high of 740 in August 1926 to 646 by March 1927).[45]

In five countries, all severely affected by the war, there was hyperinflation. These were Russia, Germany, Austria, Hungary and Poland. In Russia there was substantial inflation during the First World War, which became worse during and after the wars of intervention and civil war. According to one early series of data, under the tsarist government in 1915–16 revenue covered 24.9 per cent of expenditure, with this declining to 18.3 per cent during 1917. From July 1914 until the end of 1916 the amount of paper currency in circulation rose by 414.3 per cent and prices rose to 287, from a 1913 base of 100. By the end of 1917 paper money in circulation had risen by 1433.7 per cent since July 1914, while prices had risen to 1805 (1913 = 100). Matters deteriorated further from 1918, with revenue in 1920 covering only 13.1 per cent of expenditure, the paper money in circulation increasing to 60,979.8 per cent of the July 1914 quantity and the price index (1913 = 100) at 1,260,000. The Soviet government began to get the dire situation under control from October 1922, issuing a new currency (the chervonets) which by early 1924 had replaced the old and became known as a new rouble.[46]

In Germany there was also a lengthy period of governments not balancing revenue while printing more and more paper money. After 1919 the socialist government needed to create a national taxation system and was faced with major expenditure (including the social policies promised in the German revolution). Steven Webb in his study of hyperinflation in Germany concluded, 'Net of expenses mandated by the Versailles Treaty and the expenses taken over from the [German] states, the central government spent about the same as before the war'. Now it was on welfare, not in accelerating the output of armaments. However, after the war Germany's economic circumstances were worse. The gross budget deficits at the ends of 1920, 1921 and 1922 were 34.9, 46.8 and 56.0 per cent of revenue (with cash reparations being paid in 1921–2). Combined with these substantial budget deficits, there was also in Germany a great growth of the money supply with increasing expectations of further inflation. Explaining the hyperinflation in terms of the quantity theory of money, Constantino Bresciani-Turroni (a member of the Allied Reparations Commission) observed, 'It was only the continual increase in the issues of legal money which made possible the incessant rise in prices and the continual fall in the external value of the mark'. Between August 1922 and November 1923 wholesale prices rose at a rate of 335 per cent per month. After stabilization attempts in March 1920 and February 1923 failed, that of November 1923 succeeded. By this time hyperinfiation forced the Allies and domestic interest groups to agree to drastic government policies.[47]

The German experience was the most extreme, but it was also a part of the general serious instability of European currencies for a decade after the Armistice. There were widespread but greatly varying depreciations of currencies. This is illustrated for December 1920 and 1921 in Table 1.6, with rates of exchange in New York. These vary from the small premium for the Japanese yen in December 1920 to the huge discounts for the Finnish, Portuguese, Czech, Austrian, Hungarian, Polish and German currencies.

In many countries there was an eagerness to 'return to 1914', even if that took no account of the changed economic strengths of major participants in the international economy. Britain (in 1925), Sweden (1922), Demark and Norway (both 1926) did return to pre-war parities but their currencies appeared overvalued, as was Italy's when Mussolini increased the value of the lira in 1927. Other countries which stabilized their currencies at the pre-war rates of exchange were Switzerland (1924) and the Netherlands (1924). Elsewhere countries allowed their currencies to float down in value to a sustainable market rate. As a result the Belgian and French francs were both fixed in 1926 at substantially lower parities to the dollar than in 1914, as were the currencies of Czechoslovakia (1923) and Finland (1924). There were lesser devaluations in Spain and Portugal (1929). By 1928 there was a new stability in currencies with all major trading nations' currencies fixed in value to gold, but it was to be short-lived.[48]

The war accelerated the decline of London as the world's major banking centre and its supersession by New York. The war had effectively made sterling unconvertible to gold and this undercut sterling's position as the currency for international transactions. After the First World War, as James Foreman-Peck has observed, 'Sterling was no longer perhaps quite as good

Table 1.6 New York rates of exchange, December 1920 and December 1921

	premium + or discount – in %	
	December 1920	December 1921
Belgium	–67.6	–61.4
France	–69.3	–59.8
Italy	–81.9	–77.2
UK	–28.2	–14.9
Finland	–87.3	–90.1
Sweden	–26.8	–8.3
Norway	–44.7	–42.9
Denmark	–44.8	–27.5
Netherlands	–23.1	–9.9
Switzerland	–20.2	+0.3
Spain	–32.4	–23.9
Portugal	–90.3	–92.6
Czechoslovakia	–94.3	–93.9
Austria	–98.7	–99.8
Hungary	–99.0	–99.3
Poland	–99.2	–99.9
Germany	–94.2	–97.9
Canada	–14.4	–7.1
India	–45.5	–41.1
Japan	+1.5	–3.0
Argentina	–16.4	–19.9
Brazil	–53.5	–59.9
Chile	–32.6	–48.0
Peru	–13.8	–27.1

Source: League of Nations, *Memorandum on Currency 1913–1921*, Geneva, 1922, pp. 32–8.

as gold'. During the war sterling was weakened as the currency for funding international trade and the City of London was very restricted as an international capital market, with much business moving permanently to New York.[49]

While many British bankers suffered substantial losses because of the war, there was no series of bank failures. In Italy (1921–3), Spain (1920), Netherlands (1920), Norway (1923–8) and Austria (1924) there were financial panics, with banks folding where the central banks did not provide adequate liquidity. In contrast, inflation in Germany, Poland and Austria (up to severe deflation in 1924) ensured ample liquidity in the economies in the early 1920s. However, the dependence of German and Austrian banking on short-term credit (often to fund long-term expenditures) and US loans was the major contributor to bank crashes in central Europe and a wider financial crisis in 1931 after the international economy went into recession. The complex issue of what impact the First World War had on German banking is analysed by Hans-Joachim Voth in Chapter 7.

The war also disrupted the flow of international finance. Some of the major lenders of the pre-1914 period were entangled in war debts and reparations. There were also massive losses after the Bolshevik Revolution, 1917, for France and other countries with large holdings in Russia. The US succeeded Britain as the largest international creditor, although its outflow of capital was greatly reduced in 1921–3. Britain and France became again net capital exporters from 1921. Between 1924 and 1929 US lending totalled $6.4 billion and British lending $3.3 billion. The US was very much the key source for new investment in the decade after the end of the First World War, providing some two-thirds in the world. Germany, a major pre-war creditor, was the largest borrower of the 1920s, much of her $7.5 billion debt at the end of the decade being owed to the US. However, in the 1920s much of the US credit in Germany, other parts of central Europe and South America went to borrowers who were overextended and relied on further loans. The dangers of this were vividly displayed when the flow of US finance was stopped.[50]

THE WAR, LABOUR AND BUSINESS

The war had a major impact on the international migration of labour and, for a time, on internal labour markets. It also strengthened organized labour and the organization of business.

There was a substantial reduction in the volume of international migration after the First World War compared with the period before it. Between 1881 and 1915 some 36.64 million people were international migrants, an average of 1.05 million per year. Nearly 60 per cent of these went to the United States, while nearly 12 per cent went to Argentina, with Brazil, Australia and Canada all receiving 7–8 per cent. Between 1921–40 some 8.63 million people were international immigrants, an average of 0.43 million per year. Of these nearly 37 per cent went to the United States, while nearly 20 per cent went to Argentina, and about 12.5 per cent went to each of Australia, Brazil and Canada. The net migration to the United States fell from 4,286,265 in 1910–19 to 3,008,780 in 1920 to only 210,437 in 1930–39. This was brought about by the war, which cut off European migration, US restrictions on immigration and the massive negative effect of the early 1930s slump. The major reason for the fall was US entry restrictions, aimed especially at immigrants from eastern and southern Europe. While the literacy test under the Immigration Act 1917 did not have much of an impact, the Quota Act of 1921, the Immigration Act 1924 and the National Origins Act of 1929 did. According to research by Claudia Goldin, had this legislation been in place in the pre-war years it would have reduced immigration to about 20 per cent. The economic problems of the 1930s were even more effective in reducing immigration into the US, with the US in the 1930s even becoming an emigrant nation (there being a net flow of people out, 1932–6).[51]

While there was massive emigration from other parts of the world, notably the Indian continent, after the First World War, this continued to be marked by a massive return of people. In the case of India, the net emigration was only 18.3 per cent of the 4.6 million who left in 1911–20, and 16.3 per cent of 6.1 million departing in 1921–30 (with net immigration, the numbers returning exceeding those leaving, in 1931–5). Many Indian migrant workers went to Burma between 1913 and 1930, though wartime shipping problems reduced the numbers during part of the war, where they laboured in the docks and rice mills. Burma supplied rice to Ceylon (Sri Lanka) and Malaya, two other major destinations for Indian immigrants. War and post-war demand for rubber created additional demand for migrant labour in both Ceylon and Malaya until the mid-1920s. There was also demand for migrant labour from tea and coffee plantations in Ceylon and from tin in Malaya. In Asia, as well as the Indian migration, there was also substantial Chinese migration to Malaya and also to the Dutch East Indies, the Philippines, Siam (Thailand) and Indo-China (Vietnam).[52]

Where there was large-scale international migration it often had not only an impact on the labour markets of those concerned but also, thereby, on the labour movements. In decades before the First World War in several countries there was sufficiently large-scale emigration to reduce the available labour enough to raise unskilled wage rates. Boyer, Hatton and O'Rourke have suggested that without the huge emigration from Ireland after 1851 the level of real wages of unskilled urban workers would have been in the region of only 66–81 per cent of what it was in 1908 (assuming capital was immobile, but 89–94 per cent if capital was internationally mobile). As for urban unskilled real wages in the UK and the US, O'Rourke, Williamson and Hatton have suggested that without the migration between the two countries in 1870–1910 the UK rates would have been 12.2 per cent lower and the US rates 34 per cent higher if there had been no capital flows (and 6.6 per cent lower in the UK and 9.2 per cent higher in the US if capital was internationally mobile). As US wage rates were higher, the mass migration was a major contributor to the convergence of Anglo-American real wages rates, and in turn was part of the notable convergence of major industrial economies in the late nineteenth century. Such convergence was halted by the First World War and did not resume until after 1950.[53]

The trade unions were very conscious of the effects of mass immigration and emigration. In Britain, notably in the 1840s and 1850s, skilled unions representing engineers, carpenters and cotton spinners were among those which operated emigration funds intended to reduce the pool of the skilled unemployed and so help to maintain wage rates. The unions were also resistant to influxes of labour from abroad or from other parts of their own country. Such opposition led to serious divisions within organized labour, such as between Polish and German workers in the coalfields of the Ruhr.[54] The First World War eased the pressure of immigration on organized labour in many industrialized countries, but divisions arising from xenophobia were still marked. There were exceptions, such as France, where there was need to replace the casualties of war. After the First World War immigrant labour in France was more concentrated in sectors such as mining, iron and steel and construction than before 1914.[55]

The First World War and the post-war boom created a massive demand for labour. This removed most unemployment in belligerent nations. It also brought more women into the labour force and moved large numbers of women from what had been deemed 'women's work' into areas which had been mostly male preserves. The impact of the war more generally on women is explored in Chapter 8 by Sarah Palmer, who argues for an interpretation which includes 'simultaneous advance and setback'.

Similarly, while labour movements made massive advances during the special economic and political circumstances of the war and its aftermath, they were not simply beneficiaries. The war exposed and accentuated many deep divisions, and these played a part in the severe setbacks of the 1930s, yet in the later stages of the war and the early phases of peace organized labour played a substantial part in fashioning the post-war economic order. The roles of labour movements are the subject of Chapter 9.

In several countries the enhanced strength of labour encouraged greater unity among business interests. In Britain many employers were put on the defensive and felt marginalized as the government repeatedly consulted the trade unions and restricted the powers of business. Such pressures brought many businessmen together locally in more trade associations and, nationally, in the formation of the Federation of British Industry (FBI) in 1917, which by 1918 represented 793 firms, 152 associations and 15 government-controlled establishments.[56]

The war also gave an additional boost to concentration. In Britain government control of large sectors of industry under the Munitions of War Acts encouraged 'rationalization', as did the need for more effective competition in sectors which suffered from the wartime loss of markets. As Leslie Hannah has commented on the UK, from the late nineteenth century onwards there were substantial moves towards large-scale enterprises. The war encouraged further mergers in Britain and elsewhere, with 'rationalization' becoming a powerful urge, especially in manufacturing.[57]

The First World War has been seen as 'a watershed' in the history of transnational corporations.[58] This was because the war years saw relative weakening of the UK in international finance, the emerging strength of the US as a creditor and no longer a debtor nation, the near disappearance of Germany as a power in international business and the wholesale abandonment of the gold standard. In terms of direct investment, however, Britain continued to exceed the US until the Second World War, the British and American shares of world direct investment being estimated to be 45.5 and 18.8 per cent respectively in 1914 and 39.8 and 27.7 per cent in 1938. These percentages were of a larger estimated total amount directly invested abroad: $24.3 billion in 1938, up from $14.1 in 1914. In the former Habsburg lands German and Austrian direct investment was replaced by British and French capital, quite possibly such investment there replacing the closed pre-war opportunities of Russia.[59]

THE WAR AND ITS EFFECTS

While it can be acknowledged as a truth that the First World War was a turning point in the history of the international economy, the nature of its impact remains complex and debatable. The effect of the war itself is often difficult to disentangle from other developments. Where the war clearly did have an impact, it could nevertheless be the case that the change would have taken place without it. Indeed, the impact of the war poses a large and difficult counterfactual question of what would have happened without the war. For several areas of economic activity the likeliest answer to such a question would include the suggestion that there was not so much a sudden, sharp break with the past but rather an acceleration of existing trends.

The First World War clearly disrupted European (and so world) manufacturing output. According to one much quoted estimate, had the European rate of increase of output of manufacturing industry continued at its 1881–1913 annual average of 3.30 per cent, the 1929 level of output would have been achieved instead in 1921.[60] In a recent study Feinstein, Temin and Toniolo have pointed to the variety of patterns of growth of industrial production among the major European producers, with 1920 output varying from 35 to 128 per cent of the 1913 level (with the total Europe figure 78 in 1920 but 102 in 1924).[61] World manufacturing output, much affected by European levels, did not reach its 1913 level until 1922, its 1920 level still being more than 6 per cent lower than pre-war.[62]

The volume of world trade also grew at a markedly slower rate after the war than before it. Before 1913 world trade had grown at an annual average of 3.3 per cent, whereas in 1913–20 the average annual growth rate for world trade was 1.6 per cent.[63] Several major European exporters performed badly compared with the US, Canada and Japan. In 1929, with an index of 1913 = 100, the volume of Japanese exports was at 257.9, Canadian at 193.2, US at 158.2, while those of the UK were 81.3, Germany 91.8, Italy 122.7 and France 147.0. The relative weakening of these European countries' exports was due to the war, directly or indirectly (as in the case of France's undervalued franc), yet this pattern had been developing before 1913, with the average annual rate of growth of the volume of exports of Canada and Japan being substantially higher than Germany, Italy, France and Britain (with only the German rate higher than the US one).[64]

While the problems of industrial overcapacity, arising from the war and post-war boom, had to be faced by all, the major European economies were more committed to the old staple industries than the US, which even before 1914 was highly competitive in the inter-war growth areas. In particular, the UK, Germany and Belgium were adversely affected by their decline in exporting textiles, yet in metals and chemicals the European countries remained competitive until the Second World War. Part of European relative weakening in trade after the First World War was the result of others' policies, notably the raising of tariffs and currency depreciation (as in Japan). Such matters were often outcomes of the First World War, albeit indirect ones.[65]

The inter-war years saw the terms of trade move adversely against primary producers. By the late 1920s primary producers on average were getting 20–30 per cent fewer manufactured goods than in 1913 for the same quantity of primary goods. Some have blamed overproduction for this, and there was overproduction in wheat, sugar, coffee and rubber. However, the trend of recent writing has been to doubt whether there was a widespread problem of serious overproduction. Instead, a standard explanation has been that there was a slowing down in European demand due to a deceleration of population growth, especially in north-west Europe, and much of this in the short term was due to the First World War. Other reasons given for Europe taking fewer primary imports include sluggish post-war economic growth in Britain and elsewhere, accompanied by higher than pre-war levels of unemployment, and a continuation for a period after the war of wartime patterns of greater self-sufficiency.[66]

While the First World War saw a mushrooming of revenue-raising tariffs, it also encouraged some states after the war to impose greater trade restrictions (although, as Andrew Marrison points out in Chapter 6, there were also reductions in tariff levels). The tariffs in European agriculture have been seen as especially adverse. Ingvar Svennilson gave the verdict, 'In no other field was economic nationalism such a striking success to the detriment of general European efficiency'. He argued that these tariffs suffered from 'a double weakness': they not only failed to boost farm incomes sufficiently to encourage modernization, but they also obstructed increases in productivity through specialization as they protected less efficient producers.[67]

The international monetary system was an area where the First World War had a major impact, yet in some of its outcomes it was accelerating changes that would have occurred in any case in due course. The First World War shattered the working of the monetary system which rested on the gold standard, a system which had become extensive in the quarter-century before 1914. With the war, countries abandoned the restraint of gold, many accrued huge debts and allowed rampant inflation of their currencies. The war left a legacy of unstable exchange rates, which took a decade to resolve.

The war also ended the City of London's predominance in banking and the money markets, with New York as its successor. This was an outcome highly likely in due course, even without a major European war. Much US banking business was lost to London during the war and was not recovered later. British banking after the war faced vigorous competition from New York and, from the late 1920s, from Paris. While Britain in the 1920s resumed her role as a major overseas investor, she was surpassed by the US, which provided capital in Germany, Austria, South America, Canada and elsewhere. The massive outflow of US capital, combined with the wartime liquidation of European holdings in the US, turned the US from a debtor to a creditor nation. The war also transformed Japan from being a debtor to a creditor nation.[68]

Greater restrictions on the migration of labour, notably in the US, followed the First World War. These, also, would probably have occurred before long without the First World War.

The First World War also hardened some attitudes, which affected later economic developments. One notable example is that the wartime need for strategic supplies encouraged some countries' later moves to autarky. In the case of Britain, the war strengthened notions of imperial interdependence, with her empire expanding further as a result of the peace treaties. Later, British industry increasingly developed export markets within her empire. Stephen Broadberry, in his recent major reassessment of the productivity of British manufacturing, has described this strategy as having had long-term consequences, since the avoidance of direct competition with the leading exporters, the US and Germany, led to dependence on sales to 'remote areas that would not be natural markets as the world economy re-integrated after the Second World War'.[69]

The First World War not only accelerated the advent of the US as the major world economic power but also damaged the international economic position

Europe, and especially that of Germany and the other losers. One new development was that Europe's share of world trade, both in terms of volume and value, declined. As the terms of trade shifted in Europe's favour, the economic effect was lessened. Germany's economic recovery was poor, adversely affected by the wrangles over reparations and in particular by the French occupation of the Ruhr, 1923–5, and by the hyperinflation of 1923–4. It was (with Austria and Hungary) among the countries in which aggregate productivity did not accelerate in the 1920s. Russian economic performance was much worse than Germany's, with major disruption of her industry and the collapse of her position as a major exporter of grain to the rest of Europe. World grain markets were filled by huge supplies not only from the US but also, encouraged by the vacuum created by the First World War and turmoil in Russia, from Argentina, Australia and Canada.[70]

The relative rise of the US and the relative decline of the UK in the international economy has been seen by Charles Kindleberger and others as fateful in the world depression of the early 1930s. His influential study, *The World in Depression 1929–39* (1973) had as its theme that 'part of the reason for the length, and most of the explanation for the depth of the world depression, was the inability of the British to continue their role of underwriter to the system and the reluctance of the United States to take it on until 1936'.[71] This was a perspective from the end of the great post-Second World War boom in the international economy (its 'golden age' of 1950–73). The 1940s international agreements and new institutions (notably Bretton Woods conference, 1944, at which the International Monetary Fund and the International Bank for Reconstruction and Development were set up) had contributed to the greater stability of the post-Second World War era, in contrast to the disharmony following the First World War.

More recently there has been a renewed interest in long-run trends in the international economy with an increasingly sophisticated quantitative analysis of the post-Second World War boom. N.F.R. Crafts, with various associates, has played the major part in this. Crafts and Toniolo, while pointing to the probable need to give greater emphasis to human capital formation in explaining the rapid European economic growth after 1950, have commented on the importance of trade liberalization, demand stabilization and favourable policies and institutions in the achieving of a much better outcome than after the First World War.

The arguments of F. Janossy (outlined by Terence Mills in Chapter 2 of this volume) have been analysed by Crafts and Mills in the light of new growth theory. They have argued against Janossy's hypothesis that after exceptional growth due to reconstruction in the post-war 'golden age' European economies would return to their pre-First World War trend. This they reject for European countries, but suggest that for ten countries variants of Janossy's hypothesis do confirm the importance of reconstruction to early post-Second World War growth.[72] In the second introductory chapter to this volume Terence Mills provides further guidance in quantitative economic history techniques, with regard to examining trends.[73]

The chapters in this volume provide insights into major aspects of the impact of the First World War on the international economy. One theme which arises from many of the essays is that, while this impact was great, there has been a tendency in the past to overstate it. It was also complex.[74]

NOTES AND REFERENCES

1. W. Ashworth, *A Short History of The International Since 1850* (2nd edn, 1962; 1st edn, 1952), p. 217. A.G. Kenwood and A.L. Lougheed, *The Growth of the International Economy 1820–2000* (4th edn, 1999; 1st edn, 1971), p. 165. James Foreman-Peck, *A History of the World Economy: International Economic Relations Since 1850*, Brighton, 1983, p. 188.
2. A. Maddison, *The World Economy in the Twentieth Century*, Paris, 1989, p. 51.
3. Speech at Bangor, 28 February 1915; reprinted in D. Lloyd George, *Through Terror To Triumph*, 1915, p. 81.
4. C.H. Feinstein, *National Income, Expenditure and Output of the United Kingdom 1855–1965*, Cambridge, 1972, T126. N.K. Buxton and D.I. MacKay, *British Employment Statistics*, Oxford, 1977, pp. 78–80. A.W. Kirkaldy, *British Labour: Replacement and Conciliation 1914–21*, 1921, pp. 1–3. D.P. Koenker and W.G. Rosenberg, *Strikes and Revolution in Russia 1917*, Princeton, NH, 1989, p. 30. S. Smith, *Red Petrograd*, Cambridge, 1983, p. 10. R.B. McKean, *St Petersburg Between the Revolutions*, Newhaven, CT, 1990, p. 328. J. Kocha, *Facing Total War: German Society 1914–18*, Leamington Spa, 1984, pp. 18–19. V. Zamagni, *Economic History of Italy*, 1993, p. 223. G. Berta, 'The Interregnum: Turin, Fiat and Industrial Conflict between War and Fascism' in C.J. Wrigley (ed.), *Challenges of Labour: Central and Western Europe 1917–20*, 1993, pp. 105–24.
5. G. Hardach, *The First World War 1914–1918*, 1977, pp. 87–8 and 67–9. D.H. Aldcroft, *The European Economy 1914–1970*, 1978, pp. 17–18.
6. Hardach, pp. 27–30, 33 and 59–60.
7. For a lucid, brief discussion of 'dependency' and 'diffusionist' approaches see B. Albert, *South America and the World Economy from Independence to 1930*, 1983, pp. 17–23.
8. A.G. Frank, *Latin America: Underdevelopment or Revolution*, New York, 1969, pp. 9–10; quoted in R. Miller, 'Latin American Manufacturing and the First World War: An Exploratory Essay', *World Development*, **9**, 8 (1981), pp. 707–16 (at p. 707).
9. B. Albert and P. Henderson, 'Latin America and the Great War: A Preliminary Survey of Developments in Chile, Peru, Argentina and Brazil', *World Development*, **9**, 8 (1981), pp. 17–34 (at p. 730).
10. See, in particular, Miller, 'Latin American Manufacturing', pp. 712–14, Albert and Henderson, 'Latin America and the Great War', pp. 722–3 and Albert, South America and the World Economy, pp. 36–7, to whose work I am much beholden. Maddison, *World Economy*, p. 56.
11. L.S. Rowe, *Early Effects of the War upon the Finance, Commerce and Industry of Peru*, New York, 1920, p. 30; quoted in Albert and Henderson, 'Latin America and the Great War', pp. 724–5. See also L.S. Rowe, *Early Effects of the European War upon the Finance, Commerce and Industry of Chile*, New York, 1918.
12. As well as the items in note 9, see R. Thorp and G. Bertram, *Peru 1890–1977: Growth and Policy in an Open Economy*, 1978; R. Gravil, 'The Anglo-Argentine Connection and the War of 1914–1918', *Journal of Latin American Studies*, **9**, 1 (1977), pp. 61–85; and W. Dean, *The Industrialization of São Paulo, 1880–1945*, Austin, Texas, 1969.

13. J. Iliffe, 'The South African Economy, 1652–1997', *Economic History Review*, **52**, 1 (1999), pp. 87–103 (at p. 93). See also, for example, D. Hobart Houghton, 'Economic Development, 1865–1965', p. 17, in M. Wilson and L. Thompson (eds), *The Oxford History of South Africa*, Vol. 2, 1971, and for a recent restatement of the war's importance: 'manufacturing only "took off" when shipping shortages during the First World War gave an impulse to import substitution', B. Waites, *Europe and the Third World*, 1999, p. 135.
14. A.G. Hopkins, *An Economic History of West Africa*, 1973, pp. 184 and 262–3. More generally, J. Forbes Munro, *Africa and the International Economy 1800–1960*, 1976, pp. 120–23.
15. League of Nations, Economic and Financial Section, *Memorandum on Production and Trade 1913 and 1923–1926*, Geneva, 1928, pp. 58–61. W.A. Lewis, *Economic Survey 1919–1939*, 1949, pp. 149–53.
16. D. Lloyd George, *War Memoirs*, 1934, p. 1269. A. Offer, *The First World War: An Agrarian Interpretation*, Oxford, 1989, is an impressively wide-ranging analysis.
17. A speech to miners' representatives, the London Opera House, 29 July 1915; Lloyd George, *Through Terror to Triumph*, pp. 178–9.
18. Hardach, *First World War*, pp. 124–7. P.E. Dewey, 'Food Production and Policy in the United Kingdom, 1914–1918', *Transactions of the Royal Historical Society*, **5**, 30 (1980), pp. 71–80. P. E. Dewey, *British Agriculture in the First World War*, 1989. E.H. Whetham, *The Agrarian History of England and Wales*, Vol. 9, *1914–1939*, Cambridge, 1978.
19. Hardach, *First World War*, pp. 131–5. Norman Stone, *The Eastern Front 1914–1917*, 1975, pp. 208–9 and 284–6.
20. Hardach, *First World War*, pp. 14 and 33. For the 20 per cent estimate see Offer, *First World War*, pp. 61–2.
21. Offer, *First World War*, pp. 23–68.
22. Hardach, *First World War*, pp. 120–122.
23. Hardach, pp. 124–38. K. Buckley, *Capital Formation in Canada, 1896–1930*, Toronto, 1955, pp. 20–25.
24. J.M. Critz, A.L. Olmstead and P.W. Rhode, '"Horn of Plenty": The Globalization of Mediterranean Horticulture and the Economic Development of Southern Europe, 1880–1930', *Journal of Economic History*, **59**, 2 (June 1999), pp. 316–52.
25. Calculated from figures in Table E11, B.R. Mitchell, *European Historical Statistics 1750–1975*, 2nd edn, 1981, pp. 430–432.
26. B. Supple, *The History of the British Coal Industry*, Vol. 4, 1987, pp. 86–8.
27. R.W. Ferrier, *The History of the British Petroleum Company*, Vol. 1, Cambridge, 1982, pp. 158–261, 638 and 674. S. Howarth, *A Century in Oil: The Shell Transport and Trading Company 1897–1997*, 1997, pp. 103–4. M. Kent, *Oil and Empire*, 1976, pp. 8–14 and 137–57. S.H. Longrigg, *Oil in the Middle East*, 3rd edn, 1968, pp. 33–47. T.A.B. Corley, *A History of the Burmah Oil Company 1886–1924*, 1983, pp. 228–42. Foreman-Peck, *History of the World Economy*, pp. 204–5.
28. Kenwood and Lougheed, *Growth of the International Economy*, pp. 211–12 and 300. I. Svennilson, *Growth and Stagnation in the European Economy*, Geneva, 1954, pp. 168–74 and 312–15.
29. League of Nations, *Memorandum on Production and Trade*, pp. 46–54.
30. League of Nations, *Memorandum on Currency 1913–1921*, Geneva, 1922, p. 6.
31. C.H. Feinstein, P. Temin and G. Toniolo, *The European Economy Between the Wars*, Oxford, 1997, pp. 28–32.
32. D.H. Aldcroft, *From Versailles to Wall Street 1919–1929*, 1977, pp. 78–96. D.H. Aldcroft, 'Destabilizing Influences in the European Economy in the 1920s' in C. Holmes and A. Booth (eds), *Economy and Society: European Industrialisation and its Consequences*, Leicester, 1991, pp. 46–8. D.H. Aldcroft, *Studies in the Interwar European Economy*, 1997, pp. 1–29.
33. H.G. Moulton and L. Pasvolsky, *World War Debt Settlements*, 1927, pp. 129–30, 140–141 and 388–409. The quotation (at pp. 400–401) is from Mellon's statement to the Ways and Means Committee of the House of Representatives, 4 January 1926.

34. D. Lloyd George, *War Memoirs*, Vol. 1 (1933), p. 74. For his account of the financial crisis in London, see pp. 100–123.
35. Hardach, *First World War*, pp. 139–41. K.E. Born, *International Banking in the Nineteenth and Twentieth Centuries*, Leamington Spa, 1983, pp. 185–6.
36. T. Seabourne, 'The Summer of 1914' in F. Capie and G.E. Woods (eds), *Financial Crises and the World Banking System*, 1986, pp. 77–116. E.V. Morgan, *Studies in British Financial Policy, 1914–25* (1952), pp. 3–32. S.D. Chapman, *The Rise of Merchant Banking*, 1984, p. 209. N. Fergusson, *The World's Banker: The History of the House of Rothschild*, 1988, pp. 965–7. D. Kynoch, *The City of London: Illusions of Gold 1914–1945*, 1999, pp. 3–22.
37. Morgan, *Studies in Financial Policy*, pp. 12–24. On British purchasing in the US, see K. Burk, *Britain, America and the Sinews of War 1914–1918*, 1985, pp. 13–27.
38. G. Cassel, *Money and Foreign Exchange After 1914*, 1922, p. 1. Hardach, *First World War*, p. 142.
39. Morgan, *British Financial Policy*, p. 98.
40. League of Nations, *Memorandum on Currency*, pp. 7–10. For differing estimates of notes and coins circulating in Britain see A.G. Pigou, *Aspects of British Economic History 1918–1925*, 1947, p. 241 and Morgan, *British Financial Policy*, p. 222. See also Mitchell, *European Historical Statistics*, pp. 705–15. More generally, see A.L. Bowley, *Prices and Wages in the United Kingdom 1914–1920*, Oxford, 1921.
41. K. Borchardt (tr. P. Lambert), 'Germany's Experience of Inflation' in his *Perspectives on Modern German Economic History and Policy*, Cambridge, 1991, p. 135 (German edn, 1982).
42. For a brief discussion of such problems, see Mitchell, *European Historical Statistics*, pp. 771–84. League of Nations, *Memorandum on Currency*, p. 108.
43. League of Nations, *Memorandum on Currency*, pp. 7–8. Pigou, *Aspects of British Economic History*, pp. 161–83 and 236.
44. J.D. Pilgrim, 'The Upper Turning Point of 1920: A Reappraisal', *Explorations in Economic History*, **11**, 1974, pp. 271–98. D.H. Aldcroft, *From Versailles to Wall Street 1919–1929*, 1977, pp. 68–77.
45. B. Eichengreen, *Elusive Stability: Essays in the History of International Finance, 1919–1939*, Cambridge, 1990, pp. 27–30. Aldcroft, *Versailles to Wall Street*, pp. 145–51. League of Nations, *International Currency Experience: Lessons of the Interwar Period*, Geneva, 1944, pp. 116–22 (the author of most of this was R. Nurkse). D.T. Jack, *The Restoration of European Currencies*, 1927, pp. 113–26, 135–6 and 143–8.
46. S.S. Katzenellenbaum, *Russian Currency and Banking 1914–1924*, 1925, pp. 56–7, 69 and 74–5. See also R.W. Davis, *Development of the Soviet Budgetary System*, Cambridge, 1958, p. 9 (in which the paper money in circulation figures are revised down somewhat). S.G. Wheatcroft and R.W. Davies, 'The Crooked Mirror of Soviet Economic Statistics' in R.W. Davies, M. Harrison and S.G. Wheatcroft (eds), *The Economic Transformation of the Soviet Union, 1913–1945*, Cambridge, 1994, pp. 24–37. R. Munting, *The Economic Development of the USSR*, 1982, pp. 53–4.
47. S.B. Webb, *Hyperinflation and Stabilization in Weimar Germany*, Oxford, 1989, pp. 23–43 and 65–74. C. Bresciani-Turroni, *The Economics of Inflation: A Study of Currency Depreciation in Post-War Germany*, 1937, p. 398 (Italian edn, 1931). See also H. James, *The German Slump*, Oxford, 1986, C.-L. Hottfrerich, *The German Inflation 1914–1923*, Berlin, 1986, T. Balderston, *The Origins and Course of the German Economic Crisis, 1923–1932*, Berlin, 1993 and G.D. Feldman, *The Great Disorder*, Oxford, 1993.
48. Foreman-Peck, *History of the World Economy*, pp. 228–35. Feinstein, Temin and Toniolo, *The European Economy Between the Wars*, pp. 45–8. R. Munting and B.A. Holderness, *Crisis, Recovery and War: An Economic History of Continental Europe, 1918–1945*, 1991, pp. 9–10. Aldcroft, 'Destabilizing influences in the European Economy in the 1920s', pp. 43–57. For the case that sterling was overvalued see J. Redmond, 'The Sterling Overvaluation of 1925: A Multilateral Approach', *Economic History Review*, 1984, pp. 520–532 and for the contrary view, K.C.P. Matthews, 'Was Sterling Overvalued in 1925?', *Economic History Review*, 1986, pp. 572–87.

49. Foreman-Peck, *History of the World Economy*, p. 236. R. Roberts, *Schroders: Merchants and Bankers*, 1992, pp. 154–5.
50. Aldcroft, *From Versailles to Wall Street*, pp. 239–49. C.P. Kindleberger, *The World in Recession 1929–1939*, 1973, pp. 54–7.
51. Kenwood and Lougheed, *Growth of International Economy*, pp. 49 and 171. H.A. Gemery, 'Immigrants and Emigrants: International Migration and the US Labor Market in the Great Depression' in T.J. Hatton and J.G. Williamson (eds), *Migration and the International Labor Market 1850–1939*, 1994, pp. 175–99.
52. A.J.H. Latham, *The Depression and the Developing World, 1914–1939*, 1981, pp. 135–46. A.J.H. Latham, *Rice: The Primary Product*, 1998, pp. 28–30.
53. G.R. Boyer, T.J. Hatton and K. O'Rourke, 'The Impact of Emigration on Real Wages in Ireland, 1850–1914' and K. O'Rourke, J.G. Williamson and T.J. Hatton, 'Mass Migration, Commodity Market Integration and Real Wage Convergence: The Late Nineteenth Century Atlantic Economy' in Hatton and Williamson (eds), *Migration and the International Labor Market*, pp. 221–39 and 203–220. J.B. de Long, 'Productivity Growth, Convergence, and Welfare: A Comment', *American Economic Review*, **78** (1988), pp. 1138–54.
54. E.H. Hunt, *British Labour History 1815–1914*, 1981, p. 205. J.J. Kulczycki, *The Foreign Worker and the German Labor Movement: Xenophobia and Solidarity in the Coal Fields of the Ruhr, 1871–1914*, Oxford, 1994.
55. P. Sicsic, 'Foreign Immigration and the French Labor Force, 1896–1926' in Hatton and Williamson (eds), *Migration and the International Labor Market*, pp. 119–38.
56. C.J. Wrigley, 'The First World War and State Intervention in Industrial Relations, 1914–18' in C.J. Wrigley (ed.), *A History of British Industrial Relations*, Vol. 2, Brighton, 1986, pp. 23–70. A.J. McIvor, *Organised Capital*, Cambridge, 1996, pp. 146–79.
57. L. Hannah, *The Rise of the Corporate Economy*, 2nd edn, 1983, pp. 27–31 and 43–7. C.J. Wrigley, 'The Ministry of Munitions: An Innovatory Department' in K. Burk (ed.), *War and The State*, 1982, pp. 32–56.
58. By the eminent historian of transnationals, M. Wilkins in her 'European and North American Multinationals 1870–1914: Comparisons and Contrasts', *Business History*, **30**, 1988, pp. 8–45 (at p. 11).
59. J.H. Dunning and H. Archer, 'The Eclectic Paradigm and the Growth of UK Multinational Enterprise 1870–1983', *Business and Economic History*, **16**, 1987, pp. 19–49. A. Teichova and P.L. Cottrell (eds), *International Business and Central Europe, 1918–1939*, Leicester, 1983.
60. W.A. Lewis, 'World Production, Prices and Trade, 1870–1960', *Manchester School*, **20** (1952); cited in Svennilson, *Growth and Stagnation in the European Economy*, p. 19.
61. Feinstein, Temin and Toniolo, *The European Economy Between the Wars*, p. 60.
62. Svennilson, *Growth and Stagnation in the European Economy*, p. 305.
63. Aldcroft, *From Versailles to Wall Street*, pp. 305–6.
64. Maddison, *Dynamic Forces in Capitalist Development*, pp. 316–8. Feinstein, Temin and Toniolo, *The European Economy Between the Wars*, p. 10.
65. Svennilson, *Growth and Stagnation in the European Economy*, pp. 168–96. P. Fearon, *The Origins and Nature of the Great Slump 1929–1932*, 1979, pp. 13–14.
66. Aldcroft, *From Versailles to Wall Street*, pp. 218–31 and 291. Foreman-Peck, *A History of the World Economy*, pp. 198–204. Lewis, *Economic Survey 1919–1939*, pp. 149–52.
67. Svennilson, *Growth and Stagnation in the European Economy*, p. 90.
68. For valuable surveys see P.J. Cain and A.G. Hopkins, *British Imperialism: Crisis and Deconstruction 1914–1990*, 1993, pp. 40–43 and Fearon, *The Origins and Nature of the Great Slump*, pp. 16–18.
69. S.N. Broadberry, *The Productivity Race: British Manufacturing in International Perspective, 1850–1990*, Cambridge, 1998, p. 210. F.V. Meyer, *Britain's Colonies in World Trade*, 1948, p. 10.
70. Svennilson, *Growth and Stagnation in the European Economy*, pp. 169–71. Feinstein, Temin and Toniolo, *The European Economy Between the Wars*, pp. 71–8.
71. C.P. Kindleberger, *The World in Depression 1929–1939*, 1973, p. 28.
72. N.F.R. Crafts and G. Toniolo, 'Postwar Growth: An Overview' in N.F.R. Crafts and G.

Toniolo (eds), *Economic Growth in Europe Since 1945*, Cambridge, 1996, pp. 20–32. N.F.R. Crafts and T.C. Mills, 'Europe's Golden Age: An Econometric Investigation of Changing Trends of Growth' in B. Van Ark and N.F.R. Crafts (eds), *Quantitative Aspects of Post-war European Economic Growth*, Cambridge, 1996, pp. 415–31.

73. In particular see his essay 'An Economic Historians' Introduction to Modern Time Series Techniques in Econometrics' in the introductory section of S.N. Broadberry and N.F.R. Crafts (eds), *Britain in the International Economy 1870–1939*, Cambridge, 1992, pp. 28–46.

74. For an excellent analysis of the demographic impact on one country, see J.M. Winter, *The Great War and the British People*, Cambridge, 1986.

2. Recent developments in modelling trends and cycles in economic time series and their relevance to quantitative economic history

Terence C. Mills

1. INTRODUCTION

Economic historians interested in the quantitative examination of trends and cycles in long-run data such as industrial production, wage rates and price levels have, over the past few years, become increasingly acquainted with certain techniques of time series econometrics. Such techniques include, for example, unit root testing procedures, distinguishing between trend and difference stationary processes, modelling integrated and cointegrated processes, and formulating error correction mechanisms.[1]

For the purposes of the present chapter, we assume familiarity with the basic techniques of unit root and cointegration testing, and with the ideas of difference and linear trend stationarity. Our aim is to introduce some recently developed extensions to these ideas and techniques which we think are of potential relevance for economic historians and to illustrate these extensions with examples drawn from the literature on long-run economic growth, which will also provide insights into the impact of the two World Wars, particularly World War I, on output in the industrialized economies.

2. TRENDS OF MANY VARIETIES

Researchers studying the growth and cyclical behaviour of industrialized economies are immediately faced with the problem of separating cyclical fluctuations from longer-term, or secular, movements. The difficulties in doing this are well appreciated by economists and economic historians alike, but the methods of trend and cycle decomposition often used are essentially *ad hoc*, designed primarily for ease of computation without real regard for the statistical properties of the time series (or set of series) under analysis.

The underlying model in such analyses is typically one in which a time series y_t, observed over the period $t = 1,2,\ldots,T$, is decomposed additively into a trend, μ_t, and a cyclical component, ε_t, which are assumed to be statistically independent of each other, i.e.

$$y_t = \mu_t + \varepsilon_t, \quad E(\mu_t \varepsilon_s) = 0, \quad \text{for all } t, s \tag{2.1}$$

y_t is often the logarithm of the series under consideration, while the data are usually observed annually. The extension to, say, quarterly or monthly observations with the incorporation of a third, seasonal, component is, conceptually at least, straightforward.

The trend and cycle components are, of course, unobservable, and hence need to be estimated. The methods of estimation that have traditionally been employed are termed *ad hoc* above because they do not arise from any formal statistical analysis of y_t or its components. The simplest model for μ_t that we might consider is the linear time trend

$$\mu_t = \alpha + \beta t \tag{2.2}$$

which, if y_t is indeed measured in logarithms, assumes constant trend growth. Estimation of the regression model

$$y_t = \alpha + \beta t + \varepsilon_t \tag{2.3}$$

by ordinary least squares (OLS) then produces asymptotically efficient estimates of α and β, although the variances of these estimates will be biased unless the errors (i.e., the cyclical component, ε_t) are both serially uncorrelated and homoskedastic. Given such estimates $\hat{\alpha}$ and $\hat{\beta}$, the trend component is then

$$\hat{\mu}_t = \hat{\alpha} + \hat{\beta} t$$

and the cyclical component is obtained by residual as

$$\hat{\varepsilon}_t = y_t - \hat{\mu}_t$$

Note that the trend component will only be efficiently estimated in small samples, an important proviso given the limited number of observations often available on historical economic time series, if the cyclical component is, *inter alia*, serially uncorrelated. This is unlikely to be so if cycles are, in fact, present in the data, in which case generalized least squares (GLS) or an equivalent (feasible GLS) technique is required for efficient trend estimation.[2] Although the linear trend model has been used on occasions, economic historians have typically rejected the view that trend growth is constant through time, preferring models that allow for variable trend growth rates. The linear trend model can readily be adapted to allow trend growth to vary across cycles, or growth phases as they are sometimes referred to, the terminal years of which are chosen through *a priori* considerations. Thus, if T_1 and $T_2 = T_1 + \tau$ are the terminal years of two successive cycles, the trend growth rate across the cycle spanning the years T_1 and T_2 is given by the least squares estimate of β in the regression

$$y_t = \alpha_\tau + \beta_\tau t + \varepsilon_{\tau t}, \quad t = T_1, T_1 + 1, \ldots, T_2 \tag{2.4}$$

More efficient estimates of trend growth across cycles can be obtained by extending the model (2.4) in at least three ways. The first is to incorporate the models for individual cycles into a single composite model, where it is assumed that the end points of the cycles are at times $T_1, T_2, \ldots, T_{m+1} = T$:

$$y_t = \alpha + \beta t + \sum_{i=1}^{m} \gamma_i d_{it} + \sum_{i=1}^{m} \delta_i t d_{it} + \varepsilon_t \tag{2.5}$$

where the d_{it}, $i = 1,2,\ldots,m$, are 0–1 dummies, taking the value 1 in the ith cycle and the value 0 elsewhere. The second extension is to estimate (2.5) by feasible GLS to take account of possible serial correlation in the cyclical error component ε_t. This will allow hypothesis tests of, for example, a constant growth rate across the sample period ($H_0: \delta_1 = \delta_2 = \ldots = \delta_m = 0$) to be carried out efficiently.[3]

Thirdly, note that equation (2.5) does not allow the trend function to be continuous: even if H_0 is not rejected, the presence of non-zero γ_is will result in horizontal shifts in the trend. Since common sense suggests that the trend function should be smooth, continuity can be imposed by considering the class of segmented or breaking trend models.[4] A segmented linear trend can be written as

$$y_t = \alpha + \beta t + \sum_{i=1}^{m} \delta_i \varphi_{it} + \varepsilon_t \tag{2.6}$$

where the functions φ_{it} are given by

$$\varphi_{it} = \begin{cases} t - T_i, & t > T_i \\ 0 & \text{otherwise} \end{cases}$$

and extensions to allow for higher order trend polynomials and, indeed, combinations of polynomials of different orders, are straightforward.[5] We note, however, that using higher order polynomial trends fitted to the complete sample, rather than to segments, does not appear to provide sensible trend-cycle decompositions for most typical economic time series.

A potential drawback of these models is that the 'break points' $T_1,\ldots,T_m$ often have to be determined *a priori*, so that such choices could be subjectively biased. However, it is possible in some cases (typically when the number of breaks is small) for these break points to be estimated along with the other parameters of the model.[6]

We illustrate the fitting of these trend models by considering the series for annual UK output (gross domestic product (GDP) at factor cost, measured in logarithms) over the period 1855 to 1997 shown in Figure 2.1, where the impact of World War I or, more precisely, its aftermath, is clearly observed, much more so indeed than World War II. It is apparent from this plot that a linear trend would be inappropriate (we provide formal evidence that this is so later), but a segmented linear trend, having breaks at 1918 and 1921, is a plausible contender, i.e., if output can be decomposed as $y_t = \mu_t + \varepsilon_t$, then the trend function μ_t is

$$\mu_t = \alpha + \beta t + \delta_1 \varphi_{1t} + \delta_2 \varphi_{2t} + \varepsilon_t$$

where $\varphi_{it} = t - T_i$ if $t > T_i$, $i = 1,2$, and 0 otherwise, and $T_1 = 1918$ and $T_2 = 1921$. Fitting this model by GLS, to take account of serial correlation in the cyclical component, yields:

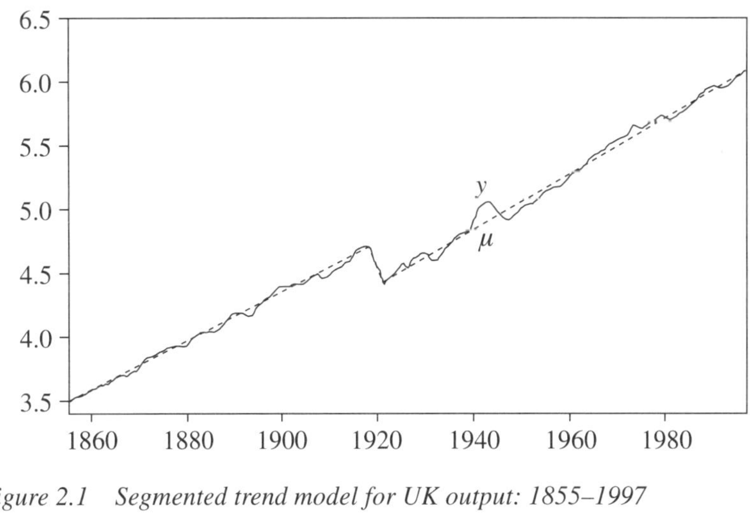

Figure 2.1 Segmented trend model for UK output: 1855–1997

$$y_t = 3.474 + 0.196t - 0.1099\varphi_{1t} + 0.1125\varphi_{2t} + \hat{\varepsilon}_t$$

This model has some simple and easily interpretable properties. Trend growth is 1.96 per cent per annum up to 1919 and (1.96 – 10.99 + 11.25) per cent = 2.22 per cent from 1922, the level of trend output falling 27% in the intervening three years. The component $\hat{\varepsilon}_t$ can be modelled by a second-order autoregressive process whose parameters imply that output exhibits stationary cyclical fluctuations around the trend growth path, the cycles having an average period of eight years. The fitted segmented trend component is shown superimposed on the output series in Figure 2.1.[7]

These break points were, of course, determined 'endogenously' by visual inspection of the data: a procedure found to be useful by most data analysts in most disciplines! As stated above, it is possible to determine break points in a more formal statistical manner. This is demonstrated within the context of a second example, where the basic model (2.6) is used to test various hypotheses about long-run economic growth.[8]

Our starting point is the framework of Maddison's 'epochs' in growth. Maddison sees the World Wars as interruptions to the growth process, with a successful reconstruction of what became the Organization for Economic Co-operation and Development (OECD) economies ushering in a Golden Age of growth between 1950 and 1973, when the stagflationary shocks of the 1970s intervened.[9] It seems clear that Maddison regards all these as exogenous shocks, rather than realizations from the tail of the distribution of the underlying data generating process of the time series. We might interpret these views as implying a segmented trend model of the form of (2.6) with $m = 5$ breaks: the first four breaks being at $T_1 = 1914$, $T_2 = 1919$, $T_3 = 1939$ and $T_4 = 1950$. The last break, at T_5, is allowed to occur at some point between 1950 and 1979, depending on the country being investigated, and may be determined by fitting models for different values of T_5 and selecting the 'optimal' break point that maximizes goodness of fit.[10]

Given this selected value of T_5, we may then take the analysis a stage further by considering other views of the growth process. For example, a very well-known historical view of the process of economic growth was put forward by Janossy and has been much discussed by writers on West Germany.[11] Janossy emphasized that the phase of 'super growth' after World War II primarily reflected reconstruction, and argued that there would be a return to growth on a 'historically normal' path. More recently, Abramowitz and Nelson and Wright have also reviewed long-run European growth within a catch-up and convergence framework, emphasizing the increased potential for technology transfer.[12]

The hypothesis common to all these authors is that, while there might be a phase of abnormally rapid growth during reconstruction, the eventual growth path for European countries would involve a superior performance to that which might have been forecast on the basis of early twentieth-century experience, i.e., pre-World War I. This allows two variants of the pure Janossy hypothesis also to be tested. The first of these, which might be called a 'modified Janossy' hypothesis, sees the eventual growth rate returning to its original size but with income levels on a higher path than would previously have been possible, rather than on the same path as Janossy supposed. The second version, which might be called a 'reverse Janossy' hypothesis, predicts that when growth returns to normal it will be along a trend growth path which can be extrapolated back to the point at which interruption occurred, but which exhibits faster growth than would have been possible before the interruption. Both these variants would reflect the greater accumulation of technological capability in post-war Europe.

The precise algebra of these specifications can be spelt out as follows. After the final break, the trend model becomes

$$y_t = \alpha + \beta t + \sum_{i=1}^{5} \delta_i (t - T_i) + \varepsilon_t$$

which can be written as

$$y_t = \alpha + \beta t + \left(\sum_{i=1}^{5} \delta_i\right) t - \sum_{i=1}^{5} \delta_i T_i + \varepsilon_t$$

If $\Sigma_{i=1}^{5} \delta_i = 0$, output *growth* returns to pre-1914 rates, i.e., the path of y is *parallel* to the trend level extrapolated from 1914: this is the modified Janossy hypothesis. Conditional upon this restriction, the path of y will be the *same* as the extrapolated path if $\Sigma_{i=1}^{5} \delta_i T_i = 0$: this is the pure form of the Janossy hypothesis.

The 'reverse Janossy' hypothesis has the backwards extrapolated final trend joining an earlier segment at a break point. A join point at 1914 (T_1), for example, implies the linear restriction $\Sigma_{i=2}^{5} \delta_i (T_1 - T_i) = 0$, whereas a join point at 1939 (T_3) implies that $\delta_4 (T_3 - T_5) + \delta_5 (T_4 - T_5) = 0$ must hold.

Figures 2.2, 2.3 and 2.4 present logarithms of output per capita for the period 1870 to 1989 for the US, Germany and Canada, respectively, with fitted segmented trends superimposed. The final breaks are estimated to be at 1958, 1955 and 1954 (although only for Germany is the break significant). The three trends are examples of the pure Janossy, reverse Janossy and modified Janossy hypotheses. Note that in each model the fitted trend has been estimated using a feasible GLS technique to account for autocorrelation in the cyclical component ε_t, while in each case the respective hypotheses have been tested and found to be acceptable, with all acceptable (including zero) restrictions being imposed.

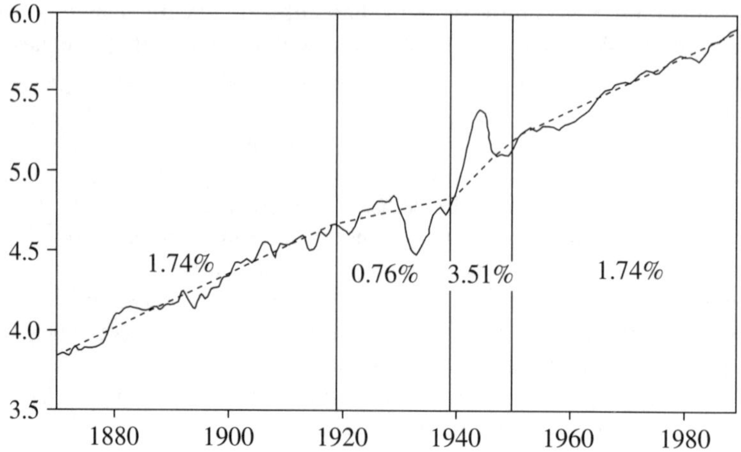

Figure 2.2 US output per capita: an example of the 'pure Janossy' hypothesis

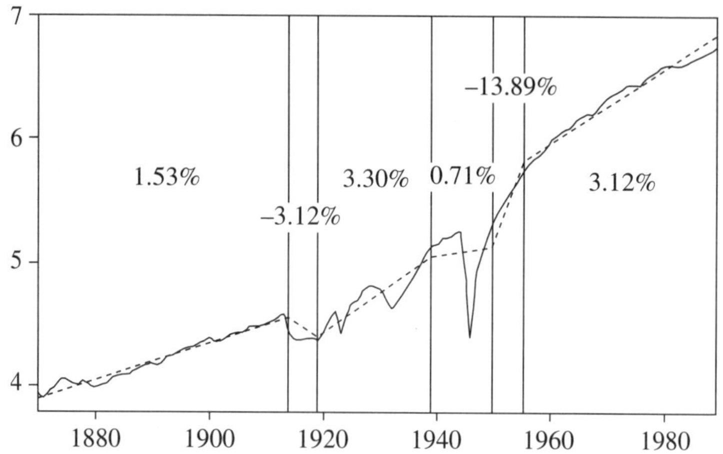

Figure 2.3 Germany output per capita: an example of the 'reverse Janossy' hypothesis (join point 1914)

For the US, output per capita returns to the pre-1914 trend of 1.74 per cent growth per annum after 1950, is not affected by World War I, and there is no Golden Age after World War II. In contrast, German trend output per capita declines substantially during World War I, recovers during the inter-war period, and then undergoes a rapid increase in the early 1950s before returning after 1955 to a trend rate of growth that is substantially higher than that

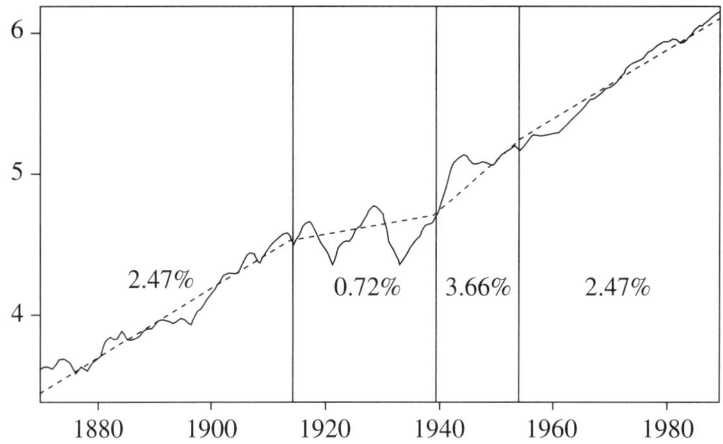

Figure 2.4 *Canada output per capita: an example of the 'modified Janossy' hypothesis*

existing pre-World War I, although extrapolating this final trend backwards does meet the initial trend at 1914. Canada returns to its pre-1914 growth rate of 2.47 per cent after 1954, although the trend line is above (but of course parallel to) the pre-1914 trend. It suffers a downturn during World War I that continues throughout the inter-war period. Thus it is clear that the impact of World War I differs significantly in the three countries, as might be expected given their vastly different experiences during this period.

3. TESTING FOR UNIT ROOTS IN SEGMENTED TREND MODELS

An important potential drawback of the linear trend model and its extensions is that trend growth across cycles is regarded as being deterministic, so that all fluctuations in y_t must be attributable to the cyclical component. Furthermore, any fluctuation from trend is only temporary: since the cyclical component ε_t is estimated by the residual from a regression, it must have zero mean and be stationary, so that any shocks to y_t that force it away from its trend path must dissipate through time.

It would obviously be desirable if alternatives to deterministic trends existed and methods were available to discriminate statistically between different decompositions. This is particularly so given that the allocation of fluctuations to components, and the determination of whether such fluctuations have permanent or transitory effects, can be heavily dependent upon the decomposition chosen. Such alternatives are readily available and may be formalized by considering the segmented trend model in rather more detail. To this end, consider (2.6) again

$$y_t = \alpha + \beta t + \sum_{i=1}^{m} \delta_i \varphi_{it} + \varepsilon_t \qquad (2.6)$$

where we now explicitly assume that the cyclical component ε_t is an autoregressive process of order p: it is convenient to express this as

$$\varepsilon_t = \rho \varepsilon_{t-1} + \sum_{i=1}^{p-1} \phi_i \Delta \varepsilon_{t-i} + u_t \qquad (2.7)$$

where $\Delta\varepsilon_{t-i} = \varepsilon_{t-i} - \varepsilon_{t-i-1}$ and u_t is independent and identically distributed with zero mean and variance σ^2.

The models in Section 2 have all assumed that $\rho < 1$, so that ε_t is stationary and does not contain a unit root. Given the importance of the above discussion, the ability to be able to test the unit root null of $\rho = 1$ against the stationary alternative is paramount. Note that under $\rho = 1$, (2.6) and (2.7) become

$$\Delta y_t = \beta + \sum_{i=1}^{m} \delta_i D_{it} + \omega_t \qquad (2.8)$$

and

$$\omega_t = \sum_{i=1}^{p-1} \phi_i \omega_{t-i} + u_t \qquad (2.9)$$

where $\omega_t = \Delta\varepsilon_t$ and the $D_{it} = \Delta\varphi_{it}$ take the value unity when $t = T_i$ and zero elsewhere. Thus, up until T_1, y_t has an average rate of growth of β, while between T_i and T_{i+1}, $1 \le i \le m$, the average rate of growth is $\beta + \delta_1 + \delta_2 + \ldots + \delta_i$.

Testing for a unit root within a segmented trend model is a non-standard procedure for which there is no single optimal technique. The basic problem is the appearance of the regressors $\varphi_{1t}, \ldots, \varphi_{mt}$ in (2.6): otherwise it would be a standard unit root test. Critical values of tests of the statistic $\hat{\rho} - 1$, for example, are thus dependent upon the number of breaks, m, and the timing of these breaks, $T_1, \ldots, T_m$. For $m = 1$ and T_1 known, tables of critical values are available.[13] In the examples given in Section 2, however, $m > 1$, and this, we feel, will be the typical case when long runs of economic time series are analysed. We thus consider three approaches that seem to be useful, illustrating each of them in turn. The first approach considers the following 'reduced form' regression:[14]

$$\Delta y_t = \pi y^*_{t-1} + \alpha + \beta t + \sum\nolimits_{i=1}^{m} \delta_i \varphi_{it} + \sum\nolimits_{i=1}^{k} \gamma_i \Delta y_{t-i} + u_t \qquad (2.10)$$

where $y^*_{t-1} = K_t y_{t-1}$, $K_t = T/(T_i - T_{i-1})$ if $T_{i-1} < t \leq T_i$, $i = 1, \ldots, m + 1$, $T_0 = 0$ and $T_{m+1} = T$. $\pi = 0$ thus corresponds to $\rho = 1$, and the limiting distribution of the t-test of this null hypothesis depends only on m, the number of breaks, but not on the timing of these breaks. Critical values are available for $m = 2$: the 0.05 and 0.025 values are –4.75 and –5.00.

Equation (2.10) with $k = 1$ was estimated for the UK output series shown in Figure 2.1 to test whether there is a unit root in the cyclical component after fitting the segmented trend with breaks at $T_1 = 1918$ and $T_2 = 1921$. With $T_0 = 1854$ and $T = 1997$, y^*_t is equal to $(143/64)y_t$ for $1855 \leq t \leq 1918$, $(143/3)\, y_t$ for $1919 \leq t \leq 1921$, and $(143/76)\, y_t$ for $t \geq 1922$. The t-statistic on $\hat{\pi}$ is –5.24, thus conclusively rejecting the unit root hypothesis. This is in stark contrast to the inference drawn from fitting a simple linear trend, for this yields a conventional Dickey–Fuller statistic of only –2.52, from which we certainly could not reject a unit root.

Critical values of the asymptotic distribution for $m > 2$ are not yet available, and there is also the question of how accurate these critical values would be with samples of the length usually available. A second approach is thus to use Monte Carlo simulation to compute critical values case by case. A convenient way of doing this is to use the following framework.[15] Under the null hypothesis of $\rho = 1$, feasible GLS estimates of the parameters of (2.8) are consistent and efficient. Since the additional lags of ω_t are only necessary to account for residual autocorrelation effects on the estimate of ρ in the actual application, when we conduct a Monte Carlo simulation we may assume *a priori* that all the φ_i are zero. The 'unit root process'

$$y_t = y_{t-1} + \left(\ddot{\beta} + \sum\nolimits_{i=1}^{m} \ddot{\delta}_i D_{it}\right) + u_t, \quad y_0 = 0, \quad t = 1, 2, \ldots, T \qquad (2.11)$$

can then be simulated n times with u_t drawn from, say, a normal distribution with variance $\hat{\sigma}^2(\hat{\beta}$, the $\hat{\delta}_i$, and $\hat{\sigma}^2$ are the GLS estimates of the parameters of (2.8) under $\rho = 1$).

Each simulated y_t series can then be regressed on the vector $(1, t, \varphi_{1t}, \ldots, \varphi_{mt})$ to yield a residual series, $\hat{\varepsilon}_t$, which can then be tested for a unit root using the t-statistic in the auxiliary regression of $\Delta\hat{\varepsilon}_t$ on $\hat{\varepsilon}_{t-1}$. The n t-statistics can then be gathered together in a frequency distribution from which appropriate critical values can be read off.

To obtain the actual unit root test statistic, equation (2.6) can be estimated and the residuals used in a second regression of the form of (2.7), with the lag order p chosen appropriately. The t-statistic on $\hat{\rho}-1$ can then be compared with the empirical distribution obtained from the simulation. Alternatively, the reduced form (2.10) can be estimated, but with y_{t-1} replacing $\hat{y}^*_{t-1}$, and the t-statistic on $\hat{\pi}$ used (see equation (2.12) below).

To show the feasibility of this approach, we consider again the 'five-break' model for US output per capita. Estimates of β, $\delta_1,\ldots,\delta_5$, and σ^2 were obtained by estimating (2.8) and (2.9) with $p = 4$. Equation (2.11) was then simulated with these estimates $n = 10{,}000$ times with $T = 130$. Each simulated y_t series was then regressed on the appropriate set of regressors and the subsequent residuals subjected to a unit root test. The 10,000 test statistics were then gathered together in an empirical frequency distribution, from which critical values were calculated. For example, the 0.10, 0.05 and 0.01 values were –4.99, –5.30 and –5.96, respectively. Equation (2.6) was then estimated for the actual US output series and the residuals used to construct a unit root test by estimating the regression (2.7), the test statistic being calculated to be –5.23. Comparing this with the percentiles of the empirical distribution of the statistic, we see that the unit root null is rejected at almost the 0.05 level, confirming the appropriateness of our trend estimation procedure in Section 2.

This approach was also used to test the unit root hypothesis for the trends fitted to Germany and Canada. Since the final break occur at different years, the empirical distributions of the test statistics are a little different from those for the US (sampling variation would also play a part in explaining these variations). The actual test statistics are calculated to be –6.62 for Germany and –5.47 for Canada, thus again allowing the rejection of the unit root null hypothesis.

A third approach to the problem is to use a model selection criterion to discriminate between the (segmented) trend stationary model given by (2.6) and (2.7) and the difference stationary model (2.8) and (2.9). One such criterion, known as the Bayes likelihood ratio criterion (*BLR*), is completely consistent, in that both type I and type II errors tend to zero as the sample size tends to infinity, as well has having excellent finite sample properties.[16] It is calculated using the reduced form regression from (2.6) and (2.7)

$$\Delta y_t = \pi y_{t-1} + \alpha + \beta t + \sum_{i=1}^{m} \delta_i \varphi_{it} + \sum_{i=1}^{p-1} \gamma_i \Delta y_{t-i} + u_t \tag{2.12}$$

and the 'auxiliary' regression

$$y_{t-1} = \tilde{\alpha} + \tilde{\beta} t + \sum_{i=1}^{m} \tilde{\delta}_i \varphi_{it} + \sum_{i=1}^{p-1} \tilde{\gamma}_i \Delta y_{t-i} + \tilde{u}_t \tag{2.13}$$

Defining σ^2 as the error variance from (2.12), $\tilde{\sigma}^2$ as the error variance from (2.13) and $M = m + p + 2$ then, with $B = M(\tilde{\sigma}^2 / \tilde{\sigma}^2)$, the *BLR* can be written as

$$BLR = B^{-\frac{1}{2}} \exp(B\hat{\pi}^2 / 2)$$

The difference stationary model is then 'favoured' over the trend stationary model if $BLR < 1$. The actual value of *BLR* can be interpreted as the posterior odds of favouring one of the models: for example, $BLR = 0.5$ implies posterior odds in favour of a unit root of 2:1.

The *BLR* criterion was computed for the US, German and Canadian output per capita series. In each case the posterior odds in favour of the segmented trend model was in excess of 300:1, thus again confirming the appropriateness of these fitted trends.

4. COMMON TRENDS AND COMMON CYCLES

It has become a commonplace in applied time series econometrics to investigate cointegration between a group of integrated series, i.e., to determine whether they share some common stochastic trends that 'drive' the long swings in the individual series, so that at least one linear combination exists which has no long swings and is therefore stationary. Looked at from a more general perspective, cointegration is an example of a common feature: some distinctive characteristic, or feature, of a set of time series, such as trends, cycles or seasonality, is said to be common if a linear combination of the series fails to have the feature even though each of the series individually does have it.[17]

As a simple example of the model underlying the idea of a common feature, consider two stationary time series, y_{1t} and y_{2t}, that are generated by the model

$$\begin{aligned} y_{1t} &= \lambda w_t + \varepsilon_{1t} \\ y_{2t} &= w_t + \varepsilon_{2t} \end{aligned} \qquad (2.14)$$

where w_t is serially correlated but ε_{1t} and ε_{2t} are not. Now,

$$Y_t = y_{1t} - \lambda y_{2t} = \varepsilon_{1t} - \lambda \varepsilon_{2t}$$

will be serially uncorrelated, even though both y_{1t} and y_{2t} are individually serially correlated: w_t is thus a common serial correlation feature, contained in both the individual series but not in the linear combination Y_t. If y_{1t} and y_{2t}

are output growth rates of two countries, say, then w_t may be thought of as a business cycle component, imparting serial correlation into the growth rates, that is common to both countries.

The presence of a common feature can be tested in the following way. Suppose (2.14) is extended to

$$y_{1t} = x_t\beta_1 + z_t\gamma_1 + \varepsilon_{1t}$$
$$y_{2t} = x_t\beta_2 + z_t\gamma_2 + \varepsilon_{2t}$$

where z_t is the feature and x_t is a vector of other important variables. To test whether this feature is common to both series, we test whether there is a λ such that $Y_t = y_{1t} - \lambda y_{2t}$ does not have this feature. An optimal estimate of λ is the two-stage least squares (2SLS) estimate in the model

$$y_{1t} = \lambda y_{2t} + x_t\beta + \varepsilon_t \tag{2.15}$$

where the instruments are x_t and z_t. A Lagrange Multiplier test of whether this estimate, $\hat{\lambda}$, produces a common feature is given by $T \cdot R^2$ from the regression of e_t, the 2SLS residuals, on x_t and z_t: this statistic is asymptotically distributed as χ^2 with $r - 1$ degrees of freedom, where r is the number of variables in z_t.

We illustrate these ideas by considering whether there is a common business cycle feature in US and Canadian output per capita growth, which might plausibly be expected given the close geographical proximity and historical development of the two countries. Figure 2.5(a) shows annual growth rates for the two countries from 1870 to 1989, measured as logarithmic differences (i.e., they are the differences of the series shown in Figures 2.2 and 2.4). The cyclical movements of the two series are apparent, with portmanteau statistics for autocorrelation, estimated over the first 12 lags, being 31.9 and 31.5, respectively, both significant at less than the 0.005 level.[18] Equation (2.15) was estimated by 2SLS with x_t containing just a constant and z_t containing one lag of both growth rates, i.e., $z_t = (y_{1,t-1}, y_{2,t-1})$. The estimate $\hat{\lambda} = 1.012$, having a standard error of 0.118, was obtained. The Lagrange Multiplier test statistic for a common feature was calculated as $T \cdot R^2 = 3.48$, distributed as χ^2 with one degree of freedom, so that it is insignificant at the 0.05 level. When additional lags of the growth rates were included in $z_t, \hat{\lambda}$ hardly altered, and the $T \cdot R^2$ statistics were never remotely significant. Since $\hat{\lambda}$ is insignificantly different from unity, Figure 2.5(b) plots $Y_t = y_{1t} - y_{2t}$, in which no cycles are apparent. This is confirmed by the autocorrelation portmanteau statistic, which is now only 17.9, and by the fact that no sample autocorrelations of Y_t are individually significant: the growth rate differential is thus white noise and the two economies share a common business cycle feature.

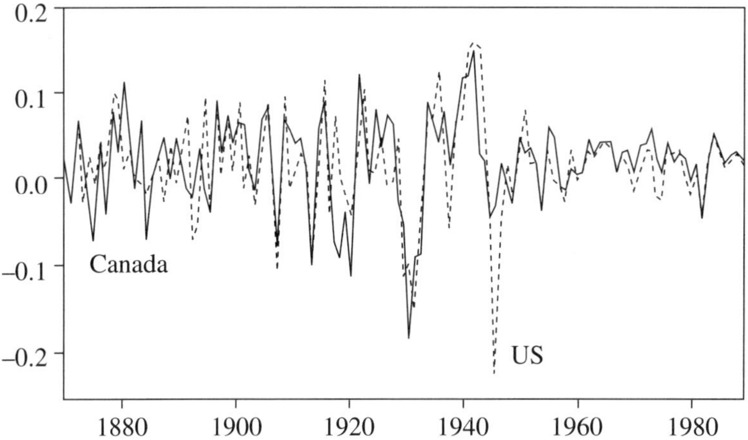

(a) Growth rates

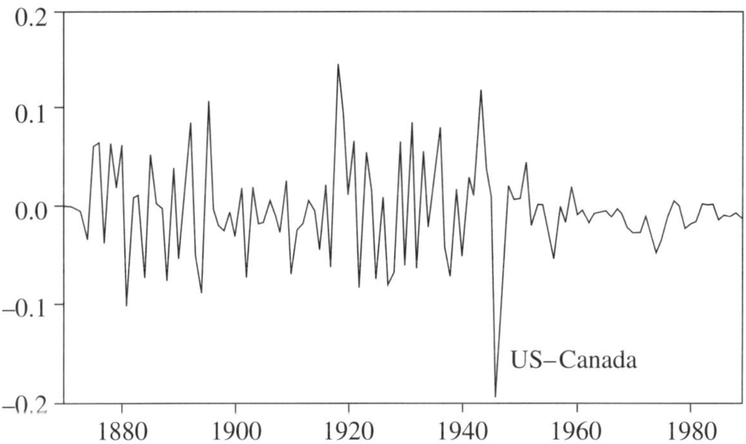

(b) Common business cycle

Figure 2.5 US and Canadian output per capita growth

This example has assumed that the only common feature is that of a business cycle component in the (stationary) growth rates, and has implicitly assumed that the (logarithmic) levels of the series are not cointegrated, which, given the context of the example, must be questionable. The question thus naturally arises whether cointegration and common cycles can be analysed together.[19] Suppose that y_{1t} and y_{2t} are $I(1)$ processes that are cointegrated with cointegrating parameter α, so that $Z_t = y_{1t} - \alpha y_{2t}$, is stationary ($I(0)$) and may be called the error correction term. It is then possible that Δy_{1t} and Δy_{2t} may contain a common cycle as well as their levels containing a common trend. However, in this case Δy_{1t} and Δy_{2t} may be related not just to their own past values but also, through the error correction term, to their past levels, this being an implication of Granger's Representation Theorem.[20] For Δy_{1t} and Δy_{2t} to contain a common cycle feature, $Y_t = \Delta y_{1t} - \lambda \Delta y_{2t}$ must be uncorrelated with all past levels of y_{1t} and y_{2t}, i.e., that Y_t must be an *innovation*.

Conditional on cointegration existing, a test of a common cycle is to regress Δy_{1t} on Δy_{2t} and x_t using 2SLS (cf. equation (2.15)), but with the extended list of instruments (z_t; Z_{t-1}). Y_t is then constructed using the estimate $\hat{\lambda}$ so obtained, and the residuals from the regression are then regressed on (z_t; Z_{t-1}) to obtain a $T \cdot R^2$ test statistic as before.

Letting y_{1t} and y_{2t} now be the logarithmic levels of Canadian and US output, standard tests of cointegration are able to reject non-cointegration at less than the 0.01 significance level, and a maximum likelihood estimate of the cointegrating parameter is $\hat{\alpha} = 1.275$. The error correction is then $Z_{t-1} = y_{1,t-1} - 1.275 y_{2,t-1}$, which is then used in testing for a common cycle.

The 2SLS estimate of λ is 0.909, with a standard error of 0.108, which is again insignificantly different from unity. The $T \cdot R^2$ statistic is now calculated to be 14.8 which, with one lag of Δy_{1t} and Δy_{2t} contained in z_t, is distributed as χ^2 with two degrees of freedom. The statistic is obviously significant and this is entirely due to the presence of Z_{t-1} as a regressor, the extent of the relationship being seen from the following regression

$$Y_t = \underset{(0.038)}{-0.130} - \underset{(0.028)}{0.100}\, Z_{t-1}, \quad T \cdot R^2 = 11.65$$

where standard errors are shown in parentheses. Thus, while the growth differential is uncorrelated with past growth rates of both countries, it is correlated with past disequilibria in the cointegrating relationship between the output levels so that, when a common trend in the levels is accounted for, the common cycle in growth rates disappears.

5. CONCLUSIONS

This chapter has discussed some recent developments in time series econometrics, in particular segmented trends and common cycles, that we feel have considerable potential for the analysis of the types of series that quantitative economic historians frequently encounter. Examples have been provided that illustrate these developments in practice and these show that the impact of the World Wars can be very different depending on which countries are being investigated. The UK, for example, underwent a major shift in trend output growth *after* the end of World War I, whereas Germany experienced a major shift in output per capita during the war, as did Canada, and a major acceleration after World War II, which Canada did not. The US, on the other hand, was unaffected by either war, as was the business cycle relationship between the US and Canada.

NOTES

1. Reviews of this literature written for an economic historian audience have been provided by Mills (1992, 1996).
2. See Canjels and Watson (1997) for detailed analysis of this model.
3. See Crafts, Leybourne and Mills (1989).
4. These models were popularized by Perron (1989) but are, in fact, a special case of grafted polynomials: see, for example, Fuller (1976, ch. 9.2).
5. For example, Capie and Mills (1991) and Crafts and Mills (1994a) use combinations of constant (zero order, i.e., flat) and linear trends to model money and real wages respectively, while Crafts and Mills (1994b) and Mills and Crafts (1996a) use constant, linear and polynomial segments to model industrial production.
6. Examples of how this may be done can be found in Crafts and Mills (1994b) and Mills and Crafts (1996a), and a detailed econometric theory is developed in Bai and Perron (1998).
7. Mills (1994) provides more details of the model and its estimation. Note that the segmented trend, although continuous, is not 'smooth' (it is not differentiable at the break points). An alternative model that allows the trend to move smoothly from one 'regime' to another is the *smooth transition* model, successfully fitted to industrial production between 1700 and 1913 in Crafts and Mills (1997). However, such a model produced a much poorer fit than the segmented trend to the output data being used here. Other types of trend models have been fitted to this series, in particular, the *basic structural model*. Mills and Crafts (1996b) provide a review of this model in the context of the current example.
8. This example is based upon the analysis of Crafts and Mills (1996): see also Mills and Crafts (2000) for various extensions. The data base is that of Maddison (1991): Crafts and Mills (1996) use 17 countries in their analysis.
9. See Maddison (1991, 1995).
10. This procedure was first proposed by Gallant and Fuller (1973) and has recently been shown to produce a consistent model selection by Phillips and Ploberger (1994).
11. See, for example, Dumke (1990). The original reference is Janossy (1969).
12. Abramowitz (1986); Nelson and Wright (1992).
13. Perron (1989) develops the appropriate testing procedure and provides tables of critical values. When T_1 cannot be assumed to be known, and must be determined endogenously, Banerjee, Lumsdaine and Stock (1992), Zivot and Andrews (1992) and Perron (1997) all provide solutions.
14. This approach has been developed by Park and Sung (1994).
15. See Campbell and Perron (1991).
16. See Phillips and Ploberger (1994).
17. The concept of common features was introduced by Engle and Kozicki (1993), who developed the testing technique outlined below.
18. These are the statistics proposed by Ljung and Box (1978), here distributed as χ^2 with 12 degrees of freedom on the null hypothesis of no autocorrelation.

19. This has been considered by Vahid and Engle (1993): see also Mills (1998).
20. See Engle and Granger (1987).

REFERENCES

Abramovitz, M. (1986), 'Catching-up, Forging Ahead, and Falling Behind', *Journal of Economic History*, **36**, 385–406.

Bai, J. and P. Perron (1998), 'Estimating and Testing Linear Models with Multiple Structural Changes', *Econometrica*, **66**, 47–78.

Banerjee, A., R.L. Lumsdaine and J.H. Stock (1992), 'Recursive and Sequential Tests of the Unit-root and Trend-break Hypotheses: Theory and Evidence', *Journal of Business and Economic Statistics*, **10**, 271–87.

Campbell, J.Y. and P. Perron (1991), 'Pitfalls and Opportunities: What Macro-economists Should Know About Unit Roots', in O.J. Blanchard and S. Fisher (eds), *NBER Macroeconomics Annual*, pp. 141–201, Cambridge: MIT Press.

Canjels, E. and M.W. Watson (1997), 'Estimating Deterministic Trends in the Presence of Serially Correlated Errors', *Review of Economics and Statistics*, **79**, 184–200.

Capie, F.H. and T.C. Mills (1991), 'Money and Business Cycles in the U.S. and the U.K., 1870–1913', *Manchester School*, **59** Supplement, 38–56.

Crafts, N.F.R., S.J. Leybourne and T.C. Mills (1989), 'The Climacteric in Late Victorian Britain and France: A Reappraisal of the Evidence', *Journal of Applied Econometrics*, **4**, 103–17.

Crafts, N.F.R. and T.C. Mills (1994a), 'Trends in Real Wages in Britain, 1750–1913', *Explorations in Economic History*, **31**, 176–94.

Crafts, N.F.R. and T.C. Mills (1994b), 'The Industrial Revolution as a Macroeconomic Epoch: An Alternative View', *Economic History Review*, **47**, 769–75.

Crafts, N.F.R. and T.C. Mills (1996), 'Europe's Golden Age: An Econometric Investigation of Changing Trend Rates of Growth', in B. van Ark and N.F.R. Crafts (eds), *Quantitative Aspects of Postwar European Economic Growth*, pp. 415–31, Cambridge: Cambridge University Press.

Crafts, N.F.R. and T.C. Mills (1997), 'Endogenous Innovation, Trend Growth, and the British Industrial Revolution: Reply to Greasley and Oxley', *Journal of Economic History*, **57**, 950–956.

Dumke, R.H. (1990), 'Reassessing the Wirtschaftswunder: Reconstruction and Postwar Growth in West Germany in an International Context', *Oxford Bulletin of Economics and Statistics*, **52**, 451–90.

Engle, R.F. and C.W.J. Granger (1987), 'Co-integration and Error Correction: Representation, Estimation and Testing', *Econometrica*, **55**, 251–76.

Engle, R.F. and S. Kozicki (1993), 'Testing for Common Features', *Journal of Business and Economic Statistics*, **11**, 369–80.

Fuller, W.A. (1976), *Introduction to Statistical Time Series*, New York: Wiley.

Gallant, A.R. and W.A. Fuller (1973), 'Fitting Segmented Polynomial Regression Models Whose Join Points have to be Estimated', *Journal of the American Statistical Association*, **68**, 144–7.

Janossy, F. (1969), *The End of the Economic Miracle*, White Plains: IASP.

Ljung, G.M. and G.E.P. Box (1978), 'On a Measure of Lack of Fit in Time Series Models', *Biometrika*, **66**, 67–72.

Maddison, A. (1991), *Dynamic Forces in Capitalist Development*, Oxford: Oxford University Press.
Maddison, A. (1995), *Monitoring the World Economy 1820–1992*, Paris: OECD.
Mills, T.C. (1992), 'An Economic Historians' Introduction to Modern Time Series Techniques in Econometrics', in S.N. Broadberry and N.F.R. Crafts (eds), *Britain in the International Economy 1870–1939*, pp. 28–46, Cambridge: Cambridge University Press.
Mills, T.C. (1994), 'Segmented Trends and the Stochastic Properties of UK Output', *Applied Economics Letters*, **1**, 132–3.
Mills, T.C. (1996), 'Unit Roots, Shocks and VARs and Their Place in History: An Introductory Guide', in T. Bayoumi, B. Eichengreen and M.P. Taylor (eds), *Modern Perspectives on the Gold Standard*, pp. 17–51, Cambridge: Cambridge University Press.
Mills, T.C. (1998), 'Recent Developments in Modelling Nonstationary Vector Autoregressions', *Journal of Economic Surveys*, **12**, 279–312.
Mills, T.C. and N.F.R. Crafts (1996a), 'Trend Growth in British Industrial Output, 1700–1913: A Reappraisal', *Explorations in Economic History*, **33**, 277–95.
Mills, T.C. and Crafts, N.F.R. (1996b), 'Modelling Trends in Economic History', *The Statistician*, **45**, 153–9.
Mills, T.C. and N.F.R. Crafts (2000), 'After the Golden Age: A Long Run Perspective on Growth Rates that Speeded Up, Slowed Down and Still Differ', *Manchester School*, **68**, 68–91.
Nelson, R.R. and G. Wright (1992), 'The Rise and Fall of American Technological Leadership', *Journal of Economic Literature*, **30**, 1931–64.
Park, J.Y. and J. Sung (1994), 'Testing for Unit Roots in Models with Structural Change', *Econometric Theory*, **10**, 917–36.
Perron, P. (1989), 'The Great Crash, the Oil Price Shock and the Unit Root Hypothesis', *Econometrica*, **57**, 1361–401.
Perron, P. (1997), 'Further Evidence on Breaking Trend Functions in Macroeconomic Variables', *Journal of Econometrics*, **80**, 355–85.
Phillips, P.C.B. and W. Ploberger (1994), 'Posterior Odds Testing for a Unit Root with Data-based Model Selection', *Econometric Theory*, **10**, 774–808.
Vahid, F. and R.F. Engle (1993), 'Common Trends and Common Cycles', *Journal of Applied Econometrics*, **8**, 341–60.
Zivot, E. and D.W.K. Andrews (1992), 'Further Evidence on the Great Crash, the Oil Price Shock, and the Unit Root Hypothesis', *Journal of Business and Economic Statistics*, **10**, 251–70.

3. Manufacturing industry in the United States during the First World War

Peter Fearon

The First World War did not have the dramatic social and economic impact on the United States that it had on the European belligerents. It was not the mounting casualty lists from France but the Great Depression which provided Americans with their first major shock of the twentieth century. America had a short war, becoming a direct participant on 6 April 1917, a role that was to last for just 19 months. However, as we shall see, there had been a large-scale shift of resources into war-related industries even before Woodrow Wilson, who had been re-elected in 1916 as the President 'who kept America out of the war', joined the Allied cause. But in a conflict with such a horrifying death toll for Germany, France, Russia, Austria-Hungary and Britain, US losses, which totalled 48,000 killed in action and 2,900 missing, were relatively modest. Indeed the 56,000 Americans who died of disease outnumbered those who fell in battle.[1]

The impact of war is, however, not limited to the powerful emotions so evident in the homes of the young men who perished, distressing though they undoubtedly were. In order to analyse the economic effect of the Great War on the manufacturing sector, we must first assess America's absolute and relative position as an industrial power on the eve of the conflict, for only then can both the short- and long-run changes which resulted from the war be separated from trends already clearly in place.

THE DOMINANCE OF BIG BUSINESS

There is no doubt that the US was the world's leading manufacturing nation in 1914, by which time America's share in world manufacturing output was only slightly less than that of Britain, France and Germany combined. Moreover, this ascendancy was not a position that the new world had only recently acquired. Between 1860 and 1914 manufacturing output grew impressively at around 5 to 7 per cent each year, but most rapidly during the 1880s and also at the turn of the century. An emphasis on capital investment ensured not only increases in output but also a decline in labour costs per unit of output. The triumph of US manufacturing was not just a massive rise in output. A revolution in industrial and managerial organization transformed a rapidly urbanizing nation.

An important determinant of manufacturing growth during the half-century before 1914 was the rise to prominence of the large corporation. America pioneered big business and in the early twentieth century a number of industries were dominated by a few large enterprises. The rapidity with which the industrial structure of the country changed was remarkable. It is important to understand the structure of American business, and its relationship with government, because both played a key role in the response of the manufacturing sector to meeting war demands.

What do we mean by big business? Enterprises which fall into this category usually had capital requirements so large that they could not be run or financed by a single individual, as could the traditional family firm. Corporations relied on major finance houses to raise money from the public. These enterprises were run by boards of directors and by professional managers. In other words there was a separation between the ownership of the business, which was in the hands of the shareholders, and control which was the responsibility of management. Because of their complexity, large corporations required clearly defined management structures, with excellent lines of communication. These were essential if there was to be no ambiguity as to managerial responsibility. However, while size bought the economies of scale which were needed to reduce unit costs, an inevitable result was high fixed costs which often left business especially vulnerable during the numerous business recessions of the period. Many businesses came to dread price competition, especially during periods of depression and deflation.

Unfettered competition which coincided with widening markets, falling prices, the need to adopt new technologies and to experiment with new systems of management was a source of great anxiety. The stress, the uncertainty and the possibility of bankruptcy were powerful forces persuading business that stability had many advantages. The search for order in an uncertain competitive world was increasingly a feature of corporate life. Some of the new consumer goods industries could, to some extent, insulate themselves from competition by the use of brand names and advertising. Food processing companies, who were concentrating on urban markets – for example, Swift, Armour, Libby's and Kelloggs – used advertising, marketing and the brand image. This strategy was, of course, only available to large companies. Other devices to curb competition such as the creation of pools and trusts became the catalyst for regulatory legislation.

The decade after 1895 saw a great wave of mergers which transformed the structure of the manufacturing sector. The merger movement was partly in response to the Depression of 1893, but it also stemmed from changes in the legal system and from opportunities presented by a new market in industrial securities. On the eve of the Great War modern American manufacturing was clearly visible. The names of the giants which dominated their markets were internationally famous. Standard Oil, US Steel, American Tobacco, Swift and Company, Armour, General Electric, Westinghouse and Eastman Kodak are just a few examples of manufacturing excellence which could provide a powerful base for war expansion.

The emergence of a cadre of experienced managers used to dealing effectively with high-volume, low unit cost output was a crucial ingredient in the triumph of American manufacturing industry. Salaried managers were a new powerful class who made the key decisions on wages, employment, prices, output and delivery. Mass production and mass distribution required administrative co-ordination. Middle managers ousted financiers and even family members from the key decision-making processes in the major corporations.[2] They enabled modern capitalism to flourish.

The merger movement had occurred in spite of both growing public concern and legislation which had been specifically designed to hinder collusion and promote competition. The Sherman Anti-trust Act (1890) was a broad, indeed vague, piece of legislation which attempted to use the federal courts as a means of enforcing competitive standards on business. Contrary to expectations, the interpretation which the courts placed on this legislation encouraged the spread of integrated holding companies which were regarded as lawful since they were not cartels.

The Sherman Anti-trust Act is just one example of regulatory intervention during a period when Americans came to believe that Congress should play a more significant role in controlling the big manufacturing corporations by, for example, curbing the power of the railroads and providing a stable banking system. Among the most important pieces of legislation were the creation of the Interstate Commerce Commission (1887), the powers of which were strengthened by the Mann–Elkins Act (1910); the creation of the Federal Trade Commission (1914) and the passage of the Clayton Act (1914) which was designed to further tighten the anti-trust laws; finally the Federal Reserve Act (1913) created a decentralized system of central banking.

Through the Progressive Era Congress had an active interest in regulation, but it would be wrong to view this as simply a conflict between big business and the nation's legislature. There is no doubt that much of the legislation was politically popular but its effect on big business was limited; indeed, it was sometimes the case that regulated corporations supported and even played a part in forming the regulatory legislation.[3] The relationship between legislation and big business is, in fact, highly complex, but it is possible to see this period as one in which both sides strove for a set of rules which would provide more stability. It was in the interests both of business leaders and of Congress to provide a regulatory framework which allowed business to flourish. Regulation often took place in co-operation with big business rather than in an atmosphere of conflict. We can, therefore, see a growing relationship between the new corporate economy and the state which by 1914 had not yet evolved into a coherent model. It is important to remember in the context of the First World War that there was sometimes a close relationship between big business and the state, and that significant experimentation with regulation had taken place.[4]

MANUFACTURING INDUSTRY 1914–19

A useful guide to movements in manufacturing output can be found in the index constructed by Solomon Fabricant and reproduced as Table 3.1. This shows a substantial growth of output between 1899 and 1913, identifies 1914 as a depression year and marks out 1915 and 1916 as a period of exceptional growth. On the other hand, we can note that manufacturing output for 1916–18 is maintained at a very similar level for all three years.

Table 3.1 Index of physical output for US manufacturing industries (1899 = 100)

1912	185
1913	198
1914	186
1915	218
1916	259
1917	257
1918	254
1919	222
1920	242
1921	194
1929	364

Source: Solomon Fabricant, *The Output of Manufacturing Industries, 1899–1937*, New York, 1940, p. 44.

Americans had every reason to feel confident about a manufacturing sector which in 1914 had 7,036,247 wage earners and 964,217 salaried employees. Both figures had increased since 1909, but the expansion in the number of wage earners at 6.4 per cent was far more modest than that of salaried employees, which grew at 22 per cent.[5] The average full-time working week in manufacturing was 55 hours, a reduction from the 60 hours in 1899.[6] However, 1914 was a year of recession which forced up unemployment to an estimated 7.9 per cent of the civilian labour force. An indication of the position of manufacturing in the economy as a whole can be formed by a comparison with the farm labour force which stood at 10,145,000 on the eve of the First World War.[7]

Americans were and are highly mobile, and the growing urbanization of the nation had been fuelled mainly by a mass movement of people from rural areas where job opportunities were limited and wages relatively low. Native Americans who were fluent in English, literate and adaptable could respond to the growing employment opportunities in the manufacturing sector. They had a clear advantage over non-English-speaking immigrants, especially when competing for white-collar or management posts. Immigrants had come to the US in large numbers before 1914 and they were a source of relatively cheap labour. In both 1913 and 1914 approximately 1.1 million Europeans arrived on the eastern seaboard. Of this flow, in 1914, 227,000 were classified as non-farm-labourers and another 145,00 as craftsmen, foremen and operators.[8] Many looked immediately for factory jobs and they were a significant addition to the manufacturing labour force. A flexible labour market, with few powerful trade unions, was an important asset for US employers. When the demand for workers increased, additional numbers from Europe could virtually be guaranteed, thus ensuring that industrial expansion need not be checked because of serious labour supply constraints.

America's main manufacturing groups are listed in the 1914 *Census of Manufactures* with the number of wage earners in parenthesis, as follows: textiles (1,507,374), iron and steel (1,061,058), lumber and its remanufacture (833,529), food and kindred products (469,234) paper and printing (452,900), railroad repair shops (365,902) and stone, clay and glass (334,612). It is important to remember that they and their workers were not evenly distributed across the country, but were regionally concentrated. The most industrialized states and their average number of wage earners in 1914 were: New York (1,057,857), Pennsylvania (924,478), Massachusetts (606,698), Illinois (506,943), Ohio (510,435), New Jersey (373,605) and Michigan (271,909).[9] The remainder of the country had relatively little manufacturing and even California, the most industrialized of the western states, could muster only 139,481 factory workers.

The Census of 1914 also gives a clear indication of the power of big business. The 142,436 establishments which were owned by individuals employed a mere 707,568 people; the 78,152 corporations employed 5,649,891 workers. Of the wage earners employed by corporations, 4,167,924 worked in the New England, Mid-Atlantic and East North Central census regions.[10]

Although the US had many small manufacturing businesses, the corporations dominated output, investment and employment.

The 1919 *Census of Manufactures* reveals that the following changes had taken place. The number of wage earners in textiles (1,611,309) shows a modest increase over the 1914 figure, while iron and steel (1,585,712) had managed to increase its workforce by a staggering 524,654 persons or practically 50 per cent. Lumber (839,008) had a scarcely noticeable rise in employment, but the workforce in food and kindred products (684,672) increased by about 45 per cent. Paper and printing (509,875) experienced a modest rise of 12 per cent, while the workforce in railroad repair shops (5615,709) shows a pronounced upward movement of just over 40 per cent. On the other hand, the number of workers in stone, clay and glass (298,659) declined by 35,953. The effect of war pressures on two other manufacturing employment groups are worth recording. In chemicals the labour force rose from 299,569 in 1914 to 427,008 in 1919. During the same period the expansion in metals and metal products other than steel was from 262,154 to 339,469.[11]

These figures indicate the differing pressures on the manufacturing sector which in some cases resulted in a massive increase in employment over a short period. The 1919 Census calculated that the number of manufacturing wage earners for the country as a whole rose by 29.3 per cent between 1914 and 1919. In the highly industrialized north the increase was 28.1 per cent. The South, however, managed to increase its manufacturing workforce by 23.3 per cent while the west saw a massive rise of 71.9 per cent.[12] Absolutely the north maintained its manufacturing ascendancy, as we can see by noting the number of wage earners in each state in 1919. New York (1,228,130), Pennsylvania (1,135,837), Ohio (730,733), Massachusetts (713,836), Illinois (653,114), New Jersey (508,686) and Michigan (471,242) all increased their numbers of manufacturing workers. By 1919 California (243,692) had moved into eleventh rank in this listing, but into a higher position if the value of manufacturing output is used as an indication.[13]

Just before the First World War the US manufacturing industry had reached a level of concentration which has changed relatively little since. There was a clear link between size of the unit of production and the use of the latest technology, high levels of productivity, the attainment of economies of scale and a commitment to mass production and mass distribution. Of great significance here was the example of Henry Ford who, between 1908 and 1914, faced many of the problems which were later to plague manufacturers during the war. Massively increasing demand for the Model T Ford could not have been satisfied if the company had relied upon traditional methods of production. Apart from anything else a shortage of skilled mechanics would have presented a formidable obstacle both to lowering costs and to raising output.

Ford pioneered a manufacturing system which enabled the unskilled to produce high quality goods in large quantities. The company used unskilled US and immigrant workers: indeed in 1914 just over 70 per cent of the workforce was foreign-born. With a highly standardized product, a strict division of labour which simplified even the most complex tasks, and the use of the most sophisticated machines and machine tools, craft-based assembly was cast aside. The introduction of, and the emphasis on, continuous assembly required a total rearrangement of the work process and a new system of manufacture – Fordism – was introduced.[14] A continuous search on the part of management for improvement led to massive productivity gains, a sharp fall in costs and high levels of profit. The cost of the Model T fell from $825 in 1913 to less than $300 by the mid-1920s. As Hounshell observes, the transformation of work at the Highland Park plant, which was opened in 1912, did not strictly conform to the ideas articulated by the doyen of scientific management, Frederick W. Taylor. The Ford approach was not simply to make the worker more efficient, but to replace labour by machinery.[15] Henry Ford and his managers were quite open about what they had accomplished and manufacturers throughout the land could read about and could visit the plant to see for themselves the Ford revolution. Even before war demand had impacted upon the economy, Ford Motor Company managers had demonstrated that it was possible to respond to the challenge of heavy demand within a short period.

THE INTERNATIONAL DIMENSION

The initial effect of the war in Europe was disruptive rather than stimulating. International markets in goods and finance were paralysed by uncertainty and the valuable European market was in disarray. As many US observers shared the view that within a few months the collective madness which had seized the Old World would be over, inactivity seemed an appropriate response until sanity could be restored. Events, however, unfolded in an unpredictable fashion. By late 1914 Britain's attempts to control the seas and to enforce a blockade of the Central Powers was affecting shipping from neutral America. Neutrality, however, did not affect the willingness of US manufacturers to provide goods for the warring Europeans, and the US was dragged out of the recession which gripped industry in 1914 by foreign orders. In previous depressions exports had played a minor role in reviving the economy, but on this occasion they led the way.

Even before the war America was a major participant in international trade and, with Germany, was mounting a vigorous challenge to British commercial supremacy. US industry played a leading role in this export drive. In

1913, for the first time, overseas sales of manufactured goods were greater by value than other groups of exports, including farm products. War demand soon placed enormous pressure on the manufacturing sector. High profits were assured if the goods could be made and shipped overseas.

Table 3.2 US exports, 1914–21

		Value of exports $m			Index of finished manufacturing exports (1913 = 100)	
	Total	UK	France	Germany	Value	Quantity
1914	2365	594	160	345	94.3	86.0
1915	2769	912	369	29	100.9	163.6
1916	5483	1887	861	2	130.6	252.0
1917	6234	2009	941	–	150.4	225.0
1918	6149	2061	931	–	169.7	153.4
1919	7920	2279	893	93	174.4	179.1
1920	8228	1825	676	311	197.7	202.2
1921	4485	942	225	372	163.3	125.6

Source: *Historical Statistics*, *op. cit.*, Cols 1–4 Series U317, 325, 326, 327; Cols 5–6 Series U235, 236.

Table 3.2 shows the effect of the Great War on American exports. The total value of overseas sales, strongly influenced by rising prices, surged in 1916 and 1917 but was checked in 1918 before moving on to a peak in 1920. Most interesting are the figures for exports to the UK, France and Germany. We can note that before April 1917 the US had become an essential part of the Allied war effort and that Britain and France consumed one-third of US exports measured by value. Exports to Germany, however, were dramatically cut as early as 1915 and sank virtually to zero during the following year. These figures are for all goods at current prices but the composition of total exports was heavily influenced by the sale of finished manufactures and processed foodstuffs, for example, flour, dried and tinned foods. The index of finished manufacturing exports, which is not influenced by inflation, indicates just how rapidly the quantity of exports grew from a depressed base in 1914. Indeed, the quantity index shows that a peak was reached in 1916 from which point there was a decline until 1918 and then a rise to a new, though lower, peak in 1920. Mounting inflation ensured that export values continued to rise until the post-war depression of 1920–21.

The war caused a massive disruption to international trade and as a result Britain, the world's premier maritime nation, could no longer service many of her profitable peacetime markets. Although Europe was the principal market for US exports, trade had been shifting towards Latin America and even parts of Asia in the decade before 1914. The war greatly accelerated this movement. Once British exporters were unable to satisfy their customers, the opportunity for sales in a virtually competition-free zone beckoned. However, business was frustrated in its early attempts to exploit new export opportunities because of a serious shortage of shipping. The US merchant fleet was not only small, it had been in decline for some time. Lack of shipping space was such a cause for concern that, in 1916, Congress passed the Shipping Act. This legislation established a Shipping Board, which was empowered to own and to run a merchant fleet, and an Emergency Fleet Corporation which both purchased and built commercial vessels.[16]

The growth of the US merchant fleet was one of the success stories of the war. The gross tonnage of vessels built rose from 251,700 in 1914 to 1,080,437 in 1918 and on to 3,475,872 in 1920. Of particular interest was the substantial progress in shipbuilding which took place on the Pacific coast. In 1914 the gross tonnage produced in this region was a paltry 36,000, a figure which had risen to 518,000 in 1918 and on to 1,363,503 by 1920.[17] The massive rise in output from west coast shipyards provided many new manufacturing jobs and America emerged from the war as the world's leading shipbuilding nation.[18]

Favourable trading conditions enabled the US to increase the balance-of-payments surplus which was comfortably evident before 1914. Indeed, Washington was especially anxious that the trading advantages gained during the war should not be lost in peace. A vigorous nationalistic commercial policy ensured that the US was favourably placed to expand exports during the 1920s.[19] This decade saw a significant increase in the overseas sales of manufactured goods, led by machinery and automobiles, at a time when there was a decline in agricultural exports.[20]

War also stimulated the growth of import substitutes when essential goods were no longer available from overseas. Before 1914 Germany had manufactured more than 75 per cent of the world's supply of coal-tar-derived dyes. Artificial dyes were vital to the explosives industry and rapidly rising Allied demands led to sharp price increases which provided the incentive for the speedy development of an American-based industry. This increasingly vital sector was given the boost of protective tariff in 1916 and was further assisted by the confiscation of German patents which in peacetime had been a significant barrier to domestic growth.[21] The artificial dyestuffs industry was firmly established in 1917 and its fortune was assured.

Often a shortage of imported goods was overcome by successful experimentation with native materials. Thus, American clay replaced German clay in the linings of crucibles and furnaces. An artificial abrasive, vital for grinding optical lenses, was manufactured at Niagara Falls and replaced the natural product which had previously been imported from Greece.[22] In the battle to produce import substitutes the role of the scientist was especially important. Many large corporations had created research laboratories before 1914 and had an impressive record in their use of highly trained experts. These changes, whether they were new markets won overseas or new products manufactured at home, were not temporary. They were an important part of the strong industrial base on which 1920s expansion was built.

THE WARTIME LABOUR FORCE

American manufacturing industry had to cope with many difficulties as it responded to rapidly growing, war-oriented demands. Among the most pressing was an inadequate supply of workers. Table 3.3 confirms the statistical evidence presented elsewhere, that the early stages of the European war did not stimulate the manufacturing industry. Not only was there no rise in the number of manufacturing employees during 1915, the annual average wage in this sector actually declined. Moreover unemployment, already high in 1914, rose to 8.5 per cent of the labour force in 1915. From that point, however, there was a dramatic change. By 1918 the manufacturing industry had recruited an additional 1,957,000 workers over 1915 levels. By 1919–20

Table 3.3 United States: manufacturing sector

Year	Employees (thousands)	Annual earnings: full-time employees		Consumer price index 1914 = 100
		Money wage ($)	Real wage ($)	
1914	8,210	696	696	100.0
1915	8,210	661	660	100.1
1916	9,629	751	691	108.7
1917	9,872	883	691	127.7
1918	10,167	1,107	740	150.0
1919	10,702	1,293	750	172.5
1920	10,702	1,532	767	199.7
1921	8,262	1,346	756	178.1
1929	10,702	1,543	903	170.9

Source: Stanley Lebergott, *Manpower in Economic Growth: the American Record since 1800*, New York, 1964, pp. 514, 516, 525, 526.

that figure had swollen to an extra 2,492,000 hands. The manufacturing employment levels reached by 1918 would be quite remarkable even if the federal government had not also been a major labour recruiter during 1917 and 1918.

Once America entered the war its minuscule military presence had to be increased. There were fewer than 180,000 men in the armed forces in 1916 but the draft, introduced during the following year, added a further 2,820,000. In addition about 2 million men volunteered for service. As a result, a considerable number of young and healthy men were removed from the civilian labour force. Moreover, the federal government boosted its inadequate bureaucracy by hiring an extra 460,000 civilian employees. America's involvement in the Great War had a sudden and dramatic effect upon the labour supply, which required workers, managers and government to introduce new measures to ensure that factory output was maintained.

All parts of manufacturing did not experience equal pressure. The food sector, rubber products, chemicals, petroleum refining, iron and steel, machine making and transport equipment, especially automobiles and shipbuilding, led the way.[23] Firms within these groups enjoyed huge profits and, in general, it was the larger concerns that experienced the most marked growth. Indeed, the numbers of self-employed in manufacturing actually declined from 505,000 in 1914 to 489,000 in 1918.[24] War always favours the big industrial battalions in the fight for increasingly expensive labour and raw materials. Major contracts are won by the factory, not the workshop.

During a period of rapidly increasing demand for workers the labour force can display remarkable flexibility. First, the unemployed are absorbed and then the employed can be persuaded to increase their working hours. Intense pressure leads to the implementation of two or even three shifts which can keep plant in operation for 24 hours. However, the use of multiple shifts is not without cost as serious organizational difficulties have to be overcome to ensure that additional output is not bought at the expense of declining productivity.

Eventually jobs will be offered to those who are not normally part of the workforce. The retired and those with disabilities, who would in times of normality have been judged unemployable, find their way onto the payroll. Women, boys and girls are hired to do jobs normally done by men, sometimes even skilled men, though this often requires an investment in new machinery and carefully planned changes in factory layout.

High wages enticed married women, who had previously chosen to stay in the home, to move to the factory, and also encouraged part-time workers to become full-time. Those industries with high hourly rates of pay and long hours attracted workers in spite of the fact that migration often resulted in major housing and other social problems. Rates of pay, conditions on the job, clear information to prospective employees, together with an ability to get the most out of those without previous factory experience were among the factors which governed the attraction and the retention of labour.

Table 3.3 charts the growth in annual average earnings for the manufacturing sector. From a low point in 1915 wages began a steep rise which did not reach a peak until 1920 as employers sought to attract workers. This pattern of wage increases, and the growth in the number of manufacturing wage-earners, illustrates not only the impact of war but also the vigour of the post-war boom. Unfortunately, inflation, first evident in 1916, became a major problem. Table 3.3 shows that consumer prices which rose by 50 per cent between 1915 and 1918 had doubled by 1920. Indeed, post-war inflation was more rapid than price increases during the war.

Inflation seriously eroded the purchasing power of wages and as a result the growth in real wages was much more modest than levels of take-home pay would suggest. Some workers may have suffered from a money illusion. In other words, although they were aware of inflation as a mounting problem, they did not appreciate the extent to which price rises had reduced the value of their earnings. Their reaction was less strident than others who strove vigorously, sometimes assisted by trade unions, to increase money wages in the hope that such action, if successful, would halt or even reverse real income decline.

Although it is clear that the real monetary gains to the average manufacturing employee were modest, it should be borne in mind that some workers fared better than others. Munitions workers, for example, achieved higher rates of pay than the average. There were also other advantages which were more widely spread. The war prevented the seasonal lay-offs and the unemployment which normally accompanied business recessions. Both had been a regular feature of pre-war industrial life . The war ensured that overtime was plentiful and some families benefited greatly from the presence of more than one highly-paid wage earner. Thousands of new jobs were created in manufacturing and were eagerly seized by men and women fleeing from insecure, low-pay jobs in both urban and rural America.

Before 1914 manufacturing employers had been able to hire workers on very favourable terms. There was a constant supply of immediately employable, native-born labour, much of it migrating from rural areas. This was augmented by a flexible supply of low-wage and largely unskilled labour from Europe. When job opportunities increased in the New World, more Europeans were enticed to make the trans-Atlantic journey. When economic expansion slackened, many immigrants returned to their homeland, thus reducing the numbers of unemployed. Natural population growth was sufficient to guarantee a growing labour force, but the above-average growth in the decade before 1914 was mainly caused by immigration.[25] The war dealt a severe blow to the operation of the trans-Atlantic economy and in doing so presented employers with serious problems.

Immigration was one of the war's first casualties. Between 1905 and 1914 annual average immigration from Europe was just over 900,000 persons. In 1915 less than 200,000 arrived and numbers steadily declined until 1918 when just over 31,000 were admitted. At a time when the demand for labour was reaching unprecedented heights, one of the main sources of supply for the manufacturing sector was cut off. Before 1914 employers had argued with groups who wanted to restrict immigration that the free flow of labour from Europe was essential for US business prosperity. Some of the industries most affected by rising war-related demand, for example, steel production, meat packing and automobiles, were major employers of immigrants. How would employers respond to this labour crisis? How would factory operatives exploit their newly acquired power?

Manufacturers eased part of their labour worries by turning to the South, the nation's poorest region. Here wage differentials with the rest of the country were marked even when confined to comparable occupations. For example, an unskilled foundry worker in Alabama earned $2.50 for a 10-hour day, while his Illinois counterpart earned $4.25 for a 9-hour day.[26] The difference between the Southern rural wages and those employed as industrial workers elsewhere was even greater. As the South was the least urbanized part of the US, Northern employers had, in wage rates, an attractive bait. Both whites and blacks had been leaving the South for decades, but with the advent of war this trickle became a flood.

Between 1915 and 1920 approximately 1 million Southerners, of whom about half were black, left for more highly-paid jobs elsewhere.[27] Whites moved to a variety of locations; some to small or medium-sized towns, others to major cities. African Americans, for whom this Great Migration was a watershed, migrated almost exclusively to large conurbations. Chicago, Detroit, New York and Philadelphia all experienced significant increases in their black population. Most of the jobs available were dirty, dangerous, unpleasant and physically demanding. Indeed, they were the very tasks which had been monopolized by recent immigrants. The Chicago packing houses, for example, employed 67 blacks in 1910, but these numbers had swollen to 3,000 in 1920.[28] The Southern steel mills had a long history of employing black workers, but now Northern firms were willing to hire non-whites other than as strike breakers.[29] In Indiana, the Quarry Works had employed 189 black workers in 1915 but hired 1,295 in 1918.[30] African Americans were also able to secure jobs in the automobile industry and in shipbuilding.[31]

For Southern blacks the pull of the North extended beyond the prospect of high money wages. The racial tension in the South, where Jim Crow laws were enforced by beatings or even lynching, was becoming more oppressive.

Northern cities, even with segregated housing and the violent race riots such as those that rocked Philadelphia and East St Louis in 1917, appeared to offer greater opportunities than could ever be grasped in Dixie. Encouraging letters from family and friends who had made the journey combined with highly favourable reports in the black press, especially in the *Chicago Defender*, helped to create an enthusiasm for moving. Even the revival of cotton prices, which temporarily lifted the crop from its boll-weevil-induced misery, could not stem the flow.

Employers were attracted to black labour not just because it was cheap and they were desperate to recruit. Unlike European immigrants these workers were American-born and could understand the English language. Moreover, American manufacturing industry was used to absorbing labour which had no previous factory or foundry experience. There was, of course, a risk of serious racial tension if white hostility was pronounced, but if the most extreme intolerance could be avoided, a racially mixed workforce had advantages. To a management becoming more apprehensive about the spread of trade unions, the prospect of some shop-floor division rather than solidarity was welcome. In 1915, many employers used labour agents to advertise the opportunities which were now available in the North. However, once the Great Migration gathered momentum, agents were no longer necessary.

Women also played a key role in the war economy. Of the 9.4 million war workers, 2.25 million were female and of these 1.25 million were employed in the manufacturing sector.[32] Women moved from traditional employment into iron and steel, metal working, electrical machinery manufacture, optical goods and into munitions, the latter being especially important. The ability of management to break down complex jobs into simple repetitive tasks and the introduction of special-purpose machinery enabled the unskilled, male or female, to perform jobs previously the preserve of the skilled worker. Women workers were capable, available and were paid at half the male rate. They operated sophisticated machinery such as drills, turret lathes and grinders, acquired new skills and adapted to the discipline of factory work.[33] Black women at last found that industrial work which had been previously closed to them was available.

For a while women enjoyed higher pay than they would have received in domestic service or as shop assistants. To earn it they endured long hours and arduous conditions. However, as Alice Kessler-Harris points out, this manufacturing employment shift was temporary. In industries such as tobacco manufacture and food processing, where job opportunities had been expanding for women before 1914, we note a rise in employment during the war but then a decline to a level that would have prevailed if the war had not occurred. In industries such as chemicals and electrical goods where female jobs had been declining before 1914, the war provided a stimulus, but after

1918 pre-war trends continued.[34] War helped the fight for female suffrage, but it did not result in a permanent occupational shift to the manufacturing industry.

Paradoxically the tight labour market enabled workers to negotiate a substantial reduction in the working week. Between 1914 and 1919 the average full-time hours of work of factory employees declined substantially, from just over 55 to 50 hours per week. For most workers this did not mean a reduction in hours worked; it did mean more overtime. There was, it should be noted, great diversity in the manufacturing sector. The decline in the length of the working week in iron and steel, for example, where the 12-hour shift was still common, was much less than for other industries. There was also a marked regional variation. By 1919 workers in the North-east region had a full-time working week of 49.6 hours, whereas in the East South Central region the average was 55.3 hours.[35]

The war stimulated trade union membership. Workers had successfully unionized before 1914 and the American Federation of Labor (AFL), a loose association of unions, had been formed in 1886. The employers, too, had organized themselves and the National Association of Manufacturers (NAM), which vigorously opposed trade unions and collective bargaining, was established in 1903. Total union membership which stood at 2,687,000 in 1914 reached 3,467,00 in 1918 before peaking, two years later, at 5,048,000. About 2.8 million workers, in 1918, belonged to unions affiliated to the AFL.

Union membership in metals, machinery and shipbuilding, a key manufacturing sector, was 226,000 in 1914 and 396,000 in 1918 with all the expansion concentrated in the last two years of this period. However, a dramatic acceleration in membership came after the war and in 1920 this group of industries had 839,000 unionized workers. Although the war acted as a spur to union expansion, the most significant growth came during the post-war boom.[36]

Union organizers were helped by full employment, a confident workforce and by employers who were often prepared to give ground to organized labour. A further advantage was that the federal government, which believed that it was essential to gain the support of organized labour once the possibility of US participation in the war became more likely, guaranteed workers rights to unionize. Sam Gompers, President of the AFL, was co-opted on to the Advisory Commission of the Council of National Defense thus achieving for himself, and the movement that he represented, national respectability. Gompers and other AFL leaders became staunch supporters of the war and denounced other groups who sought to organize workers in support of peace.

The federal government's now close relationship with the AFL did not persuade all workers to abandon the strike weapon. There were often sharp differences of opinion between national officials and those closest to the membership. The number of strikes increased sharply in 1916, then rose to a wartime peak in 1917 when there were 4,450 stoppages. The number of strikes in 1918, at 3,353, was marginally fewer than the 3,789 of 1916.[37] These aggregate figures do present analytical problems. They cannot be broken down so that manufacturing alone can be considered and, furthermore, the number of man-days of work lost through strikes or lock-outs was not recorded.[38] Nevertheless, it is clear that the cause of the vast majority of disputes was a conflict over wages and hours, not union recognition.[39] As inflation began to mount, workers became conscious of the erosion of their real income and struggled to maintain purchasing power. From the government's point of view it was the disruption that strikes and lock-outs caused to key industries that was most vexing. As we shall see later, government intervention sought to assist mediation and, where that failed, to force intransigent strikers back to work.

As the economy overheated, employers realized that their recruitment problems could not be resolved simply by increasing wages, an action which in any case was inevitably met by matching offers in rival plants. Moreover, the difficulties which the hirers of labour faced were wide-ranging. They included labour poaching, absenteeism, and high levels of turnover to which can be added a rising accident rate combined with an alarming increase in worker militancy and trade union membership. For example, the Machinists' Union, which before 1914 was conservative, had become socialist by 1919.[40] The surplus of jobs had shifted the balance of power significantly in favour of the workers and threats of dismissal no longer caused great fear. Indeed, job-searching workers would often accept half a dozen positions in the course of a single day before deciding at which factory to show up on the following morning. Management bemoaned the loss of discipline that the fear of unemployment had previously guaranteed. But managers also realized that positive action on their part was essential if their labour problems were to be contained.

Progressive employers tried to provide a more welcoming environment in which to work, especially for females who, it was thought, faced factory employment with apprehension. If industrial work was considered respectable, more women might become available for training as, for example, machinists. Other employers tried to create a loyal and stable workforce by Americanizing their foreign-born employees.[41] Of greater significance, however, were the attempts made to change the way in which all factory workers were treated rather than to concentrate effort on particular groups. In this context the increasing prominence of personnel departments, which eventually wrested from foremen the control of hiring, firing and promotion, was of great long-term importance.

With the creation of employment or personnel departments labour relations became part of scientific management and trained specialists were hired to implement new theories. Many of the firms which adopted this approach also simplified their wage structures and introduced a range of welfare benefits for their workers which included lunch rooms, medical facilities and leisure programmes. Indeed we can see the birth of a movement which in the 1920s was called 'welfare capitalism' and was embraced by all progressive businesses.

Although it can be argued that the concentration of decision-making on crucial issues such as recruitment, dismissal, job evaluation and promotion in the hands of personnel managers was a crucial step forward in modern management techniques, too much emphasis should not be placed on the role of the war. Labour turnover was a serious problem even before 1914. For example, in 1913 the Ford Motor Company hired 52,445 men in order to maintain a total workforce of 13,632. During that year, 8,490 men were dismissed and 50,448 quit voluntarily.[42]

Henry Ford and his senior managers moved resolutely to combat the problem of labour turnover and also to eradicate the nascent trade unionism which was beginning to disturb other automobile manufacturers. Early in 1914 a new pay structure was introduced: The Five Dollar Day. The wage was a combination of the existing pay supplemented by a profit-sharing scheme and was available for all co-operative and efficient workers. A newly established Sociological Department investigated all workers and initially half were judged to have met the standards required for the new rates of pay. In addition to raising pay, the wage structure was rationalized and centralized and the authority of foremen to hire and fire was restricted. One result was that labour turnover declined dramatically from a high 370 per cent in 1913, to 16 per cent in 1915 before rising to 51 per cent in 1918; the latter figure, however, was inflated by the inclusion of workers who left for the armed forces.[43]

The Ford initiative succeeded in combating absenteeism, but it was a very expensive scheme and therefore could not be widely adopted. It should be noted that the Company did not rely solely on very high rates of pay. Changes in pay structure, in the role of the foreman and the creation of a Sociological Department, were seen as vital parts of an integrated package. Henry Ford moved to combat high levels of labour turnover at an early stage, but other employees did not begin to address the issue systematically until war pressure made managerial interest unavoidable.

The role of war, therefore, was to encourage business to think seriously about a range of labour problems which many had previously ignored. By 1918 significant progress had been made in the development of personnel management on which business was to build so effectively during the 1920s. As early as 1915 professional managers had replaced speculators and financiers in top management positions, with the war acting as an accelerator in the creation of centrally controlled bureaucratic businesses. Scientific management and personnel work were perceived to be an effective means of coping with pressures on resources.[44] However, relatively few companies had actually created personnel departments by 1918 and not all of those departments were models of professional excellence. The management of human resources was still in its infancy.[45]

THE ECONOMY AND THE GOVERNMENT

When Woodrow Wilson was elected President in 1912 he was a firm believer in anti-trust legislation. Indeed, during his campaign he had aroused the wrath of the steel makers by criticizing the Steel Trust which had effectively limited price competition in the industry. By 1916, however, Wilson's position had changed as war and anti-trust were seen to be increasingly incompatible. The aim of a war economy is to raise output; concern over industrial structure is a low priority. The President and other political leaders recognized the arguments that came from business lobbyists, with export interests to the fore, calling for a relaxation of the anti-trust laws and also extolling the virtues of inter-industry co-operation.[46]

Any attempt to mobilize the economy required the help of business. In contrast to the European powers, the federal government had a small civil service which had never attracted the nation's high flyers.[47] Expertise relating to productive capacity, pricing and the flow of raw materials resided almost exclusively with business executives, the corporations and the trade associations.[48] For example, when it was discovered that neither the Army nor the Navy had detailed information about the national industrial capacity, the Industrial Preparedness Committee, a subdivision of the Naval Consulting Board, undertook a detailed industrial inventory. This exercise, which was privately funded and reliant on voluntary effort, was the brainchild of Howard E. Coffin who had played a major part in standardizing automobile production. Coffin believed that industrialists had a key role – perhaps even *the* key role – to play in organizing the war economy.

By 1916 US involvement in the war was becoming increasingly likely. The Merchant Marine Act created the US Shipping Board which had the power to own, operate and regulate merchant shipping. The Council of National Defense (1916) was charged with co-ordinating industrial resources, though within carefully circumscribed limits. The Council established a National Defense Advisory Commission (NDAC) which created a number of sub-groups where industrial experts, while still retaining their private sector positions, provided the expertise to conduct a survey of the country's industrial base. Industrial executives who donated their time, and even covered their own expenses, were known as 'dollar-a-year' men.

The NDAC lacked the authority to deal effectively with the prioritization of war contracts. The determination of the two branches of the armed services to keep control over their own purchasing contributed to mobilization confusion, which led to the replacement of the NDAC with the War Industries Board (WIB) in 1917. The chaos that prevailed during the severe winter of 1917–18 led to the creation of a revitalized WIB under the chairmanship of Bernard Baruch. Amongst the wide-ranging powers of the new WIB was to conserve existing resources, to organize new sources of supply, to determine priorities and to make purchases for the Allies. The WIB was heavily dependent upon 'dollar-a-year' men and because of a limitation on its powers had to rely heavily on exhortation rather than compulsion.

With Baruch at the helm the WIB made considerable progress although it had neither the staff, the information or the technical expertise to take a really firm grip on the mobilization of the economy.[49] Great reliance had to be placed on business executives and their organizations, especially the Chamber of Commerce and trade associations. This was inevitable given the absence of a powerful federal bureaucracy, although there were dangers that many of the decisions taken owed more to industrial convenience than WIB influence.[50]

A large part, possibly most, of the rise in war manufacturing output was gained by diverting resources from civilian use. This was done much more systematically under the WIB, and the most important industry affected was automobile manufacture. Under an agreement reached with the producers, passenger car output in 1918 was only 45 per cent of the previous year's total. To the relief of the companies, the declaration of peace released them from output restrictions and they could respond to soaring demand.

The stimulation of industrial growth by the encouragement of greater standardization was an important WIB initiative. The Conservation Division of the WIB sought to reduce styles, colours and sizes in the production of a range of goods. Thus, the manufacturers of car tyres reduced the number of styles produced from 287 to 32; the number of types of steel ploughs declined from 312 to 76; the use of tin in silk dresses was eliminated and the variety of models in a wide range of goods ranging from baby carriages, typewriter ribbons, bicycles and coffins was severely curtailed.[51] Many of these war economies were retained after 1918, making the manufacturing industry much more streamlined and cost-effective than before the war.

Washington, now a friend of organized labour, enforced the 8-hour day, recognized trade unions in war contract work and supported collective bargaining. The National War Labor Board was established in 1918 to arbitrate in industrial disputes with a membership divided equally between employers and union representatives.[52] Once the war was over, however, the government's close relationship with trade unions cooled. Aggressive employers, the severe depression of 1920–21 and an unsympathetic Republican administration during the 1920s help to explain why that decade was one of serious decline for organized labour. The optimism that bolstered wartime union leaders was dashed by 1921.

Government intervention was not in place long enough to have a marked effect on the war economy. The short-run impact of controls were not terribly significant but the long-run effects were, especially as many of the agencies established during the war resurfaced during the 1930s. For example, the WIB reappeared in 1933 as the National Recovery Administration; the War Labour Board resurfaced, in 1935, as the National Labor Relations Board. Moreover, many of the key individuals who served in Washington also helped to mobilize the economy during the fight against the Great Depression. The public was convinced that co-operation between business and government was a success during the war and they believed that a peacetime crisis could also be resolved with a similar strategy.

President Wilson had suspended his belief in the competitive system because he realized the necessity of winning the full co-operation of business. Once the war was over, however, he moved quickly to dismantle the bureaucracy that had ensured co-operation between parts of the manufacturing sector, even though there was support for maintaining it in order to ensure an orderly demobilization. Within two weeks of the Armistice the dissolution of the WIB was ordered; other agencies received identical instructions and the 'dollar-a-year' men left Washington for home. The economy embarked on a vigorous inflationary post-war boom until the savage depression of 1920–21.

CONCLUSION

What was the impact of the war on the manufacturing sector? From the end of the Civil War until the onset of the Great Depression the US experienced a massive secular boom in which manufacturing played a major role. Between 1870 and 1929 the US share of world manufacturing output rose impressively from 23 per cent to 42 per cent. At the same time Britain experienced a decline from 32 per cent to 9 per cent.[53] The First World War has to be seen in the context of half a century of rapid industrial growth.

The expansion of output from America's factories between 1914 and 1919 was a seemingly impressive 26.1 per cent. However, this was not as great as the figure recorded for 1904–9, 30.2 per cent, and not much greater than the 22.2 per cent growth which occurred between 1899 and 1904.[54] The growth of manufacturing output during the war was not exceptional and was clearly in line with peacetime performance. Table 3.1 shows quite clearly that between 1916 and 1918 the volume of manufacturing output changed very little in spite of all the pressures to increase it. However, while output remained on a plateau the manufacturing labour force increased by approximately 538,000 (Table 3.3). Indeed for the period 1914–19 the average number of factory workers rose by 29.3 per cent compared with a rise of 21 per cent for 1904–9. There was clearly a slippage in labour productivity during the war as industry struggled to integrate many new workers into the factory system.

War did encourage new investment in selected parts of manufacturing. Table 3.4 shows some striking examples with the figures expressed in constant 1929 dollars to eradicate the effects of inflation. Most noticeable was the expansion in the motor vehicle industry and in activities closely associated with it: petroleum refining and tyre production. The figure for food manufacture is more impressive if allowance is made for a decline of $858,000 (1929 dollars) in the alcoholic drinks industry. The industries recorded here were in a strong position to respond to buoyant peacetime demand and did so dramatically during the post-war decade. Consumer durables, headed by the automobile, were at the very core of the 1920s boom. The increase in output from factories producing electrical machinery was no less impressive.[55] War demands provided a valuable stimulus for industries whose investment could easily be turned to satisfying civilian markets.

Table 3.4 Capital in manufacturing industries in 1929 dollars ($ million)

	1914	1919
Total manufacturing capital	36,737	46,094
Tyres and tubes	265	704
Petroleum refining	552	1,380
Iron and steel	3,911	5,292
Electrical machinery and equipment	718	1,146
Motor vehicles	991	2,480
Food and allied products	6,515	7,593

Source: *Historical Statistics*, *op. cit.*, Series P. 123, 126, 147, 158, 161, 168, 173.

Big business had a good war. The public suspicion of the corporations had moderated by 1918 as the business community was believed to have played an essential role in the effort for victory. Moreover, the anti-trust philosophy of the Wilson administration had run out of energy. The corporate culture was now accepted by the general public, who saw more advantages than disadvantages from the dominance of the corporations.[56] Many 'dollar-a-year' men left Washington with a feeling that co-operation between business and government had worked. Politicians, executives and other decision-makers not only accepted the co-operation that trade associations brought but even welcomed them as a vital part of the model that would underpin the new capitalism of the 1920s.

The manufacturing labour force expanded during the war and did not contract after the Armistice. Indeed, the factory workforce was the same size in 1929 as it had been a decade earlier, although there was a change in composition as some occupations declined and others recruited. During this decade factory output increased by 60 per cent, so that productivity growth was impressive. The war played a part here in encouraging investment, in making scientific management more popular and by persuading firms to modernize their employment practices by setting up personnel departments. The emphasis on standardization and the avoidance of waste which was impressed on management in 1918 remained part of strategic thinking once the war was over.

However, the war must be seen as a stimulating rather than an innovative force. A near contemporary expressed the view that the war developed no new basic process. Although management was encouraged to look more closely at mass production during the period of intense activity, the mechanical processes that enabled the 1920s boom to occur were in place before the war.[57] Military demands were placed on an economy that was already highly productive and technologically advanced.

In the short-term the influence of the war was a distorting one. Extra production of war-related output was gained by shifting resources out of relatively low priority activities. However, the war did encourage some initial redistribution of manufacturing activity. For example, the South experienced an increase in shipbuilding, cigarette manufacture and cotton textile production. In addition, government subsidies encouraged the establishment of a wood chemical industry which continued after the war. The conversion of large powder plants which utilized cellulose to rayon production was also very beneficial to this under-industrialized region after 1918.[58] If the WIB had been given more authority, however, the dispersion of manufacturing activities away from the overcrowded North-east towards the South and the Pacific region would have been even more pronounced.

Even without the war the US manufacturing sector would have expanded and done so in a more orderly manner, especially in relation to prices. In the longer term the US benefited from an expanded merchant fleet and from newly acquired export markets. The war, however, was sufficiently destabilizing to generate a major post-war depression in 1920–21. The effects of war may also have played a significant role in the onset of the Great Depression in 1929. From the first of these shocks the manufacturing sector made a quick and spectacular revival. The second ensured that large parts of the factory system did not experience full recovery until the Second World War.

NOTES AND REFERENCES

1. W.E. Leuchtenberg, *Perils of Prosperity*, Chicago, 1958, p. 9.
2. A.D. Chandler, *The Visible Hand. The Managerial Revolution in American Business*, London, 1977, pp. 484–91; E.W. Hawley, *The Great War and a Search for a Modern Order. A History of the American People and their Institutions, 1917–1933*, New York, 1979, pp. 5–8.
3. G. Kolko, *The Triumph of Conservatism: A Reinterpretation of American History, 1910–1916*, New York, 1963.
4. M.A. Eisner, *The State in the American Political Economy*, New Jersey, 1996, pp. 106–22.
5. *Abstract of the Census of Manufactures*, 1914, Department of Commerce, Washington DC, 1923, Table 205.
6. *Historical Statistics of the United States, Colonial Times to 1970*, Bureau of the Census, Washington DC, 1975.
7. S. Fabricant, *Employment in Manufacturing, 1899–1939*, NBER, New York, 1943, p. 14.
8. *Historical Statistics*, op. cit., Series c 125, 129.
9. *Abstract Census of Manufactures*, 1919, op. cit., Tables 10, 211.
10. *Abstract Census of Manufactures*, 1919, op. cit., Tables 198.
11. *Abstract Census of Manufactures*, 1919, op. cit., Table 10.
12. *Abstract Census of Manufactures*, 1919, op. cit., Table 187.
13. *Abstract Census of Manufactures*, 1919 op. cit., Tables 187, 188.
14. S. Meyer III, *The Five Dollar Day. Labor, Management and Social Control in the Ford Motor Company 1908–1921*, Albany, New York, 1981, pp. 11–23, 47–55; D. Hounshell, *From the American System to Mass Production, 1800–1932*, Baltimore and London, 1984, pp. 217–51.
15. Hounshell, op. cit., pp. 249–53.
16. D.M. Kennedy, *Over Here. The First World War and American Society*, Oxford, 1980, pp. 301–11.
17. Historical Statistics, op. cit., Series Q459–462.
18. G. Hardach, *The First World War 1914–18*, Harmondsworth Penguin, Middlesex, 1977, pp. 44–6.
19. Kennedy, op. cit.
20. H.B. Lary, *The United States in the World Economy*, Washington DC, US Department of Commerce, 1943, pp. 59–60.
21. G.B. Clarkson, *Industrial America in the World War. The Strategy Behind the Line 1917–1918*, Boston, 1924, pp. 412–14.
22. Clarkson op. cit., pp. 417–18.
23. S. Fabricant, *Employment in Manufacturing, 1899–1939*, NBER, New York, 1943, pp. 211–12.
24. S. Lebergott, op. cit., p. 516.
25. M.R. Darby, *Labor Force, Employment and Productivity in Historical Perspective*, Institute of Industrial Relations, University of California, LA, 1984, p. 11.
26. C. Marks, *Farewell – We're Good and Gone. The Great Black Migration*, Bloomington, 1989, p. 113; J. Jones, *The Dispossessed. America's Underclass from the Civil War to the Present*, New York, 1992, pp. 88, 146–7, 213.
27. J.M. Clark, *The Costs of the World War to the American People*, New York, 1931, p. 257; A. Meier and E. Rudwick, *From Plantation to Ghetto*, New York, 1976, p. 235.
28. Marks, op. cit., p. 121.
29. H.R. Northrup, *Organized Labor and the Negro*, New York, 1944, p. 174.
30. D. Brody, *Steelworkers in America. The Non Union Era*, New York, 1960, p. 186.
31. Northrup, op. cit., pp. 186–7, 210–212.
32. N.A. Wynn, *From Progressivism to Prosperity. World War I and American Society*, New York and London, 1986, pp. 139–40.
33. M.W. Greenwald, *Women, War and Work. The Impact of World War I on Women Workers in the United States*, London, 1980, pp. 6–8, 15–22.

34. A. Kessler-Harris, *Out to Work. A History of Wage–earning Women in the United States*, Oxford, 1982, pp. 219–24.
35. L. Wolman, *Hours of Work in American Industry*, NBER, Bulletin 71, 27 November 1938, New York, p. 1.
36. *Historical Statistics of the United States*, op. cit., Series D941, 944, 952, 955.
37. *Historical Statistics of the United States*, op. cit., Series 977–79.
38. F. Peterson, *Strikes in the United States 1880–1936*, Washington DC, Bureau Labor Statistics, Bull No. 651 N.D., pp. 35–40.
39. P.K.L. Edwards, *Strikes in the United States 1881–1974*, Oxford, 1981, p. 37.
40. D. Montgomery, *Workers' Control in America*, Cambridge, 1979, p. 99.
41. D. Nelson, *Managers and Workers. Origins of the Twentieth Century Factory System in the United States, 1880–1920*, 1995, 2nd edn, pp. 157–9.
42. J. Shaw Peterson, 'AutoWorkers and their Work, 1900–1933', *Labor History*, **22** 1981, p. 229.
43. Meyer, op. cit. pp. 100–111, 115–21, 162.
44. D. Nelson, *Frederick W. Taylor and the Rise of Scientific Management*, London, 1980, p. 201.
45. S.M. Jacoby, *Employing Bureaucracy, Managers, Unions and the Transformation of Work in American Industry, 1900–1945*, New York, 1985, p. 147; Nelson, op. cit., p. 167.
46. T. Freyer, *Regulating Big Business. Antitrust in Great Britain and America 1880–1990*, Cambridge, 1992.
47. T.C. Cochran, *Challenges to American Values. Society, Business and Religion*, Oxford, 1985, pp. 60–78.
48. P.A.C. Koistinen, 'The "Industrial–Military Complex" in Historical Perspective: World War I', *Business History Review*, **XLI**, 4, 1967, p. 380.
49. Eisner, op. cit., p. 132.
50. R.D. Cuff, *The War Industries Board. Business Government Relations during World War I*, Baltimore and London, 1973, p. 269; Eisener, ibid., p. 133.
51. B.M. Baruch, *American Industry in the War. A Report of the War Industries Board*, New York, 1941, pp. 64–7. This volume contains a lengthy account of the WIB Commodity Sections; Clarkson, op. cit., pp. 219–25.
52. G. Soule, *Prosperity Decade. From War to Depression: 1917–1929*, London, 1947, pp. 66–73.
53. F. Hilgert, *Industrialisation and Foreign Trade*, League of Nations, 1945, p. 11.
54. E.E. Day and T. Woodlief, *The Growth of Manufacturers 1899–1923*, Dept of Commerce, Census Monographs VIII, Washington DC, 1928, pp. 34–7.
55. P. Fearon, *War Prosperity and Depression. The US Economy, 1917–45*, Deddington, Oxford, 1987, pp. 53–5.
56. L. Galambos, *The Public Image of Big Business in America, 1880–1940*, London, 1975, pp. 186–7.
57. D.S. Kimball, 'Industry' in *Recent Economic Changes in the United States*, New York, 1929, Vol. 1, pp. 80–81.
58. G.B. Tindall, *The Emergence of the New South 1913–1945*, Baton Rouge, 1967, pp. 53–60.

4. Impact of the First World War on the Lancashire cotton industry and its workers

Alan Fowler

The British economy as it developed over the course of the nineteenth century was still largely in place at the outbreak of the war in 1914. Britain's industrial structure was dominated by the basic industries of cotton, coal, iron and steel, shipbuilding and heavy engineering. The industries which were to come to dominate the twentieth century, electrical, chemical, car, were considerably less important in Britain than in other major economic powers (Kirby, 1981). There has been debate among economic historians about the success or failure of the British economy before 1914. The key issues in this debate have centred on the question of the over-commitment of the British economy to the staple industries, the failure to invest in new technology in those industries, the failure to develop new industries, the role of the entrepreneur in the British economy, and the reliance on free trade and on Empire. All this is set against a background of economic liberalism which espoused a minimal role for the state (Pollard, 1994). Economic historians have attempted to explain the relative decline of the British economy in the twentieth century by seeking the genesis of that decline. The debate has centred on whether or not the British economy was in decline before 1914 and whether the economic dislocation of the war was the catalyst for change. The cotton industry provides a major case study for this debate. Cotton had been the key industry of the British industrial revolution and in 1914 still remained the premier export industry of the British economy.

IMPACT OF THE WAR ON THE COTTON INDUSTRY

Prior to 1914 Lancashire had seen over a century of economic progress, or so it seemed to contemporaries. After 1920 the history of the industry was largely one of economic decline and depression with the industry's eventual demise in the 1970s. The century prior to 1914 in reality had not been entirely one of uninterrupted economic progress (Farnie, 1979). There had been several deep depressions during the nineteenth century. Still part of the popular folk memory in 1914 were the events of the cotton famine of the 1860s. It was the Edwardian expansion of the industry that left contemporaries on the eve of the Great War feeling so self-confident:

> ... Lancashire was arrogant, Lancashire talked cotton, thought cotton, dreamed cotton. To the typical cotton man the Manchester Royal Exchange, the Liverpool Cotton Exchange and Paradise – if anyone were so foolish as to bring Paradise into the connection – ranked in that order (Bowker, 1928, p. 19).

The Lancashire cotton trade was of a highly specialized nature. The industry was horizontally rather than vertically organized and could be described as a series of linked industries. The process started in Liverpool where the raw cotton merchants were based. The preparatory trades, carding and combing, worked on the raw cotton but were located within the spinning mills. Spinning and weaving were separate industries based in south and north Lancashire. The finishing trades were based in south Lancashire and east Cheshire. The final product went to the Manchester merchants who dominated the Manchester Royal Exchange and the Chamber of Commerce. The specialization went even further, in fact, with the spinning town of Oldham concentrating on production of coarse yarn, while in Bolton fine yarn was produced. There was a similar division in weaving where coarse cloth was produced in Blackburn, medium cloth in Burnley and the finer products in Nelson. The towns even varied in the type of raw cotton they used. Oldham used American cotton, while Bolton used the finer Egyptian variety. The labour force within the various trades was also highly differentiated. While some of the preparatory processes in cotton involved both a male and female labour force, the spinners were aristocrats of labour and were exclusively male. In weaving both men and women were employed and uniquely for the period received equal rates of pay (Farnie, 1979; Tyson, 1968; Board of Trade, 1918).

There were three important developments during the period of the war itself which determined subsequent events within the cotton industry. The initial impact of the war was economic dislocation resulting in high levels of unemployment and short-time working for the operatives. In August 1914 it appeared as though the whole trade would have to stop since at one point 75 per cent of mills were closed (Bolton Spinners, 1914). The government was forced to act to save the industry by, on the one hand, guaranteeing payments for contracts and thus saving many firms from bankruptcy and also offering relief to displaced operatives as part of its national programme to relieve those affected by the outbreak of hostilities. The Lancashire cotton trade unions all had unemployment pay funds, and the government assisted the unions in providing for members thrown out of work (Bolton Spinners, 1914; Chapman and Kemp, 1915).

From 1915 onwards the industry suffered a shortage of labour as the demand for recruits to the army and eventually conscription, introduced in 1916, took its toll of mill workers. The situation was especially acute in spinning because of a shortage of piecers. Piecers assisted the spinner in his task, and new entrants to the industry would begin their working lives as little piecers, moving on to become big piecers and hoping for an eventual place as a spinner. It was the young men employed as piecers who were initially attracted and then drafted into the army, causing an acute labour shortage. Traditionally women had never worked in this sector of the industry and it was only with reluctance that the spinners accepted women into the spinning room at the behest of the government (Bolton Spinners, 1915; Foulger, 1988). The industry was also faced with other problems as a direct result of the war. Dyestuffs became difficult to obtain since Germany had been a major supplier of dyes before the war. Shipping routes were dislocated because of the hostilities affecting both the importation of raw cotton and the export of finished goods (Bolton Spinners, 1915).

From 1917 a new situation emerged with the shortage of raw cotton imports threatening a repeat of the cotton famine of the 1860s when the American Civil War had interrupted the supply. The shortage of raw cotton was a direct result of the German U-boat campaign which disrupted shipping. This in turn led to escalating costs of raw cotton, and it seemed the price of raw cotton would spiral out of control. The government was forced to intervene by temporarily closing the Liverpool Futures Market in raw cotton and setting up a Cotton Control Board. This Board was to dominate events in the industry until the end of the war (Bolton Spinners, 1917; Henderson, 1922).

Profits within the industry were maintained during most of the war and in fact rose dramatically in 1918 to the surprise of contemporaries. The effect of the shortage was to force up prices and enhance profits. The operatives, however, did not fare so well, as unemployment, short-time working and the failure of wages to keep pace with wartime inflation reduced standards of living.

LANCASHIRE'S MARKETS: THE WAR AND ITS AFTERMATH

Estimates suggest that in 1913 about 80 per cent of the cotton fabrics manufactured in the United Kingdom were for shipment abroad, representing nearly a quarter of Britain's exports by value. A 1918 Report commented:

> The British cotton industry is the largest of the worlds textile industries. The immense volume of its output, the capital invested, the number of operatives employed and the inherent strength of its position in international trade all combined to place it in the first rank of British industries (Board of Trade, 1918, p. 45).

Lancashire's key market was India, which took approximately 40 per cent of her exports. The second most important export markets were Latin America and China, each representing around 10 per cent of total exports. In Latin America exports were largely dependent on peasant consumers. Because of the extreme poverty of the peasantry, the Chinese market was purely an urban one. Lancashire also exported to Europe and the Dominions where the markets were mainly urban (Board of Trade, 1918).

India was crucial to Lancashire before 1914 but was also an important factor in the British economy. In 1913 India took 16 per cent of all British exports, the largest component of which was textiles. Britain was the largest export market for Indian raw materials. However, the majority of Indian exports went to countries outside the Empire, in Europe and America. It was precisely these countries with which Britain had a trade deficit. Thus, India's trade surplus with the rest of the world enabled Britain to meet its debts in Europe and America. India's deficit with Britain enabled Britain to manage its international trade and play a vital role in the international economy based as it was on the gold standard and free trade. Therefore, the balance of trade between Britain and India, in which Britain was the beneficiary, was crucial in maintaining its central role within the international economy. Furthermore, Britain could not have sustained this situation without Lancashire's exports to India (Chatterji, 1992).

The prosperity of the Indian peasantry was essential to Lancashire's success. However, the incomes of the Indian peasantry fluctuated considerably, dependent like all peasant incomes on crop prices often determined by the weather. Representing approximately 40 per cent of the total exports of Lancashire, this volatile market could determine the fortunes of the whole industry and by implication have repercussions on the British economy (Board of Trade, 1918).

The success of the cotton industry was dependent on access to Indian markets on terms similar to those of the expanding indigenous industry. In the 1890s an import duty on Lancashire cotton into India had been introduced by the Liberal Government. Lancashire, the home of Liberalism, retaliated by withdrawing support for the Liberals at the 1895 General Election. The incoming Conservative Government introduced an equivalent excise duty on the Indian cotton industry to offset any advantage. So blatant was the measure that it became a *cause célèbre* in India, with the nationalists arguing that Manchester had more influence on Indian policy than the native population.

The war offered India an opportunity to redress what they saw as this great wrong (Chatterji, 1992).

Britain looked to the Empire to support the war effort with both men and munitions and with money. In 1917 the Indian Government offered a gift of £100 million to help Britain fight the war. However, the gift could not be made without the Indian Government raising revenue powers. One of the least unpopular ways to do this was to increase the tariff on imported cotton cloth from Lancashire. What outraged Lancashire was there was to be no equivalent rise in revenue duty on the Indian cotton industry. The settlement of 1896 was being destroyed. Lancashire began a furious lobby of the wartime government. Austen Chamberlain, Secretary of State for India and Lloyd George both received deputations from Lancashire which included the Chamber of Commerce, the main employers' organizations and leading trade unions as well as Lancashire MPs. Chamberlain argued that Lancashire would be little affected by the change as there was virtually no competition between the Lancashire and Indian cotton industries. He argued that India produced cotton cloths under 30 counts, coarse cloths, while Lancashire exported cloths above 20 counts and there was therefore only a small overlap in the products. Chamberlain was aware that Lancashire had little understanding of the politics involved in the revenue changes. He considered that their suggestion of a similar rise in the excise duty on Indian-produced cloth was impractical. Chamberlain stood firm, indicating he would rather resign than implement the policy Lancashire wanted. There can be no doubt about the strength of feeling in Lancashire which correctly recognized that this decision was a historic turning point in which the balance of influence on the Indian government had swung against them. Lancashire carried the battle into the House of Commons where the vast majority of Lancashire MPs were opposed to the government. A motion critical of the government was defeated, but some 40 per cent of MPs voted with the Lancashire malcontents – a significant event in the wartime coalition government. The vote, however, made clear the government's determination to subordinate Lancashire's interest to the more general one of winning the war. In future it would be Bombay rather than Manchester which determined policy with regard to Lancashire's major market (*Cotton Factory Times*, 1917).

In contrast there appears to have been little contemporary comment over Lancashire's decline in the Indian market during these years. By the middle of 1917 exports of cloth to India had fallen to two-thirds of their pre-war figure. Partly pre-war exports had created a surplus of cotton cloth, partly peasant incomes fell due to a poor monsoon season, partly wartime panic affected credit. From the summer of 1917 there was a more serious fall in Lancashire exports to India. The poor monsoon conditions continued, there was a shortage of shipping space and the influenza epidemic in 1918 exacerbated matters. At the same time the adverse terms of trade for agricultural products during the war further reduced peasant incomes. Importantly, the war years had seen some expansion of the Indian industry as well as a rise in imports from Japan. Lancashire's share of imports to India fell from 97 per cent to 77 per cent, while Japan's rose from 1 per cent to 21 per cent (Dupree, 1996; Tomlinson, 1979),

Table 4.1 Indian mill production compared with imports from the United Kingdom and Japan (cloth, thousand yards)

		Imports	
Year	Indian production	United Kingdom	Japan
1913–14	1,164,292	3,104,311	8,901
1919–20	1,639,779	967,127	75,953

Source: Pearse, 1930, p. 191.

Essentially a European phenomenon, the war had stimulated the development of textile industries all over the world. Industrialization in turn had led to the growth of economic nationalism. The impact of protection was something Lancashire had no control over and was to be responsible for the loss of the majority of her former markets in the inter-war years. As well as the growth of the Indian home industry and Japanese competition, China, Brazil and the Balkans all began to develop textile industries. Of all these changes, however, the most significant was the undermining of Lancashire's position in the Indian market.

THE COTTON CONTROL BOARD AND STATE INTERVENTION

Historians have always seen the First World War as a turning point in the history of state intervention in British economy and society. It is generally argued that the war witnessed the end of traditional *laissez-faire* attitudes towards the state. Indeed, so ingrained were these attitudes that Britain was the only participant to rely on raising its armed forces by voluntary means at the outbreak of the war. Despite proclaiming 'business as usual', the government intervened in the economy from the earliest days of the war, but historians have normally seen the rise of Lloyd George as a watershed in government intervention during the war. It was Lloyd George, as Minister of Munitions, who turned on its head the notion of the government as simply another buyer in the market, particularly in the munitions industry. Attention has largely focused on the munitions industry and the labour force required for that industry. The fortunes of the cotton industry which necessitated the importation of raw cotton from either America or Egypt were effectively determined by state control of shipping space. Determining what could be imported led of necessity to government involvement and control in the productive processes of the industry. The cotton industry has received far less attention from historians than other industries, but provides a case study of state intervention of a different character.

The shortage of raw cotton in the summer of 1917 led to the establishment by the Board of Trade of the Cotton Control Board, which has been described as 'unique amongst war controls' (Henderson, 1922, p. 12). Despite its official status the Board was a representative of the industry rather than an organization belonging to Whitehall. The Board, which initially consisted of 12 members largely drawn from the industry, met in Manchester. Four representatives were drawn from employers' organizations, four from the trade unions, two from the merchants of Liverpool and Manchester and two were government nominees, although one of the latter, Sydney Chapman, was a former Professor of Economics at Manchester University. It was chaired by Sir Herbert Dixon, who was the head of the largest employer in the industry, the Fine Spinners' and Doublers' Association (Henderson, 1922).

The Board's initial concern was to tackle the problem of the reduced supply of raw cotton. They therefore devised a scheme whereby firms were only allowed to use a percentage of their spindles and looms. Firms in the spinning industry were allowed to use 60 per cent of their spindles. Firms using American cotton could operate a further 10 per cent of the spindles on payment of a levy. Those using Egyptian cotton could operate at full capacity, but only on payment of a levy for the use of more than 60 per cent of their spindles. This reflected the fact that the German U-boat campaign interrupted the supply of American cotton to Lancashire to a greater extent than the supply of Egyptian cotton. The position was further complicated by the need to use shipping space from America to bring munitions and troops to Europe. Shipping between Egypt and Britain represented a different situation. Troops and munitions had to be shipped to the Middle East and there were no goods other than cotton which needed to be shipped back. The weaving industry was subject to similar regulations to those applied to the Egyptian spinning sector. Of course, some weaving firms would not be able to operate at 100 per cent capacity because the supply of yarn was reduced (Henderson, 1922).

Implementation of the policy led to short-time working and unemployment for the operatives, forcing the Board to consider not only the rationing of raw cotton but also the social consequences of such a policy. The government was already concerned about industrial unrest, general during 1917, and therefore relief of unemployed operatives necessitated the introduction of some system of unemployment pay. The levy paid by employers was used to provide funds for unemployment pay for the operatives, although there was no provision made for those working short-time (Henderson, 1922).

The other crucial decision the Board made was that operatives were not to be permanently unemployed but instead were to be laid off on a temporary basis, in other words there was to be a rota system. Weekly unemployment pay was set at 25/- (£1.25) for men and 15/- (75p) for women, which represented a substantial reduction in income for some workers. The rota system was adopted because of pressure from the trade unions, but according to the Board it discouraged operatives from seeking work in other industries. It is not clear that cotton operatives were easily transferable to other occupations despite a national shortage of labour in the latter part of the war.

The 1918 German spring offensive intensified the crisis for the cotton industry. The government's priority now became one of transporting men and munitions from the USA to Britain. In the circumstances of 1918 cotton was at the bottom of the list when decisions were being made about shipping space. For a period of two months the import of raw cotton was suspended completely. The government was becoming increasingly concerned with effective use of labour, which brought the rota system used by the Cotton Control Board into the spotlight (Henderson, 1922). The Cotton Control Board decided that because of the shortage and stocks of raw cotton were at an all-time low, there would have to be further reductions in production. A new formula was devised whereby firms would have to pay levies on all machinery in use. The operatives' contribution to solving the crisis was in the form of increased short-time working: in the American spinning industry in Oldham the working week was cut to 40 hours. This did not have the force of law but, because the Cotton Control Board was responsible for distribution of raw cotton, they were able to implement the policy (Henderson, 1922).

The tripartite relationship between government, employers and trade unions within the Cotton Control Board came under extreme pressure at this moment of crisis. In response to government pressure the Board decided to end the rota system which provided unemployment allowance funded by the levies for those full-time operatives temporarily laid off. The consequence of the ending of the rota system would have been full-time unemployment for some operatives. Operatives were aware, unlike the government, that moving labour from textiles to industries of shortage was not always easy. An attempt to establish an aircraft factory near Oldham in late 1917 was aborted because of a lack of surplus labour in the area. The decision to end the rota system, therefore, led to a large-scale public protest by the cotton unions. The rota system had been popular in Lancashire because it built on traditions of short-time working in the industry when there was a depression in trade. The system had enabled the burden of unemployment to be shared equally among operatives and had been seen as a fair solution to the problem. The cotton unions lobbied the President of the Board of Trade, Sir Albert Stanley, and the agitation appears to have made the government hesitate. The situation eased in the summer of 1918 as the military threat receded and the government was able to release shipping space, thus increasing the supply of American raw cotton. The Cotton Control Board were able to relax the short-time hours restrictions in American spinning. However, the rota system was still replaced. Reluctantly most of the cotton unions accepted the situation. The exception was the spinners' union who decided to take strike action (Fowler, 1987; Henderson, 1922).

It has been suggested (Singleton, 1994) that the Lancashire cotton industry failed to make the contribution to the war effort between 1914–18 that it could have made. In particular contrast has been drawn between the reduction in the industry's capacity and demand for labour between 1939 and 1945 which enabled resources, especially labour, to be used more effectively for the war effort. To many contemporaries a contraction of the cotton industry between 1914 and 1918 was unthinkable and this view did influence public policy. Hubert Henderson, Secretary to the Cotton Control Board, commented:

> … many other industries might be curtailed … under the stress of war. This might indeed be done deliberately by government … which was done with the building industry which employs … more work people than cotton. But for the work people engaged in the cotton mills of … Lancashire the problem was not so easy. … In what alternative employment was it conceivable that this enormous population, with its peculiar habits, traditions, psychology could have been absorbed? All the munitions factories within reach of the homes of the cotton operatives could not have absorbed more than a small fraction of them. The army had already in its grasp the bulk of men of military age (Henderson, 1922, p. 3).

The cotton industry had a history of state intervention, particularly with regard to hours of work for women and children. However, the Cotton Control Board was the first attempt to control production in the industry. It did its job as a public body, largely staffed by members of the industry, superimposing state control on an industry which remained in private ownership. The Board set out to ensure the continuation of the cotton industry and to provide a 'fair' distribution of resources. It was to provide the model for future forms of state intervention in the twentieth century, was able to draw on both sides of industry and for the most part to contain the conflict between capital and labour in its operations. However one major failing was the continued pretence that the Board had nothing to do with the wage question, when the reality was that its whole operation was central to the issue of wages in the industry.

WAGES AND HOURS

The Lancashire cotton operatives were the first factory proletariat in the world and over a century of industrialization had produced a labour force with a long history of trade unionism and experience of factory legislation. They had been in the forefront of the establishment of building societies, savings clubs, co-operatives as well as trade unions. By the end of the nineteenth century they were one of the most prosperous sections of the British working class. The hours of work of operatives were tightly controlled, formally for women and in reality for men. By 1914 the working week stood at 55.5 hours. However, work still started at 6 o'clock in the morning as it had done at the beginning of the nineteenth century, with a half-hour break for breakfast when many of the women operatives would return home to prepare meals and rouse younger children. At midday there would be an hour's break for dinner. The reduction in the working week had secured the operatives more leisure time on Saturdays where work stopped at noon. The holiday period for operatives had also increased, and by 1914 they enjoyed 12 or 13 days which included a whole week in the summer when towns would stop at different periods for the Wakes holiday. Although the operatives were not paid for holidays, many were able to put aside money in savings clubs for their week's holiday in a seaside boarding house. Blackpool, the world's first seaside town to cater for working-class consumers, had been created for their benefit by 1900 (Walton, 1998).

Contrary to popular notions of high wages, average wages in the industry were low, near the poverty level of 'round about a pound a week' but, because in many cases more than one member of the family worked, this raised family living standards. Women formed a majority of the labour force, but what was particularly unusual about Lancashire was that there was a significant group of married women in the workforce including married women with children. The half-time system of education meant that children aged from 12–14 years old also worked and contributed to family prosperity. The weaving industry was the major employer of women and men and women did the same tasks and were paid on the same wage list. Theoretically men and women received equal pay based on a wage list detailing the piece rates for the production of different cloths. In reality there was some differentiation in tasks or cloths woven and generally men had a higher weekly wage. Overall the effect was to bring the family incomes of many up to the levels of those enjoyed by families of labour aristocrats (Walton, 1987; White, 1978).

Despite its long history, trade unionism within the industry only became effective in the 1880s with the reorganization of the Amalgamated Association of Operative Cotton Spinners, the reform of the Amalgamated Weavers' Association and the founding of the Amalgamated Association of Card, Blow-ing and Ring Room Operatives. The process was completed by the creation of a political pressure group and factory reform organization, The United Textile Factory Workers' Association and the setting-up of a newspaper to cater specifically for cotton operatives, the *Cotton Factory Times* (Clegg, Fox and Thompson, 1964; Turner, 1962).

It was the leaders of these organizations who presented themselves before the Royal Commission of Labour in the 1890s and who impressed Sidney and Beatrice Webb as they pursued their studies of contemporary trade unionism. Their philosophy of trade unionism was straightforward: that trade unions should have a large bank balance when they entered an industrial dispute so that their members could not be starved back to work on employers' terms as they had been earlier in the century. Their officials were products of self-help and technically very able wage calculators, as much of their time was spent calculating their members wages to ensure they had been paid according to the agreed wage list (Webb and Webb, 1901).

The growth of trade unionism had resulted in one of the most advanced systems of collective bargaining in Britain. The two main employers' organizations were the Federation of Master Cotton Spinners' Association and the Cotton Spinners' and Manufacturers' Association, the former representing employers engaged in spinning and the latter in weaving. Employer organization at a county- or industry-wide level had followed the growth of trade union organization rather than preceded it, which somewhat disadvantaged the employers, so that at the beginning of the twentieth century labour and capital in cotton were on more equal terms than they had been for most of the preceding century. This may well have encouraged collaboration between the two sides of industry over such issues as the supply of raw cotton or cotton duties in India. However, the industry could still produce classic struggles between capital and labour and participated fully in the labour unrest of the Edwardian period (McIvor, 1996; White, 1978, 1982).

Lancashire was not central to the war economy and the movement of wages of the operatives reflected this fact. They lagged behind the munitions workers and real wages fell during the war. This created a sense of grievance initially seen in the conflict with the Cotton Control Board in 1918, but emerging more clearly in the post-war industrial unrest. By January 1917 wage rates were only 10 per cent above those of 1914, while the cost of living had risen by 46 per cent. From 1917 there was a catching-up process for many workers and by 1919 wages in most industries had risen by 95 per cent on the 1914 levels. In cotton wage rates had only advanced by 57 per cent by the end of the war compared with a rise in the cost of living of 103 per cent. Significantly, differences between wage rates and wage earnings disappeared. Earnings for most of the war had kept ahead of wage rates, reflecting the shortage of labour. The greatest shortage was in the spinning room among the piecers. It was this group, largely young men aged 18–25, who had volunteered or been conscripted into the armed forces. Because they were a lower-paid group, their elimination from statistics raised the average earnings per head in the industry. However, this small gap between earnings and wage rates in cotton spinning closed by 1918, the result of the end of the rota system for unemployment and the growth of short-time working (Bowley, 1921; Rowe, 1924).

Table 4.2 Changes in cotton wage rates and earnings

Year	Wage rates	Wage earnings	Cost of living
June 1914	100	100	100
Feb. 1916	105	110	(1916) 146
Feb. 1917	110	121	(1917) 176
Jan. 1918	133	142	(1918) 203
Nov. 1918	157	157	(1918) 203

Sources: Wages – Bowley, 1921, p. 179; Cost of living – Clegg, 1985, p. 568.

The establishment of the Cotton Control Board in June 1917 created an entirely new set of circumstances for collective bargaining in the industry, despite the fact that in theory the Board was to have nothing to do with wages. The reality was that employers saw the levies they paid to the Board, which were then passed on to the operatives as unemployment pay, as payments in lieu of wages and were only prepared to continue paying the levies if wage advances were restricted (Henderson, 1922; Fowler, 1987).

Wage negotiations in the cotton industry in 1915 and 1916 had been arbitrated by the government's Committee of Production. The committee, led by Sir George Askwith, had responsibility for arbitrating between employers and labour. Initially the government was concerned to keep wages down in order to hold back wartime inflation, although from 1917 the Committee took a more generous attitude to labour in an attempt to avert labour unrest. However, collective bargaining in the cotton industry was to come under the influence of the Cotton Control Board even though it was not initially envisaged that the Board would have such role. The effect of this was to centralize wage negotiations, bringing spinning and weaving together for the first time in the history of the industry. Wage negotiations took place in the autumn of 1917 and the spring of 1918 and it was Sir Herbert Dixon, Chairman of the Cotton Control Board, who acted as arbitrator. To bring pressure on the trade unions to accept wage offers, the Cotton Control Board announced that it was prepared to suspend the levy system until the wage question had been settled.

This threat to unemployed cotton operatives was sufficient to achieve a negotiated settlement largely on employers' terms in both 1917 and 1918. However, the settlement in the spring of 1918 left the operatives resentful, and industrial unrest broke out. The Spinners' Amalgamation balloted for strike action in August. Ostensibly, the spinners took action over the Cotton Control Board's decision to end the rota system because of the shortage of raw cotton and government pressure to release labour. Underlying this issue, however, was discontent over the wage settlement of the spring of 1918 and what operatives felt was a lack of similar sacrifice on the part of the employers whose profits had surpassed their pre-war levels. Although the operatives had received a substantial advance on wage rates in the spring of 1918, the gains to those in spinning had been offset by the onset of short-time introduced by the Cotton Control Board. The effects were greatest in Oldham, the centre of the American cotton spinning sector. Because of short-time working, wages in spinning in Oldham were only 13 per cent above the 1914 wage level (Henderson, 1922; Fowler, 1987).

One of the key developments in industrial relations during the war was the establishment of the shop stewards' movement in the engineering industry. The local nature of trade unionism in Lancashire meant that unofficial organization generally had not been a feature in the cotton industry. However, a shop stewards' movement did develop among Oldham spinners, which is partly explained by the fact that, as spinners of American cotton, they had been the most affected by the shortage of raw cotton imports. Oldham spinners had a long tradition of industrial militancy and since the 1880s Oldham had been the cockpit of industrial conflict in Lancashire (Turner, 1962). Falling real wages and the ending of the rota system of short-time working fuelled industrial militancy in Oldham. The Spinners' Amalgamation voted by 10,998 to 2,526 to take strike action against the abolition of the rota system in August 1918. The government faced a difficult situation. To declare the strike illegal and put the union leaders in prison, when the strike was seen to be caused by the influence of shop stewards rather than official leaders of the union, was likely to inflame the situation. They therefore decided to make the payment of strike pay rather than the strike itself illegal. The strike ended as a result of intervention by Lloyd George, who promised a government enquiry. The enquiry was held in the Town Hall in Manchester, but with the war nearly over and the cotton supply situation improving all the time it was somewhat academic. The enquiry found little evidence to question the Cotton Control Board's decision to end the rota. Union criticism concentrated on the failure to compensate operatives for short-time working, arguing that the money paid in levies to the Board was in lieu of wages and therefore 'belonged' to the operatives. The enquiry was sympathetic, although its terms of reference restricted it from making recommendations and suggested the real solution to the problem from the operatives' point of view would be an increase in wages (Fowler, 1987).

The cotton operatives only effectively caught up with wartime rises in the cost of living in the immediate post-war period. The operatives' unity in presenting claims for wage advances collapsed in this period. The Weavers' Amalgamation claim in December 1918 was referred to the Court of Arbitration, an interim body that replaced the Committee of Production. A settlement of 50 per cent on wage rates was rushed through, effectively restoring real wages to their 1914 level.

Meanwhile, the Spinners' Amalgamation and the Cardroom Amalgamation, making a similar claim for a wage advance, pressed their case with strike action. The strike coincided with the 1918 election campaign which clearly worried the Coalition Government concerned as it was about the impact of the action on its fortunes in Lancashire. Lloyd George intervened for the second time in three months and called the leaders of the employers and unions to Downing Street. He was successful in persuading both sides to accept the arbitration award in weaving as the basis for a settlement in spinning and the two-week strike ended before the election day (Fowler, 1987; Wrigley, 1990).

Lancashire operatives also achieved a significant reduction in hours of work in 1919 from 55.5 to 48 hours per week, which ended the 6 o'clock start when work began before breakfast, and was especially important in an industry where so many married women with children were employed. In seeking the hour's reduction the cotton operatives were part of a wider movement in British industry for the 8-hour day. The demand was encouraged by the expectations of Lloyd George's promised 'land fit for heroes' and an increased preference for leisure with the end of the war. So important was the issue for all cotton operatives that the cotton unions had united in the first industry-wide strike to secure the reduction. As importantly, they also secured a wage advance so that the reduced hours did not have to be compensated with increased productivity to maintain the weekly wage. Employers were finally minded to accept the operatives' demands because they were convinced that government would shortly be legalizing the 48-hour working week, although this in fact did not happen (Fowler, 1987).

The cotton operatives on the eve of the war were among the most prosperous groups of industrial workers, albeit that prosperity was based on family income rather than individual wages. The war period saw their living standards fall dramatically because of shortages of supply of raw cotton caused by disruption to shipping. While employers were keen to maintain production and profits, the operatives were more concerned with equitable distribution of the work available. To this end they accepted the rota system for unemployed workers, short-time working and wage rates that fell behind wartime inflation, so that employers could make levy contributions to the Cotton Control Board. By the end of 1918 the position changed. Industrial action was necessary to restore the cotton operatives' 1914 position with regard to wages and to secure the 48-hour working week. The major legacy of this period for industrial relations was thc growth of state intervention, in the form of the Cotton Control Board, in disputes between capital and labour. State intervention in negotiations between employers' organizations and trade unions were to become a familiar feature of the inter-war years, but the pattern had been established between 1914 and 1918.

PROFITEERING, SPECULATION AND NEW TECHNOLOGY

In 1914 the weaving industry was still largely in the hands of private family firms, so information about profitability is not readily available, although employers constantly stressed that they were not making large profits. In contrast, the spinning sector was largely dominated by limited liability companies. Pre-war dividends averaged around 5–7 per cent in spinning, but peaked during the pre-war boom of 1905–7 at nearly 16 per cent (Walton, 1987). Although dividends fell during the early period of the war, the cotton spinning industry, to the surprise of contemporaries, remained very profitable especially during 1917 and 1918 when the Cotton Control Board rationed and distributed raw cotton. By 1918 dividends had reached the level of the 1905–7 boom at approximately 16 per cent (Robson, 1957). The *Cotton Trade Review*, the industry's bible, commented on 1918:

> The Lancashire cotton industry during the past year has experienced the most prosperous period in its history. More money has been made than in any previous twelve months (Bowker, 1928, p. 31).

A year later the same journal reported:

> The year 1918 was a record year for profits but 1919 has been even better. It is probable that in 1920 all previous figures will be beaten (Bowker, 1928, p. 33).

While the profits in spinning were probably greater than those in weaving, by the end of 1919 both were enjoying unprecedented levels of prosperity. A contemporary commented:

> Lancashire earned and spent on a prodigal scale. Not one but a score of men do I know who spent their lives in a four roomed cottage, who now either bought up a

country estate or set about building a mansion ... places like St. Anne's on Sea or Southport took on a new ostentation from cotton money (Bowker, 1928, p. 35).

In 1919, as Lancashire was able to receive more raw cotton and re-enter markets from which it had been excluded by the wartime shortage of shipping space, a major restocking boom took place. This was part of the general post-war boom shared by the whole of British industry.

Profits in spinning led to a massive speculative spree with many larger firms being recapitalized or financially restructured. These changes did not involve any new investment in the industry, but required profits to continue at their 1919 peak in order to continue to pay out dividends on a far greater nominal capital than the pre-war period. Specific to Lancashire was a system whereby new shares were bought 'on call' which enabled shareholders to pay only half the value of the share initially, the rest being described as 'on call'. The difference between the share value and the money paid by the shareholder was raised by the company borrowing from the banks. The whole edifice was based on the assumption that post-war profit levels would continue throughout the 1920s. However, the bubble burst in the summer of 1920 and the cotton industry moved into a trade depression that was to last effectively until 1940 (Dupree, 1996; Porter, 1979).

Although the profits in 1918 and 1919 were real enough, the boom attracted a speculative element out of proportion to the industry's ability to provide long-term returns. To some extent the speculation was fuelled within Lancashire from profits made during and immediately after the war. However, speculators from outside Lancashire, especially from London, were attracted to what became a bandwagon. Speculation was centred on the spinning industry, especially those companies involved in spinning American cotton. Some 46 per cent of the spinning industry changed hands, though only a little over 10 per cent of weaving was affected. Bolton avoided the worst of the speculation partly because of the leadership of Sir Herbert Dixon who saw events in Lancashire in 1919–20 repeating the catastrophe of the South Sea Bubble (Bowker, 1928; Committee on Industry and Trade, 1928; Dupree, 1996; UTFWA, 1923). The sector most affected were the great limited liability spinning companies in Oldham. The older and more inefficient firms were not particularly the object of speculation, and paradoxically this was to leave them in a better position to deal with a downturn in trade. The speculation was greatest in the most modern factories, particularly those that had introduced ring spinning, because they commanded the highest price and profits. Consequently, the most technically efficient mills were prone to become the most financially desperate. The post-war speculation left the industry heavily in debt during the 1920s when interest rates were kept high to enable Britain to return to the gold standard. Many Lancashire banks were heavily involved in the speculation because of the 'on call' system of share finance, and their policy was a major factor in the failure of industrial capacity to contract in the 1920s. The banks sustained Lancashire companies in the vague hope that there would be an upturn, and this compounded rather than helped the industry's problems (Bamburgh, 1988; Dupree, 1996; Porter, 1979).

War in the twentieth century has been seen by some historians as an agent of technological change and modernization. The war did not provide an engine for any technical changes in the cotton industry, although there were limited changes in labour practices. Technological developments had taken place prior to the outbreak of hostilities and had been mostly introduced not by the Lancashire cotton industry but by its competitors, particularly America.

The machinery in use in the Lancashire cotton industry had hardly developed at all from that in the mid-nineteenth century. The industry was predominantly the self-actor mule spindle in spinning and the Lancashire loom in weaving. Technological developments had resulted in the production of much more efficient ring spinning and the Northrop or automatic loom, but these technologies had not been widely adopted in Lancashire. America, in contrast, had embraced the new technology, partly reflecting the higher cost of labour in the United States but also the fact that a protected home market enabled the production of coarse yarns and cloths in long runs suited to that home market. Contemporaries argued that American producers did not need the flexibility of Lancashire, which produced a range of goods suited to different markets (Board of Trade, 1918; Marrison, 1996).

There has been much debate about why Lancashire failed to embrace ring spinning and the Northrop automatic loom (Mass and Lazonick, 1990; Sandberg, 1974). Between 1900 and 1914 the productive capacity of the industry had expanded by a quarter, but the investment was largely in mule spinning and Lancashire looms. While Lancashire entrepreneurs have been criticized for the lack of investment in new technology before 1914, it has been argued, on the other hand, that Lancashire entrepreneurs acted rationally in their own interests. Certainly, contemporaries saw no contradiction in continued use of the traditional plant.

> We are satisfied that the machinery and plant used in the cotton trade are on the whole highly efficient and that British spinners and manufacturers keep fully abreast of modern inventions (Board of Trade, 1918, p. 51).

Potentially the profits made by the Lancashire cotton industry during and immediately after the war could have been used to introduce new technology to make the industry more competitive. Instead these profits formed part of the capital involved in the massive speculation of 1919–20. That speculation had left the most technically advanced mills with burdens of debt so great that further expansion was unthinkable and contraction out of the question while there was a glimmer of hope that they could recoup losses by continued production. The factories left with the traditional technology were simply not in a position to provide investment for new machinery out of profits and, because of the depression of the 1920s, unable to attract new capital. Indeed, the dearth of capital was to spell ruin for some investors who found that money for shares 'on call' was demanded in situations where they could not meet the obligations (Greenwood, 1951).

It was the wartime profits which led to the speculative frenzy and that speculation which impeded investment in new technology within the cotton industry. In no sense did World War I provide a stimulus to technical change in the Lancashire cotton industry. Nor did the war alter the structure of the cotton industry, seen by some historians as the main obstacle to the investment in new technology (Lazonick, 1986, 1990, 1992). Instead the industry continued with the use of traditional technology against competitors who were far more productive. The response of the cotton employers was to turn their attention not to their capital investment, but to their labour force.

THE COTTON INDUSTRY IN THE INTER-WAR YEARS

The European war of 1914–18 had stimulated the growth of cotton production outside Europe and started a fundamental transformation of the international trade in textiles. Lancashire was slow to recognize this, as one of the more perceptive observers of the inter-war period remarked:

> They never asked themselves why countries like India and China which grow raw cotton and wear cotton clothes and which were weaving cotton cloth whilst our ancestors walked about in the skins of wild beasts, should continue to send the cotton over the seas to be manufactured into cloth or should buy from Europe cloth made of American cotton. (Utley, 1931, p. 24–5)

The inter-war years transformed the Lancashire cotton industry. Capacity fell by approximately a third while production was almost halved (see Table 4.3).

The industry was beset by unemployment, short-time work and wage cuts for the operatives and was never to return to its pre-1914 pre-eminence. The cause of this change was simple – a fall in exports, especially the loss of the Indian market. The two key players in this development were India and Japan. Home production in India developed behind protective tariffs while at the same time Japan gained a foothold in the Indian market, so that by 1939 Japan had replaced Lancashire as the main exporter of cotton cloth to the Indian market and indeed to the world market (Board of Trade, 1946).

Table 4.3 Lancashire cotton industry, 1912–38

Year	Cloth produced (m/n sq. yards)	Cloth exported (m/n sq. yards)	Spindles (million)	Looms (thousand)
1912	8,050	6,913	61.4	786
1924	6,046	4,444	63.3	792
1930	3,500	2,472	63.2	700
1938	3,126	1,499	42.1	495

Source: Board of Trade, 1946, p. 6.

A major response to this international situation was to look again to the state to deal with the industry's problems. State intervention during the war, in the form of the Cotton Control Board, had been seen as successfully saving the industry from crisis. It was in this context that the industry subsequently looked to the state to solve its problems. By 1928 it was clear that the legacy of the war and post-war boom would have to be dealt with. The Bank of England, concerned about the over-commitment of the Lancashire banks to the industry, negotiated the establishment of the Lancashire Cotton Corporation which took over responsibility for those firms previously in the hands of the banks (Bamburgh, 1988). This took place against the background of the Mond–Turner talks between the leading employers and the TUC which extolled the virtues of rationalizing British industry as a means of meeting foreign competition. The Lancashire Cotton Corporation set about the task of rationalizing the industry. In 1936 the government introduced legislation – the Cotton Spinning Industry Act – which took machinery out of use and compensated employers. Employers' compensation was raised by a levy on the industry modelled on the one introduced by the wartime Cotton Control Board. However, there was no rationale about how this process was organized. Ring spindles as well as mule spindles went to the scrap yards. Finally, in 1939 the Cotton Industry Act was introduced with the aim of a further reduction in capacity. Modelled on the Cotton Control Board, the responsible agency under the Act was never fully established because of the outbreak of World War II. While the industry looked to government to solve its problems and compensate companies and firms withdrawn from production, there was little state concern with the plight or future of the cotton operatives who received no government compensation. However, in weaving, following the continued intervention of the Ministry of Labour, legislation was introduced in 1934 which legalized weavers' wages, a rather neglected piece of social legislation. (Dupree, 1996; Fowler, 1987, 1988).

Many economic historians, as well as contemporaries, have emphasized the low wages of Lancashire's competitors in the inter-war years and seen this as crucial in Japan's success story. A major study of the world textile industry by the International Labour Office in 1937 placed great emphasis on Japan's lower labour costs, while not denying that the country possessed other substantial advantages. It argued that productivity was higher in Lancashire, but not to the extent that it would offset the lower wages in Japan. However, it has been pointed out that arguments that depend entirely on low wages fail to explain why Japan rather than India replaced Lancashire (Mass and Lazonick, 1990). Neither is it true that Lancashire's wage bill in the inter-war years was inflexible. Substantial wage reductions took place between 1921–32 and there was a further wage reduction in weaving in 1935 (Fowler, 1988). A contemporary study of the industry argued that if wages had fallen even further it would have made little difference to Lancashire's competitiveness and the key lay in the failure to raise productivity levels (Jewkes and Gray, 1935). Attempts to raise productivity centred on weaving and the issue of 'more looms'. 'More looms' was the term coined to increase the number of Lancashire looms an operative minded from four to six or even eight with a commensurate cut in the piece rate but a proposed increase in the wage earned because of increased productivity. Although the trade unions generally opposed the introduction of the 'more looms' system, it was established in the 1930s with little noticeable effect on the industry's competitiveness. Nor did 'more looms' represent new technology (Fowler, 1988).

Cotton operatives had achieved a reduction in hours worked by the end of the war, and employers looked to this reduction in hours as well as wage rates as an explanation for Lancashire's lack of competitiveness. Although the employers sought to increase hours in 1928 and 1932, they were unsuccessful as it was difficult to maintain their arguments when so many operatives were on short-time working. However, social convention did affect the extent to which employers in cotton were able to extend production on existing machinery. Attempts to introduce a double shift into the cotton industry were fought off by union activity and community feeling against such a system in an industry where so many women were employed.

A more effective response to increased competition would have been the introduction of new technology in the form of ring spinning and the automatic loom. However, resources for large-scale investment were not available in the inter-war years, while the constraints of the shift system may not have helped (Economic Advisory Council, 1930).

The Great War was a watershed for the Lancashire cotton industry. Events were set in motion by the war from which the industry was never able to recover and which led to its eventual demise. The long-term effect was to centre the production of cotton on those countries or areas where cotton was grown and labour cheaper. It is difficult in this context to see how Lancashire could have retained its pre-1914 eminence.

REFERENCES

Bamburgh, J. (1988), 'Rationalisation of the British Cotton Industry in the Inter-war Years', *Textile History*, **19**, 83–102.

Board of Trade (1918), *Departmental Committee to Consider the Position of the Textile Trades after the War*, London, UK: HMSO.

Board of Trade (1946), *Working Party Report Cotton*, London, UK: HMSO.

Bolton Operative Cotton Spinners (1914–1918), *Annual Report.*

Bowker, B. (1928), *Lancashire Under the Hammer*, London: Hogarth Press.

Bowley, A.L. (1921), *Prices and Wages in the United Kingdom 1914–1920*, London: Oxford at the Clarendon Press.

Chapman, S.J. and D. Kemp (1915), *The War and the Textile Industries*, London: Royal Statistical Society.

Chatterji, B. (1992), *Trade, Tariffs and Empire: Lancashire and British Policy in India 1919–1939*, Delhi, India: Oxford University Press.

Clegg, H. (1985), A *History of British Trade Unions since 1889 Vol. 11 1910–1933,* Oxford, UK: Clarendon Press.

Clegg, H., A. Fox and A.F. Thompson (1964), *A History of British Trade Unions Since 1889 Vol. 1 1889–1910*, Oxford, UK: Clarendon Press.

Committee on Industry and Trade (1928), *Survey of the Textile Industries*, London: HMSO.

Cotton Factory Times (1917), 9 March and 16 March.

Dupree, M. (1996), 'Foreign Competition and the Inter-war Period', in M.B. Rose (ed.), *The Lancashire Cotton Industry – A History Since 1700*, Preston, UK: Lancashire County Books, pp. 265–95.

Economic Advisory Council (Clynes' Report) (1930), *Report on the Cotton Industry*, London, UK: HMSO Cmd 3615.

Farnie, D.A. (1979), *The English Cotton Industry and the World Market 1815–1896*, Oxford, UK: Clarendon Press.

Foulger, W. (1988), *Work and Gender – Ideology in the Lancashire Cotton Industry 1910–1920*, MA, Manchester Polytechnic.

Fowler, A. (1987), 'War and Labour Unrest', in A. Fowler and T. Wyke (eds), *The Barefoot Aristocrats: A History of the Amalgamated Association of Operative Cotton Spinners*, Littleborough, UK: George Kelsall, pp. 14–146.

Fowler, A. (1988), 'Lancashire Cotton Trade Unionism in the Inter-war Years', in J.A. Jowett and A.J. McIvor (eds), *Employers and Labour in the English Textile Industries, 1850–1939*, London, UK and New York, US: Routledge, pp. 107–26.

Greenwood, W. (1951), *Lancashire*, London, UK: Robert Hale.

Henderson, H.D. (1922), *The Cotton Control Board*, Oxford, UK and New York, US: Clarendon Press.

International Labour Office (ILO) (1937), *The World Textile Industry Economic and Social Problems*, Geneva, Switzerland: International Labour Office.

Jewkes, J. and E.M. Gray (1935), *Wages and Labour in the Lancashire Cotton Spinning Industry*, Manchester, UK: Manchester University Press.

Kirby, M.W. (1981), *The Decline of British Economic Power since 1870*, London, UK and Boston, US: George Allen & Unwin.
Lazonick, W. (1986), 'The Cotton Industry', in B. Elbaum and W. Lazonick (eds), *The Decline of the British Economy*, Oxford, UK and New York, US: Clarendon Press, pp. 18–50.
Lazonick, W. (1990), *Competitive Advantage on the Shop Floor*, London, UK and Cambridge, US: Harvard University Press.
Lazonick, W. (1992), *Organisation and Technology in Capitalist Development*, Aldershot, UK and Brookfield, US: Edward Elgar.
McIvor, A.J. (1996), *Organised Capital Employers' Associations and Industrial Relations in Northern England 1880–1939*, Cambridge, UK and New York, US: Cambridge University Press.
Marrison, A. (1996), 'Indian Summer 1870–1914' in M.B. Rose (ed.), *The Lancashire Cotton Industry: A History since 1700*, Preston, UK: Lancashire County Books, pp. 238–64.
Mass, W. and W. Lazonick (1990), 'The British Cotton Industry and International Competitive Advantage: The State of the Debates', *Business History*, **32**, 4, 9–65.
Pearse, A. (1930), *The Cotton Industry of India*, Manchester, UK: International Federation of Master Cotton Spinners' and Manufacturers' Association.
Pollard, S. (1994), 'Entrepreneurship 1870–1914', in R. Flood and D. McCloskey (eds), *The Economic History of Britain since 1700, Second Edition Vol. 2 1860–1939*, Cambridge, UK and New York, US: Cambridge University Press, pp. 62–89.
Porter, J.H. (1979), 'Cotton and Wool Textiles', in N.K. Buxton and D.H. Aldcroft (eds), *British Industry Between the Wars*, London, UK: Scolar Press, pp. 25–47.
Robson, R. (1957), *The Cotton Industry in Britain*, London, UK and New York, US: Macmillan.
Rowe, J.F.W. (1924), 'Wages in the Cotton Industry 1914–1920', in *Economic Journal*, **34**, 200–210.
Sandberg, L. (1974), *Lancashire in Decline*, Columbus, US: Ohio State University Press.
Singleton, J. (1994), 'The Cotton Industry and the British War Effort 1914–1918', *Economic History Review*, 2nd Series, **47**, 3, 601–18.
Tomlinson, J.D. (1979), 'The First World War and British Cotton Piece Exports to India', *Economic History Review*, 2nd Series, **32**, 4, 494–506.
Turner, H.A. (1962), *Trade Union Growth, Structure and Policy. A Comparative Study of the Cotton Unions*, London, UK: George Allen & Unwin.
Tyson, R.E. (1968), 'The Cotton Industry', in D.H. Aldcroft (ed.) *The Development of British Industry and Foreign Competition, 1875–1914*, London, UK: George Allen & Unwin, pp. 100–127.
United Textile Factory Workers' Association (1923), *Inquiry into the Cotton Industry 1921–22*, Blackburn, UK: UTFWA.
Utley, F. (1931), *Lancashire and the Far East*, London, UK: George Allen & Unwin.
Walton, J. (1987), *Lancashire: A Social History 1558–1939*, Manchester, UK: Manchester University Press.
Walton, J. (1998), *Blackpool*, Edinburgh, UK: Edinburgh University Press.
Webb, S. and B. Webb (1901), *Industrial Democracy*, London, UK: Printed by the authors.
White, J.L. (1978), *The Limits of Trade Union Militancy: The Lancashire Textile Workers, 1910–1914*, London, UK and Westport, US: Greenwood Press.
White, J.L. (1982), 'Lancashire Cotton Textiles', in C. Wrigley (ed.), *History of*

British Industrial Relations 1875–1914, Brighton, UK: Harvester Press, pp. 209–29.

Wrigley, C. (1990), *Lloyd George and the Challenge of Labour: The Post War Coalition 1918–1922*, London, UK and New York, US: Harvester Wheatsheaf.

5. The impact of the First World War on Japan

Kenneth D. Brown

By the time the First World War began in 1914, Japan was already on the way to becoming the first modern nation in Asia. Over the half-century following the restoration of imperial power in 1868 a country which appeared, in Western terms at least, to be relatively backward, acquired many of the characteristics of more developed contemporary societies. The background to this was the positive role played by the state in determining broad national goals and in establishing the economic and social infrastructures conducive to modernization. In a comparatively short space of time the system of landholding was reformed, educational provision extended, local government reorganized, the armed forces modernized, national government democratized and industrialization fostered. There was still a long way to go, however, as one of Japan's most perceptive Western residents, Lafcadio Hearn, acknowledged. 'Nearly all the phases of modern life,' he wrote in 1904, 'yield evidence that the disintegration of the old society has been superficial rather than fundamental'.[1] Another Westerner, Clive Holland, agreed, observing in 1913 that:

> Although modern Japan is so changed from what it was even twenty-five or thirty years ago, and although 'modernity' and all that the word may be held to imply, has so great and apparently irresistible an attraction for the more highly educated and official classes, the workaday life of the countryside, of the shops, fields and factories has little to do with … Western civilization.[2]

Furthermore the juxtaposition of the old and the new sometimes gave rise to uneasy internal tensions or represented little more than unsatisfying compromises between East and West. Thus, neither the promulgation of a written constitution nor the establishment of an elected bicameral legislature, both based on Western models, did much to remove effective power from the hands of the *genro*, unelected imperial advisers and string-pullers drawn from the clans which had engineered the restoration of the young Meiji Emperor in 1868. Similarly neither the establishment of the Diet nor the spread of educational provision were accompanied by much freedom of thought or organization.

Both the content of the school curriculum and the training and placement of teachers were centrally determined. The right to vote was confined to only a very small proportion of adults, all of them male, while successive imperial rescripts laid down a social code devoid of notions of rights but very emphatic about the duties and responsibilities of citizenship. Less subtle methods of controlling dissent took the form of the 1900 Peace Police Law which gave the Home Ministry extensive powers to monitor and prohibit political activity. Again, social relationships, whether between men and women, employers and employees, or society at large and its outcastes or *burakamin*, still rested primarily on Japanese rather than Western concepts, despite some tentative manifestations of labour organization and even a women's movement after 1900.

A similar mix of old and new was apparent in the economy. With strong government encouragement Japan had acquired a railway system, modern business and financial institutions, some advanced industry and technology, and had become more urbanized. At the same time a growing involvement in international trade gave her 2.3 per cent of the world's total manufacturing exports by 1913.[3] The pace of industrialization was stepped up quite deliberately after the war against Russia in 1904–5 exposed the strategic limitations of the economy, particularly in regard to heavy industry. Partly as a result, Japan's share of total world manufacturing output grew from 2.0 to 2.7 per cent between 1900 and 1913.[4] On the other hand, the bulk of industrial output continued to take the form of traditional products, particularly textiles. Equally, while accelerating industrialization was mirrored after 1905 by a decline in the absolute numbers engaged in the primary sector, the majority of people still continued to live on and derive their livelihood from the land, mainly in the form of rice cultivation.

The drive for industrial modernization also had adverse financial implications. Virtually bereft of natural resources (save some coal and a little copper), Japan had to import most of the raw materials needed by heavy industry. The ensuing payments deficit was further exacerbated by food imports, required by rising rates of population growth. An increase of 4 million people over the 1890s was followed by a further rise of 6 million in the next decade, carrying the total to about 49 million on the eve of the Great War.[5] Although technical changes in the methods of rice cultivation had raised both output and yields from the late nineteenth century, they could not keep up with such a rate of population expansion. By 1914 Japan, previously a food exporter, was buying food, even rice, from overseas. This added further to the trade deficit already generated by the demands of heavy industry. Together, the value of imported crude foodstuffs and raw materials rose almost fourfold at current prices between 1901 and 1913.[6] Not surprisingly, surpluses were achieved on the current account in only two years between 1903 and 1914, while in the last full year of peace, 1913, the total deficit on commodity trade stood at almost ¥5000m.[7]

Nevertheless, Japan's conscious drive to establish itself as an independent modern state had gained significant credibility from two sources. First, the country had announced its emergence as a potent military force, humiliating the Chinese in Korea and southern Manchuria in the 1890s and establishing a substantial presence on the Asian mainland. This was followed by another successful and even more startling feat of arms against one of the Great Powers, Russia, in the war of 1904–5. This comprehensive victory – the first by an Asian over a European nation – perhaps contributed, albeit indirectly, to the outbreak of the 1914–18 war. It certainly helped to divert Russia's attention away from the Far East and back to the Balkans, where her support encouraged the Serbs to reject the ultimatum presented by the Austrians after the assassination of the Archduke Franz Ferdinand. Second, Japan signed a formal treaty in 1902 with Great Britain, revised in 1905 and then renewed in 1911 for a further ten years. Seen by the British mainly as providing a counterweight to Russian ambitions in the East, the agreement effectively gave Japan a free hand in Korea. Much more important from the Japanese perspective, however, its very existence was interpreted as a token of acceptance by the Great Powers.

It was perhaps inevitable that the treaty should ultimately assume an anti-German character. From 1905 onwards Japan made successful attempts to improve relations with both Russia and France, all the while fearful lest the German influence and presence in China should upset her own ambitions, thereby encouraging the resurgence of Chinese nationalism.[8] Nevertheless, there was nothing automatic about Japan's allegiance in 1914, since the treaty did not require her to take Britain's part when war was declared against Germany. Indeed, both Britain and Germany hoped to prevent the fighting from spreading to the Far East. Very quickly, however, Britain invoked the treaty by calling for Japanese naval support in the Pacific. Although there were those in Japan, especially on the army's general staff, who advised caution in the belief that Germany would win, the foreign minister pursuaded his cabinet colleagues to issue an ultimatum to Germany on 17 August 1914. In this way Japan joined the First World War on the side of the Entente against the Central Powers. Her military involvement was peripheral, extending merely to some minor activity against German interests in Asia and the provision of the naval support requested by the British against German commerce raiders in the Pacific. Both during the war itself and in the complex tangle of decisions and events which eventually brought it about, therefore, Japan's contribution was indirect and marginal. Yet, the effects of the conflict on Asia's only independent participant were far-reaching. Arguably, its economic, social and diplomatic repercussions became links in a chain of events which stretched forward to Hiroshima and Nagasaki.

The immediate effect of the outbreak of war was economic dislocation in Japan. Overseas commercial and financial arrangements were thrown into disarray because it was no longer possible to arrange transactions and settle bills through the established channels of expertise in London. A severe business and industrial depression lasted into early 1915. As the full ramifications of total war for the major combatants gradually became apparent, however, Japan proceeded to experience a boom of considerable magnitude. Invisible income expanded greatly as the national merchant fleet more than doubled to 3 million tons. Not only did this allow a greater share of Japan's trade to be carried by its own ships – an increase from 57 to 87 per cent over the war years – thereby saving invisible expenditure, but the provision of shipping services to other countries also provided a valuable source of income. Japan's net income from freights was less than ¥40m in 1914: by 1918 it was over ¥450m. As for commodity trade, average annual exports over the four war years were some ¥330m larger than imports, although between 1911 and 1914 imports exceeded exports by an annual average of ¥65m.[9]

Primarily these increased exports reflected a substantial expansion of Japan's manufacturing base. Overall industrial investment during the war multiplied 17 times as enhanced profits were ploughed back into new developments. The total number of business corporations increased from 17,000 to 26,000.[10] Consequently employment in the industrial sector rose, from 4,100,000 to 6,300,000 people between 1910 and 1920. Industrial production during the war grew at more than 9 per cent per year, although this aggregate figure disguised rates which varied enormously between industries: the annual growth rate in machine tools, for instance, was 28.0 per cent, compared with 10.7 per cent in metals and a mere 4.1 per cent in spinning.[11] The enhanced significance of manufacturing in the economy was symbolically recognized in 1925 when it was brought under the aegis of a newly created ministry and removed from its previous mentor, the Ministry of Agriculture and Commerce.

This industrial expansion occurred mainly because the war disrupted established trade patterns and hugely increased world demand for certain strategic commodities. It thereby opened up new markets overseas, even for relatively undeveloped industries which had hitherto been uncompetitive in international terms. At the same time the war freed important segments of the Japanese home market from foreign competition. Japan's first significant contacts with the Western powers in the 1850s and 1860s had been followed by a number of treaties, most of which incorporated clauses governing trade relationships on terms unfavourable to the Japanese. Known as the *Ansei* (Unequal) Treaties, these had effectively prevented the protection of indigenous manufacturers against competition from cheaper foreign imports. Even their revision in the early twentieth century had been partial and ineffective but now, by restricting the inflow of foreign goods, the war acted like a tariff and permitted some degree of import substitution. Chemical production was one major beneficiary. Pre-war Japan had been almost totally reliant on imports for dyestuffs, drugs and fertilizers. With foreign supplies much restricted, the government established a chemical research laboratory in 1914 and passed a law to encourage the domestic industry. There began indigenous manufacture of Bakelite, rayon, plate glass and also of soda by electrolysis.

As for overseas markets, some industries benefited by supplying to the Allies goods which had previously been purchased from enemy powers. These ranged all the way from the relatively trivial, such as children's toys, to the much more significant, chiefly processed foodstuffs and woollen clothing, the demand for which was suddenly and dramatically increased by war needs. Cotton, already expanded and modernized before 1914, was well placed to take advantage of the virtual cessation of exports from Britain, the world's major supplier. A strong position was consolidated in India, as well as in China and the USA, for reasons explained by the British consul in Osaka.

> Not only did Japanese manufacturers find themselves freed from competition in their main market – China – but, owing to the incapacity of England and other regular suppliers ... they were able to build up a great trade in substitute goods with markets ... to which they had not previously found entry.[12]

The industry's labour force rose by almost two-thirds between 1914 and 1919 while cotton yarn output increased almost 20 per cent (Table 5.1). An important knock-on effect of this was the stimulus given to domestic engineering by the need to produce locally the textile machinery previously imported from Britain.[13]

The most spectacular expansion of all, however, occurred in the heavy industries, particularly iron, steel and ships, for all of which international demand reached new heights under the pressure of war. Heavily dependent for iron and steel before 1914 on British and German imports, now respec-

Table 5.1 Japan: industrial outputs

	1913	1920
Cotton yarn (mn lbs)	607.2	726.8
Raw silk (mn lbs)	30.9	48.2
Coal (mn tons)	21.3	29.2
Finished steel (000 tons)	255.0	533.0
Cement (000 tons)	645.0	1353.0

Source: Allen, G.C. (1981), *A Short Economic History of Japan*, London: Macmillan, p. 107.

tively embargoed and blockaded, the Japanese demand for heavy metal could be met only by an expansion of indigenous production. The home requirement for iron alone rose by about half between 1913 and 1919, while the amount of steel consumed increased from 924,000 to 1,165,000 tons.[14] The demand for coal inevitably climbed in response – by almost a half – and some of this was met by Japan's own mines, which raised their output by about 37 per cent between 1913 and 1920 (Table 5.1).

Much of the iron and steel was absorbed by the massive expansion of the shipbuilding industry. Between 1913 and 1918 the number of yards rose from six to 45 with the result that launchings of 55,000 tons in 1913 were up to 646,000 tons by 1919. In turn, this boosted the demand for engineering products such as engines, turbines and boilers. Altogether the contribution of the metals sector to total manufacturing output rose five and a half times between 1900 and 1920, that of machinery slightly over four and a half times (Table 5.3). Fixed capital formation in machinery, which had been growing steadily since 1903, rocketed from ¥367m in 1914 to ¥1,245m by 1918, remaining above ¥1,000m a year until 1922.[15]

In these ways the war served to reinforce the emphasis on modern heavy industry which government had been trying to encourage even before 1914. Even so, it is important to keep wartime developments in perspective. The number of factory workers in Japan actually declined after 1921 and the output levels achieved in iron, cotton and coal during the war were not regained until the second half of the 1920s. Furthermore, the light industries still dominated manufacturing in terms of both output and employment (Table 5.2). As is evident from Table 5.3, therefore, it was the relative significance of metals and machinery which rose, so that by the time the war ended they were responsible for more than 20 per cent of total manufacturing output, compared with only 4.5 per cent in 1900.

But if fundamental change in the structure of Japan's industrial base still lay a decade in the future, some of the changes associated with industrial

Table 5.2 Japan's industrial structure

	1914		1919	
	Light	Heavy	Light	Heavy
Employees	267,000	149,000	1,288,000	428,000
Production	¥1,005m	¥367m	¥4,782m	¥2,106m

Source: Nakamura, T. (1983), *Economic Growth in Prewar Japan*, New Haven, CT, p. 180. Heavy industry is defined as chemicals, metals, machinery, cement and lime.

Table 5.3 Japan: shares of real manufacturing output (%)

	1900	1920
Food products	47.2	30.6
Textiles	25.5	27.8
Metals	1.4	7.8
Machinery	2.9	13.7
Chemicals	9.0	8.9
Others	14.0	11.2

Source: Franks, P. (1992), *Japanese Economic Development*, London: Routledge, p. 55.

expansion during the war were undoubtedly of long-term significance. One was a substantial and enduring dissemination of electric motive power, especially for textile, chemical and metal production, where traditional methods proved increasingly unequal to the task of satisfying enhanced demand (Table 5.4).

Table 5.4 Percentage of horsepower derived from electric prime movers

	1914	1919
Spinning/weaving	22.2	54.6
Chemicals	27.4	54.9
Metals	46.9	74.1
Machinery	61.8	67.8

Source: Nakamura, *Economic Growth*, p. 188.

Another was the trend towards larger-scale industrial organization. The total number of firms with capitalizations in excess of ¥5m increased from 62 to 368.[16] Prominent among these were the enterprises owned by the *zaibatsu*, the financial–industrial conglomerates which had led the way in pre-war industrialization by bringing together financial, supply and marketing contacts. Their influence and significance in the economy was much boosted by the war. Their increased profits not only enabled them to buy up smaller firms which lacked adequate financial resources, but also to widen the range of their own activities. Firms such as Okura, Asano, Furakawa and Fujita all expanded after 1914, the latter three into banking particularly, and their ranks were supplemented by newcomers such as Hitachi and Nissan. The main *zaibatsu* beneficiaries, however, were the big four, Mitsui, Sumitomo,

Mitsubishi and Yasuda, with the first three moving decisively into heavy industry, the last concentrating more on banking. Mitsubishi created nine new companies, including Mitsubishi Shipbuilding, Mitsubishi Internal Combustion Engine, and Mitsubishi Steel, while Mitsui extended its operations to include shipbuilding, chemicals and synthetic fabrics.[17] Thc *zaibatsu* were also able to extend their commercial activities through the medium of trading companies, and by the end of the war Mitsui Bussan controlled over a third of the nation's merchant fleet and handled a fifth of all cotton exports. From this base, the *zaibatsu* proceeded to dominate the post-war Japanese economy, because, in the words of one expert:

> of the magnitude … and very wide range of their interests. These comprised mining, metals, mechanical engineering, electrical apparatus and machinery, textiles, paper, cement, glass, chemicals, shipbuilding, shipping, foreign and domestic trade, banking and insurance. It was difficult, indeed, to find any form of large scale economic activity in which the *zaibatsu* had not an important share.[18]

Ownership of numerous strategically related but operationally distinct enterprises helped the *zaibatsu* to survive the depression which set in when the end of the war deprived Japan of both the protection and the stimulus it had provided. As the post-war restocking boom petered out, Japan was exposed once more to the full rigours of overseas competition, made all the sharper by the relative sluggishness of the international economy in the 1920s. Merchant shipping was hit by a general decline in world demand, warship building by the Washington naval agreement, which restricted capital ship construction. Both had knock-on effects on engineering, iron and steel. The intensification of competition in limited markets showed just how far Japan still had to go in order to catch up with the most advanced industrial countries, exposing the comparative inefficiency of much its manufacturing activity. As early as 1919 commodity imports once more exceeded exports, although the continued sale of services overseas maintained a positive overall balance until 1920. By 1924, however, the net deficit was just short of ¥700m.[19] Unable to cope without the cushion of war, many firms struggled. Suzuki and Fujita were among the major casualties, while Kawasaki sustained heavy losses on some of its engineering enterprises. Government action in the form of revised tariffs, the encouragement of rationalization and better quality control, the establishment of a new ministry of Commerce and Industry, and other forms of direct intervention, helped to create a fiercely competitive but sheltered home market in which only the most efficient could survive. At the same time, major companies continued to invest heavily in training skilled workers and recruiting professional managers, a strategy which had been developed in response to wartime scarcities. In the 1920s those enterprises which weathered the depression, particularly the *zaibatsu*, were able to perform reasonably well in the home market, even if, with the exception of cotton and silk, they could not yet compete very well in international terms. In these ways were laid the foundations of the economic competitiveness which ultimately led to the substantial growth of exports in the 1930s. Even in the 1920s, however, progress in the heavy industries in particular enabled Japan to become less reliant on overseas suppliers for machinery, chemical products and metal manufactures.

A third long-term development which was accelerated, though certainly not initiated, by the war was the growing size of the actual units of production in industry. Already by 1914 factories accounted for more than a half of total output and by the end of the war the proportion had risen to almost two-thirds (Table 5.5). This of course rather begs the question of what constituted a factory, for it must be stressed that the majority of Japanese workers throughout the war and post-war period were employed in units of less than five people. Nevertheless, the trend was unmistakable. In 1909 there were just over 1,000 factories with workforces of more than 100 people: by 1920 the number had doubled. Large factories had 53.8 per cent of those employed in factories with more than five workers, compared with 42.0 per cent in 1909.[20] The pattern was most marked in the heavy industries, although large-scale production was appearing also in traditional activities such as cotton spinning and weaving. In 1913, for example, the spinning industry by itself accounted for almost three-quarters of all those working in units of more than 500 workers, while the heavy and chemical industries had only about a fifth. By 1919 the proportion in spinning had fallen to 65 per cent, reflecting a compensatory rise in the heavy and chemical sector to 31 per cent.[21] The number of shipyards large enough to turn out vessels weighing more than 1,000 tons rose from 5 in 1913 to 41 by 1918. At the level of the individual firm, Nagasaki shipbuilding increased its labour force from 6,371 in 1910 to 15,631 in 1918, while the number employed by Shibaura Engineering rose from 1,297 in 1911 to 4,000 by 1917.[22] Altogether the proportion of engineering firms employing more than 500 people rose from 36 per cent to 55 per cent between 1909 and 1919.[23] In the iron and steel industry the number

Table 5.5 Production in Japan (¥m)

	1914	1918
Factory production	1,518	6,544
Cottage production	1,092	3,688
Total production	2,610	10,212

Source: Nakamura, *Economic Growth*, p. 80.

Table 5.6 Japan: proportion of workers in plants of various size (%)

	Number of workers		
	5–49	50–499	500+
1914	40.0	34.9	25.1
1919	33.9	34.6	31.5

Source: Minami, R. (1986), *The Economic Development of Japan*, p. 318.

of large plants, defined as those with an annual production capacity in excess of 5,000 tons, increased from 8 to 14. Table 5.6 shows quite clearly the growing trend towards the concentration of production, although it must be borne in mind that it excludes altogether that proportion of the workforce, still over 50 per cent, which continued to work in units of less than five.

Expansion at this speed brought industrial producers hard up against the limitations imposed by shortages of raw materials, process bottlenecks and relative scarcities of skilled labour. Well before 1914 some employers in engineering and other heavy industries had been trying to wrest control of labour from the *oyakata*, usually independent contractors who recruited, supervised and paid workers on behalf of the main employer. Rising prices during the war fostered general worker discontent, while at the same time the high demand for scarce skills exacerbated labour turnover rates that were already high before 1914. In an attempt to offset skill scarcities, therefore, employers began to recruit workers directly and provided them with appropriate in-house training. To obviate the risk of these trained, skilled workers being poached by other firms, it then became necessary to offer job security, premium wages and fringe benefits as a means of securing employees' long-term commitment. Even in the textile industries, where the threat to labour supply was posed rather by the wider range of employment alternatives opening up during the war years, the major employers experimented with welfare benefits, particularly accommodation and educational provision.[24] Although much amended and revised in the light of later developments, the industrial labour strategies which emerged as a result of wartime labour pressures eventually emerged after 1945 as integral features of the much vaunted Japanese system of lifetime employment and seniority pay.

The creation of this cadre of relatively privileged workers was not merely a response to problems of labour supply during the boom years around the war. It also represented a conscious employer reaction to the first flowerings of a European-style trade union movement and its flirtation with left-wing ideologies. Given the limited extent of pre-war industrialization and the prominence within it of the cotton industry with its high proportion of women workers, it was hardly surprising that labour organization was very limited in its development. By 1914 there were only about 40 trade unions, and strikes were consequently few and far between. During the war, however, the expansion of the heavy industries helped to equalize the gender composition of the manufacturing labour force, while the growing scale of production units facilitated its organization. By 1919, therefore, the number of trade unions had risen to almost 200, and between them they organized almost 500 strikes, centring mainly on issues of recognition and the right to collective bargaining. For some employers, binding workers securely into their firms through the provision of job security, high wages, fringe benefits, and even by organizing company works councils and trade unions, was perceived as a way of heading off what they feared would develop into independent labour organizations on Western lines and with socialist ideals.[25] The post-war contraction of industry certainly weakened labour's bargaining position, but the highly competitive international and domestic manufacturing environment led many firms to continue with these types of labour policies in order to guarantee their supplies of scarce skilled workers and to protect the investment in their training. Possession of skilled labour enabled such firms to raise productivity and thus to offer better wages and benefits, turning the whole process into a self-perpetuating one of great long-term significance to productivity levels in manufacturing.

The industrial troubles which marked the years around the end of the war were part of a wider pattern of unrest in Japan, the most serious manifestation being the 1918 rice riots. Beginning with a demonstration mounted by fishermen's wives in Toyama Prefecture, protest spread swiftly, infecting 180 cities and towns in 42 of the country's 47 prefectures, and involving perhaps as many as 2 million people. Numerous casualties occurred and it required 25,000 arrests and the imposition of martial law before some 92,000 troops finally restored order over a three-week period.

The riots were the result of war-induced inflation which pushed up prices much faster than income. Overall, the wholesale price index doubled between 1915 and 1918, while rice prices tripled. Cut off from the financial expertise and resources of the City of London, Japan's unsophisticated monetary machinery proved unable to cope with the transformation of her international financial position, while rapid industrial expansion distorted the internal price structure. A huge rise in note issue by the Bank of Japan, from ¥385m in December 1914 to ¥440m in June 1918, merely exacerbated the inflationary process. Furthermore, rural workers flooding into the towns in search of work added to the pressures on general living standards. Wartime growth in Kobe, Nagoya, Kyoto and Yokahama in particular raised the proportion of the total population living in towns to 32.2 per cent by 1920, as against a pre-war figure of 27.7 per cent.[26]

All of this might be interpreted as evidence that the wealthy were the main beneficiaries of the war boom, particularly as some share of the increased national output was simply absorbed by rising population. With most of the swollen national income going to rents, dividends, interest and corporate savings, most ordinary people, it seems, were unable to derive much advantage from rising farm output. Although more food per head was being grown, a disproportionate share was taken by the wealthy few: the majority suffered from falling standards of living, hence the mass protest of 1918.

An alternative hypothesis is that by 1920 the Japanese labour market had became highly competitive, passing the stage at which wages were set at subsistence levels. The share of national income going to unskilled workers increased, real income and consumption rose, while labour's new-found confidence and prosperity expressed themselves in wider patterns of consumption, more political activity, greater job mobility and more strikes. In this scenario the rice riots and trade union activity were symptoms of frustrated expectations, not of absolute deprivation.

Neither interpretation is wholly convincing, although the short-term aggregate wage data certainly support the pessimistic rather than the optimistic view. Money wages may have risen, but in real terms aggregate incomes in manufacturing fell for both men and women during the war itself (Table 5.7). However, it is also apparent that they were considerably higher by 1922 than they had been in 1914. Furthermore, the decline prior to 1918 was not incompatible with an increase for some elements of the manufacturing labour force, those in the large-scale, modern sector, where the new types of labour strategy were most common. Morishima has estimated that in 1914 wages in enterprises employing between five and nine people were about 72 to 73 per cent of what was being paid to those working in units of over 100.[27] By the end of the war these disparities had considerably widened. The significance of this is underlined when it is remembered that the bulk of Japan's industrial workers remained in small-scale enterprises where such policies were not

Table 5.7 Index of incomes

	Real manufacturing wages		
	Men	Women	Real agricultural income
1914	100	100	100
1918	88	79	99
1922	143	145	106

Source: Nakamura, *Economic Growth*, p. 146.

operative. Even in the larger firms only a minority benefited. In this gap between relatively few privileged industrial workers in large-scale modern plants, and the majority of workers both in the modern sector and the larger non-modernized sector, lay the origin of the dual economy which became a marked feature of Japan from the 1920s onwards. It has been calculated that by 1919 the average household income of a Tokyo factory worker was 40 per cent higher than that of a non-factory worker.[28] As the dual nature of the economy became more pronounced, so differentials continued to widen to the extent that by 1932 wages in the smallest of Japan's industrial plants (defined in terms of capital) were only about a quarter of those paid in the largest.[29]

Interestingly, Table 5.7 also indicates that farm income was less volatile than manufacturing wages between 1914 and 1922, holding up quite well during the war itself. In the short-term, high levels of demand for food, both at home and abroad, allowed some of Japan's farmers to prosper. They achieved a modest growth in the per capita availability of food and, while the annual production of rice did not rise much above its pre-war levels general farm productivity did improve. Unadjusted for inflation, the figures show that agricultural output rose 137 per cent (Table 5.8). High world need, coupled with the demand from that growing proportion of Japanese who were not themselves farmers, pushed up food prices during the war. They reached record levels in 1917 and then doubled again over the following year, bringing prosperity not only to the farming communities but also to those who were able to speculate against the forward price of rice.

Nevertheless, the relative significance of agriculture in the Japanese economy declined. It remained the largest single occupation, but employment fell absolutely from 16.4 million in 1910 to 14.3 million in 1920. It is also apparent from Table 5.8 that the sector's overall importance in the economy was diminishing, since the increase in agricultural output was considerably smaller than that achieved by industry. By 1919 industrial output was well in excess of agriculture's, a reversal of the situation prevailing in 1914. This changing balance was a typical and integral part of the modernization proc-

Table 5.8 Japan: output values (¥m)

	1914	1919
Industry	1371	6738
Agriculture	1700	4038

Source: Lockwood, W. (1955), *The Economic Development of Japan: Growth and Structural Change, 1868–1938*, Oxford: Oxford University Press, p. 39.

ess, one which occurred in all modern developed societies. In Japan's case, the transition was accelerated by the war.

However, the boost provided by the war for farmers proved to be only temporary. The depressed post-war demand for primary products fell particularly severely upon Japan. In the course of the war the country had become more fully integrated into the world economy. The domestic price level, therefore, was increasingly affected by overseas events, while the developing internal market meant that such effects were more thoroughly and more swiftly transmitted throughout the national economy. With world food capacity exceeding effective demand in the 1920s, the predominantly small-scale Japanese farmers were at a particular disadvantage. Their costs remained high, and attempts to compensate for falling prices by increasing output merely depressed prices still more. Rice prices fell by more than 50 per cent in the post-war depression. In the course of the 1920s the average rent of a rice field reached 50 per cent above its product value. Matters were not helped because the Japanese government, anxious to extend its influence in Asia, was encouraging the import of rice from colonial territories in Formosa and Korea. Since this was Japan's primary agricultural product, occupying over half the cultivable land, it was hardly surprising that its price collapse forced the government to intervene in the form of the Rice Act, intended to stabilize prices. Even the 40 per cent or so of farmers who derived a secondary income from silk production struggled when its price also dropped during the depression. Although they then recovered somewhat, their overdependence on the American market was dreadfully exposed when that demand collapsed after the 1929 crash. Long before that, however, farmers had organized to voice their discontent, particularly about rents which remained high relative to their declining incomes. From 1917 onwards tenancy disputes became a constant feature of Japanese agrarian life, averaging over 2,000 a year in the early 1920s. By 1927 the number of tenants' unions had swollen to 40,000 covering an estimated 10 per cent of the farming community.

Together with the rice riots and industrial unrest, the farmers' protests were symptomatic of a general unrest apparent in Japan as the war finally came to an end. Alongside such movements went a general growth of democratic and radical sentiments which had been gaining ground ever since the start of the Taisho era in 1912. Widespread urban rioting had occurred in that year – for instance, when the army engineered the resignation of Prime Minister Saionji and his replacement by General Katsura. The protests were sufficiently strong to compel Katsura's own resignation and his successor, Admiral Yamamoto, was also forced out by popular disturbances following revelations of corruption. Identification with the victorious Entente powers had further exposed the Japanese people to more liberal ideas, and the franchise was doubled in 1919. A new Women's Association was founded in 1920 by a former member of the Blue Stocking Society and it succeeded in ending the ban on women's attendance at public meetings. Shortly afterwards, in 1924, a Women's Suffrage League was established. Another straw in the radical wind appeared in 1922 with the establishment of the *Sucheisha*, a body dedicated to ending discrimination against the *burakamin*, Japan's social outcastes. The Russian Revolution also evoked a great deal of sympathy, especially among intellectuals, in a country which had only recently been engaged in conflict against the forces of the Czar. The progress made by left-wing ideas was manifest in the foundation of the Japanese Communist Party in 1922. Members of the emerging trade unions were using language derived from Western notions of rights and socialist ideas of class struggle, even though it has been argued that their main objective at this time was to translate into the industrial context traditional notions of the employment relationship in which benevolence was required from the employer in return for loyalty and obedience from the employee.[30] It was significant in this respect that the country's leading labour body, the *Yuaikai*, a friendly society established in 1912 to foster the mutual welfare of workers, was transformed by radicals into the General Federation of Labour or *Sodemei*. Striking workers at the Kawasaki shipyards in Kobe even attempted to establish a system of workers' control in 1921.

All in all, therefore, it appeared that the effect of the war was to bring Japan still closer to fulfilling Fujii Kenjiro's pre-war prediction that a Western type of democracy would inevitably follow modernization, with popular participation in government and constitutional rights, as well as individual freedom and equality. The likelihood was enhanced still further by two other contemporary developments. One was the coming of age of the first generation of Japanese to have benefited from mass state education: the second was the declining influence of the *genro*. The deaths of Okuma and Yamagata in 1922 left only Saionji of the old ruling clique, offering at last a genuine opportunity to end the divorce which had existed between political leadership and the decision-making process. When Prime Minister Terauchi resigned following the rice riots, his successor, Kei Hara, was the first Japanese premier drawn from outside the charmed circle of the *genro*, and his appointment brought to an end 50 years of political dominance by the Satsuma and Choshu clans. Now there appeared to be a genuine opportunity for the Diet and the political parties to become real centres of political power, particularly with the 1919 franchise extension.

Such manifestations of unrest and change arising from the disruption of the war were not unique to Japan, and her experience was only a weak echo of much more disruptive forces unleashed in parts of Europe. The fact, however, that post-war Japan remained relatively stable was little consolation to those bureaucrats and other members of the ruling cliques who had long been determined to prevent modernization and industrialization in their country being accompanied by the sorts of social tensions and conflicts characteristic of those processes in the West. The war appeared to have strengthened unwelcome – because destabilizing – forces and ideas, inimical to the classical Japanese conviction that the group rather than the individual was thc basic unit of society. From this perspective the last thing Japan needed in this view was Western-style democracy or socialism with all their potential for conflict and change.

Those suspicious of democracy and radicalism were joined by two groups whose fortunes had been enhanced by the war. One was an element within the Japanese military whose supporters believed that Germany's defeat owed far less to military causes than to a failure to organize the economy adequately. This gave them a particular and growing interest in economic policy. In so doing, it also brought into new significance the armed forces' ability to influence civilian government by exercising the constitutional right to nominate their own cabinet ministers from the list of serving officers. The other group brought into prominence by the war was the business community, especially the *zaibatsu*. Their powerful economic position gave them both the desire and the ability to influence national policy in their own interests. Thus Mitsui established close working connections with the Seiyukia Party and provided important support for Prime Minister Hara, while Takaaki Kato, Prime Minister in a coalition cabinet in 1924, had close associations with Mitsubishi. In other words, wartime developments gave rise to powerful pressure group interests which, in certain circumstances, would not always work in the best interests of democracy.

In the short-term post-war Japanese social development was characterized by an uneasy compromise between populism and heavy-handedness. The further extension of the franchise in 1925 to include all males over 25, save those in receipt of public or private assistance, was tempered by the Peace Law giving government a free hand to clamp down on virtually anything it wished. Legislation to ease the rent burdens of farmers was accompanied by careful official monitoring of the tenants' union movement. As for industrial relations, the government encouraged employers to establish works councils, and also set up the *Kyochokai*, a group of scholars, civil servants and employers, mandated to devise policies conducive to workplace harmony. On the other hand, the army was sometimes used to put down strikes, and the Communist Party was suppressed as soon as it was formed.

In the long run the anti-democratic forces prevailed. However, if the economic turmoil which followed the Great Crash of 1929 aided this triumph, so, too, did the international implications for Japan of the First World War, since its repercussions were by no means confined to domestic affairs. Japan had always viewed the Far East as its own legitimate sphere of interest, a perception sharpened by the events of 1914–18. In encouraging rapid industrial development, the war highlighted both Japan's dependence on imported raw materials and the necessity of international trade as a way of paying for them. It thus appeared even more desirable to secure both markets and sources of raw materials on the nearby and mineral-rich Asian mainland. Yet these aspirations and needs were hardly acknowledged by the Versailles Peace Treaty. To an extent at least this was due to Japan's own actions during the war. The initial decision to declare war on Germany had been determined in part by the calculation that it would provide an opportunity for the consolidation of Japan's Asian interests, especially in China, which would be isolated from its usual European sources of moral, financial and diplomatic support. By the end of 1914 Japanese forces had captured the German fortress of Tsing-tau, a military operation legitimized by the president of the Chinese Republic, Yuan Shih-K'ai, who declared that the German leasehold area around Kiachow in Shantung was a war zone. However, when the Japanese went further by occupying the whole of Shantung, he demanded their total withdrawal. Japan's response was to present the so-called 'Twenty-One Demands' in January 1915. These required recognition of Japan's right to take over German interests in Shantung and the extension of the Japanese leasehold over Manchuria for 99 years. The most extreme of all effectively amounted to an abrogation of sovereignty, requiring the Chinese to employ Japanese financial and political advisers, and to allow Japanese policing of important cities. Although these were eventually withdrawn, considerable damage was done to Japan's standing abroad. Chinese resentment was natural, but far more harmful in the long run was the alienation of opinion in the United States, which reacted strongly against what was seen as opportunist Japanese bullying of a weaker neighbour. In this one act the Japanese forfeited much of the international goodwill earned by their earlier military and diplomatic activities. Nor was this much offset when they subsequently relinquished some of the territorial concessions secured by the Twenty-One Demands.

As a result of the Versailles treaty Japan gained an economic interest over former German territory in Shantung and a League of Nations mandate over German islands in the Pacific. However, this was judged by the Japanese themselves as insufficient acknowledgement either of their war contribution or of their legitimate territorial ambitions in the Far East. Nor was this the only source of their discontent with the post-war settlement. Although possession of a permanent seat on the Council of the new League of Nations implied equity with the Great Powers, Japan was largely ignored when it came to discussing the terms of the territorial settlement. Britain, France and America effectively redrew the world map between them without consulting their erstwhile Asian ally. In addition the Great Powers denied another, and to the Japanese, a more important form of parity by refusing to incorporate the principle of racial equality into the peace treaties. This confirmed Japanese suspicions that they were still not fully accepted on equal terms by the leaders of the international community, a view confirmed a few years later when the Americans imposed a ban on any more immigration from Japan. For the Japanese, this reduced them to the same status as the Chinese, a race whom they despised as inferior. A further rebuff was perceived when Britain abrogated the pre-war treaty, once described in an official Japanese government statement as the 'marrow' of imperial foreign policy.[31] It is unclear whether the British believed that they no longer required a buffer against either German or Russian ambitions in the Far East, or whether formal treaties and alliances simply seemed outmoded in the new age of international co-operation presaged by the formation of the League of Nations. Either way, the blow to Japan's pride was considerable and contributed to the subsequent deterioration of Anglo-Japanese relations.[32]

It is rarely a simple matter to untangle the complexities of the past and the task is particularly difficult in the case of so momentous an event as the First World War. The war certainly accelerated important economic change within Japan: altering – in output terms at least – the balance between industry and agriculture, boosting heavy industry and promoting the development of labour and organizational changes which were of considerable longer-term significance. It also made her far more dependent upon overseas relationships for both markets and raw materials. Japan's direct participation in the war was quite limited and, apart from the extension of the franchise, internal social change was rather limited. Women in particular remained politically powerless, while industrial labour failed to develop any genuinely independent, organized voice. Even so, the economic changes brought about within Japan by the war did generate social conflicts similar to those found in other combatant nations – civilian protests against material hardship, short-term industrial strife and longer-term rural distress. Tension was also sharpened between, on the one hand the populism and democracy associated with modernization, and the strength of tradition on the other. This was a long-standing rift within Japan, but the war added three specific contributions of its own: its impact on military thinking, its enhancement of the *zaibatsu*, and the resentful legacy of unsatisfied imperial hopes. Whether these outcomes of the Great War determined by themselves the course of subsequent Japanese history remains, of course, a matter of speculation.

NOTES AND REFERENCES

1. Hearn, L. (1904), *Japan: An Attempt at Interpretation*, Rutland, Vermont: C.E. Tuttle, p. 224.

2. Holland, C. (1913), *Things Seen in Japan*, London: Seeley, Service and Co., p. 144.
3. Maizels, A. (1963), *Industrial Growth and World Trade*, Cambridge: Cambridge University Press, p. 189.
4. Bairoch, P. (1982), 'International Industrialisation Levels from 1750 to 1980', *Journal of European Economic History*, **11**, p. 296.
5. Nakamura, T. (1983), *Economic Growth in Prewar Japan*, New Haven, CT: Yale University Press, p. 47. The first national population census in Japan was not compiled until 1920. The 1910 figure is based on the estimate made by the Cabinet Statistical Office.
6. Total imports of these commodities were worth ¥111.5m in 1901, ¥424.6m in 1913. Ohkawa, K. and M. Shinohara (eds) (1979), *Patterns of Japanese Economic Development: A Quantitative Appraisal*, New Haven and London: Yale University Press, p. 320.
7. Ibid., pp. 324, 328, 334.
8. See the discussion in Barnhart, M.A. (1995), *Japan and the World Since 1868*, London: Arnold, pp. 51–2.
9. Ohkawa and Shinohara (eds), *Patterns of Japanese Economic Development*, p. 334. This average is a more recent calculation than the slightly higher figure given in Allen, *Short Economic History*, p. 91.
10. Morikawa, H. (1992), *Zaibatsu: The Rise and Fall of Family Enterprise Groups in Japan*, Tokyo: University of Tokyo Press, p. 123.
11. Nakamura, *Economic Growth*, p. 145.
12. Quoted in Robertson, A. (1990), 'Lancashire and the Rise of Japan, 1910–1937', *Business History*, **32**, p. 88.
13. Seki, K. (1956), *The Cotton Industry of Japan*, Tokyo: Japan Society for the Promotion of Science, p. 23.
14. Yonekura, S. (1994), *The Japanese Iron and Steel Industry 1850–1990*, Basingstoke: Macmillan, p. 79.
15. Nakamura, *Economic Growth*, p. 159.
16. Morikawa, *Zaibatsu*, p. 123.
17. For Mitsui see Roberts, J.G. (1973), *Mitsui. Three Centuries of Japanese Business*, New York: Weatherill.
18. Allen, *Short Economic History*, p. 127.
19. Ohkawa and Shinohara, *Patterns of Japanese Economic Development*, p. 334.
20. Waswo, A. (1996), *Modern Japanese Society, 1868–1994*, Oxford: Oxford University Press, p. 62.
21. Morishima, M. (1982), *Why Has Japan 'Succeeded'?*, Cambridge: Cambridge University Press, p. 127.
22. Okayama, R. (1983), 'Japanese Employer and Labour Policy: The Heavy Engineering Industry in 1900–1930', in Gospel, H. and C. Littler (eds), *Managerial Strategies and Industrial Relations*, London: Heinemann, p. 162.
23. Ibid.
24. See Tamai, K. (1993), 'The Evolution of Industrial Relations in Osaka: The Case of the Textile Industry', *Journal of Economics, Osaka City University*, 3/4, pp. 117–26.
25. On this see Totten, G.O. (1967), 'Collective Bargaining and Works Councils as Innovations in Industrial Relations in Japan During the 1920s' , in Dore, R.P. (ed.), *Aspects of Social Change in Modern Japan*, Princeton: Princeton University Press, pp. 203–44.
26. *Japan Year Book* (1926), p. 52.
27. Morishima, *Why Has Japan?*, pp. 125–7.
28. Chubachi, M. and K. Taira (1976), 'Poverty in Modern Japan: Perceptions and Realities', in Patrick, H. (ed.), *Japanese Industrialization and Its Social Consequences*, Berkeley, Los Angeles and London: University of California Press, p. 401.
29. Morishima, *Why Has Japan?*, p. 111.
30. Smith, T.C., (1988), 'The Right to Benevolence: Dignity and Japanese Workers, 1890–1920', reprinted in Smith T.C. (ed.), *Native Sources of Japanese Industrialization, 1750–1920*, Berkeley: University of California Press, pp. 236–70.
31. Quoted in Ferretti, V. (1990), 'The Strategic Significance of the 1911 Anglo-Japanese Alliance', in Lowe, P. and H. Moeshart (eds), *Western Interactions with Japan. Expan-*

sion, the Armed Forces and Readjustment, 1859–1956, Sandgate, Kent: The Japan Library Ltd., p. 50.

32. Winston Churchill remarked that it was viewed as 'the spurning of an Asiatic Power by the Western World'. Churchill, W.S. (1948), *The Second World War: I. The Gathering Storm*, London: Cassell, p. 13.

6. Legacy – war, aftermath and the end of the nineteenth-century liberal trading order, 1914–32

Andrew Marrison

The 1920s were a decade of heightened national insecurity in which the legacy of the First World War was manifest not only in the interminable politico-economic wrangle over German reparations, but also in currency instability and an increased desire for economic autarky. Such factors were given further impetus by unequally rapid technological change and capacity extension in the emerging mass-production industries of the leading nations, at a time when export markets had lost their pre-war dynamism. Persistent conferences to liberalize trade relations under the auspices of the League of Nations yielded little beyond pious expressions of intent by participating countries, and by the later 1920s cynicism abounded. Policy-makers turned inwards even more violently as the world crisis of 1929–32 unfolded and ushered in what for most countries was a period of state intervention and control in the economy unparalleled in time of peace.

BEFORE THE WAR

In the 1920s, many, especially in Britain and America, looked back on the Edwardian years as an ideal in terms of economic stability and prosperity. World trade and world production had increased fairly steadily between 1870 and 1914, as the countries of Europe industrialized and as new primary producers overseas joined an expanding international economy. Expansion was underpinned by stable exchange rates during the relatively short heyday of the international gold standard, and a tremendous export of capital from Europe, especially from Britain. The image of an open international economy was reinforced by a virtual absence of regulation of the movement of labour and capital.

Whether this underlying trade stability was entirely reflected in international commercial policy is a matter of perspective. Many contemporaries who looked back to the 1860s and 1870s thought not. Falling commodity prices down to the turn of the century, reflecting falling transport costs and the superior labour productivity of the New World, triggered a protectionist reaction among European farmers.[1] Industrial rivalries were accentuated alongside political frictions. European powers sought advantage by experimenting with different forms of two-tier tariff structures and there was a series of tariff wars.[2] Thus, the conventional interpretation is that the late nineteenth century saw a 'return to protection' after the low-tariff era of mid-century, a return symbolized by Germany's 'alliance of iron and rye' (1879), the French Méline Tariff (1892), and the US McKinley (1890) and Dingley (1897) Tariffs.[3] For some contemporaries, the trade rivalries and the tariff policies associated with them were an important contribution to the origins of the war itself.

Yet these trends were not strong enough to disrupt heavily the underlying strength of world trade and growth. Examining the seven major trading countries, Capie discovers that, in a period when nominal tariff rates rose, import duty revenues nevertheless fell as a proportion of total imports, and the ratio of total imports to total output increased.[4] Studies of the USA, Italy, and Germany have shown that, when nominal tariff increases on finished manufactures are netted out for increased duties on raw materials and semi-finished inputs, the 'effective' level of protection on the finished goods was sometimes smaller than is suggested by the nominal increase.[5]

Furthermore, what seemed on the surface a rise in nominal tariff levels and bitter tariff rivalry was often blunted by a developing system of international tariff negotiation. The evolution of elaborate two-tier tariff systems – 'General–Conventional', or 'Maximum–Minimum' systems – and the proliferation of treaties embodying the unconditional most favoured nation (MFN) clause meant a large extension a country's lower-level tariff to other trading partners in a spreading process of negotiation and joint relaxation. In some ways, the tariff wars mentioned above were the exceptions, the points at which the system was tested, modified and refined.

This treaty system was centred in Europe, and most major trading countries participated. The USA, however, stayed aloof. Though the 'reciprocity' provisions of the McKinley (1891) and Dingley (1897) Tariffs were used as a retaliatory threat to wring concessions out of primary-producing countries in a handful of unimportant treaties, the US economy remained protected by what was in effect a high, non-negotiable, single-tier tariff. But even here there were small signs of change. As, after 1890, the US industrial sector developed new export potential,[6] some Americans came to recognize that national trade policy could no longer be based on simple policies of high tariffs and exclusion, and that the USA could no longer persist in high tariffs while still 'free-riding' on British free trade. Hence, the Payne–Aldrich

Tariff (1909) introduced a two-tier 'maximum–minimum' schedule in an effort to obtain access to the lower, concessionary levels of European tariffs, and the Underwood Tariff (1913) reduced tariff levels to their lowest level since before the Civil War.[7]

Nevertheless, the impact of such considerations on the political perceptions of European leaders was small. The USA was still seen in Europe as the exponent of high protectionism, unwilling to negotiate real MFN concessions, which was particularly annoying given her inexorable rise to international economic hegemony.[8] Besides, in a Britain almost obsessed with relative economic decline, domestic critics of free trade were as much concerned with German trade rivalry, a rivalry in which tariff policy was deemed to play a deliberate strategic rôle, as they were with US exclusionism. Britain's loss of pre-eminence was closely associated with the first significant revivals of political support for protectionism since the 1840s, 'fair trade' in the 1880s and Chamberlain's 'tariff reform' after 1900.[9] The Edwardian years may have been a period of comparative economic liberalism when set alongside the inter-war period, but they were already interlaced with tensions that had been growing since the low-tariff interlude of the mid-Victorian boom, already entangled within a matrix of political tensions and economic rivalries that world war could only enhance.

This chapter will concentrate mostly on the effect of war and its aftermath on commercial policy narrowly defined – that is, tariffs and prohibitions. A broader definition would encompass state policy towards export promotion and cartelization, controls on foreign direct investment, patent rights, legal structures, administrative procedures, institutional controls, sanitary and veterinary controls, regulation of foreign commercial travellers, etc. It would also prompt discussion of the industry response to tariff barriers, surplus capacity and sluggish trade – the spread of international cartel and market-sharing agreements, most notably the international steel agreement of 1926, though these were mostly in their infancy before 1929.[10] The statist impulses generated by the war and persisting thereafter can be discerned in these areas as well as in tariff policy. However, reasons of space exclude their consideration, and the obsession of contemporary observers with prohibitions and high tariffs goes some way to justifying that exclusion.

THE DIFFICULTY OF MEASURING TARIFF LEVELS

Measuring overall tariff levels is complex, and successive enquiries into the issue during the 1920s were all at pains to stress the imprecision of their results.[11] Evolving over time, a country's tariff was usually a mixture of specific and *ad valorem* duties, and could cover thousands of items, grouped into categories. The preliminary step is to convert specific to *ad valorem* rates, not easy given that market or wholesale prices fluctuate more often than specific rates are revised. Calculating changes over time requires that specific rates are converted to *ad valorem* equivalents at prices prevailing at both the beginning and the end of the period.

Thereafter, the different commodity rates of a country's import tariff must be combined into one measure. One approach is simply to average them to produce a 'nominal' or 'nominal average' tariff level. Essentially, this was the approach followed in Loveday's well-known study.[12] The 'potential' and 'general potential' tariff levels for Europe in Liepmann's classic study considered below, are also calculated in this way.[13] This method has obvious limitations if it simply combines a 10 per cent tariff on goods which are imported in small quantities with a 20 per cent tariff on goods imported in large quantities to arrive at a 'nominal average' tariff level of 15 per cent.

For any given year, this weakness can be overcome simply. The 'nominal average' tariff is adjusted by weighting each item-specific nominal rate by the volume of imports under that head to produce a 'trade-weighted average tariff'. But this is not an ideal measure of changes over time. It is an *ex post* measure of the average tariff paid on imports, not an *ex ante* measure of the *protective effect*. That is, it measures the height of the tariff *after* adjustments have taken place in exporting countries to meet the importing country's tariff. The composition of imports of the tariff-imposing country will have changed to accommodate to the tariff. In the limiting case, prohibitive tariff rates which result in zero imports of a particular good will not appear in the weighted 'nominal average'. Furthermore, exogenous changes in trade patterns will affect the ratio. For instance, tariff *rates* on all commodities could remain unchanged, but a relative shift in imports away from zero-rated raw materials to high-rated manufactures for internal structural reasons would show up as a rise in the ratio. This might be useful in assessing the welfare cost of protection to consumers in the importing country, but it would represent no change in the tariff encountered by exporters of manufactures to that country. The 'trade-weighted average tariff' is similar to the 'actual tariff level' calculated for a few European countries in Liepmann's study.[14]

A simpler and cruder way of calculating the 'trade-weighted average tariff' is to compare movements in the ratio of customs revenues to value of imports (CRIV). Again, this is far from ideal – the ratio of customs revenues to value of *dutiable* imports would be preferable, but is less generally available. Though the crude ratio has the merit of being easy to calculate over a wide range of countries, and bypasses the problem of converting specific to *ad valorem* duties, movements in it are hard to interpret. This is particularly true in a period such as the inter-war years, when prohibitions or direct controls were common. In Table 6.1 (Case A), a hypothetical country is shown intro-

Table 6.1 Effect of prohibitions or prohibitive duties on CRIV ratio of hypothetical country X

Case A: Introduction of prohibitions

	Free imports	Dutiable imports	Dutiable in year 1 but prohibited or taxed at prohibitive rate in year 2	Total dutiable imports	Total imports	Duty rate	Customs receipts	CRIV
Year 1	10000	10000	0	10000	20000	0.20	2000	10.00
Year 2a	10000	5000	5000	5000	15000	0.20	1000	6.67
Year 2b	10000	5000	5000	5000	15000	0.29	1450	9.67
Year 2c	10000	3500	5000	3500	13500	0.29	1015	7.52

Case B: Removal of prohibitions

	Free imports	Dutiable imports	Prohibited or taxed at prohibitive rate in year 1 but admitted in year 2	Total dutiable imports	Total imports	Duty rate	Customs receipts	CRIV
Year 1	10000	5000	5000	5000	15000	0.30	1500	10.00
Year 2a	10000	5000	5000	10000	20000	0.30	3000	15.00
Year 2b	10000	5000	5000	10000	20000	0.25	2500	12.50
Year 2c	10000	6500	5000	11500	21500	0.25	2875	13.37

ducing prohibitions or prohibitive duties on half of its dutiable imports. This actually leads to a *fall* in its CRIV ratio despite the fact that trade has become less liberal! The CRIV will certainly fall if prohibitions are introduced but there is no change in tariff rates on goods still imported (as shown in Year 2a), but it is important to noticc that it may also fall if the tariff on goods still imported is increased (as shown in Year 2b). Assuming no volume effect, the duty rate on goods still admitted would have to rise from 20 per cent *ad valorem* to more than 30 per cent *ad valorem* before the CRIV exhibited a rise. In Table 6.1 (Case B) prohibitions are removed and the reverse case is shown. Against a background of trade liberalization, the CRIV ratio will actually rise! Indeed, in the example shown it will not fall below the Year 1 level until the average tariff rate on all dutiable imports has been reduced from 30 per cent *ad valorem* to less than 20 per cent *ad valorem*. Furthermore, the greater the volume effect of any change in duty rate on dutiable imports, the more perverse will be the result (Year 2c in each case). It should be stressed that this hypothetical example is an extreme one, involving prohibitions or prohibitive duties on no less than 50 per cent of potential dutiable imports. At more historically accurate levels, this distortion would be less.

Without the complicating factor of a change in the incidence of prohibitions, volume effects exercise less distortion. In the example in Table 6.2, a rise in duty from 20 to 25 per cent would have to *be accompanied by* (not in itself *cause*) a shrinkage of dutiable imports by one-third before the CRIV fell below the original 10 per cent. A rise from 20 to 50 per cent would have to be accompanied by a reduction in dutiable imports by three-quarters. Since a given percentage rise in duty does not imply an equal rise in retail price, demand elasticity in the importing market would have to be extremely high for this to be a serious problem, although it should be remembered that in the troubled 1920s trade volumes might fall substantially for exogenous reasons. It should be noticed that in Table 6.2 free imports constitute half of the original import bill. Historically, they are unlikely to have been more; if they are less, the distortion is even smaller.

Prohibitions and direct controls were a pervasive feature of the war and the 1920s. It is worth remembering in what follows, therefore, that for those countries in which direct controls continued to be prominent – especially those of Central and South-eastern Europe – movements in CRIV ratios may be highly misleading. On the other hand, for those countries where direct controls were by the 1920s unimportant – the UK, Scandinavia, Belgium, Netherlands, and extra-European countries in general, etc. – they are likely to be more revealing.[15]

It should also be remembered that *ad valorem* rates on dutiable items were typically much higher than the figure revealed by the CRIV ratio. In the USA, for example, average rates on dutiable imports were always about twice as

Table 6.2 Combined effect of increase in duty and reduction in dutiable imports in hypothetical country Y

	Free	Dutiable	Duty rate	Customs revenue	Total imports	CRIV
Year 1	10000	10000	0.20	2000	20000	10.00
Year 2	10000	10000	0.25	2500	20000	12.50
	10000	9000	0.25	2250	19000	11.84
	10000	8000	0.25	2000	18000	11.11
	10000	7000	0.25	1750	17000	10.29
	10000	**6666**	**0.25**	**1666.5**	**16666**	**10.00**
	10000	6000	0.25	1500	16000	9.38
	10000	5000	0.25	1250	15000	8.33
	10000	4000	0.25	1000	14000	7.14
	10000	3000	0.25	750	13000	5.77
	10000	2000	0.25	500	12000	4.17
	10000	1000	0.25	250	11000	2.27
	10000	0	0.25	0	10000	0.00

	Free	Dutiable	Duty rate	Customs revenue	Total imports	CRIV
Year 1	10000	10000	0.20	2000	20000	10.00
Year 2	10000	10000	0.50	5000	20000	25.00
	10000	9000	0.50	4500	19000	23.68
	10000	8000	0.50	4000	18000	22.22
	10000	7000	0.50	3500	17000	20.59
	10000	6000	0.50	3000	16000	18.75
	10000	5000	0.50	2500	15000	16.67
	10000	4000	0.50	2000	14000	14.29
	10000	3000	0.50	1500	13000	11.54
	10000	**2500**	**0.50**	**1250**	**12500**	**10.00**
	10000	2000	0.50	1000	12000	8.33
	10000	1000	0.50	500	11000	4.55
	10000	0	0.50	0	10000	0.00

Table 6.3 Customs revenue as % of import values: 1900–13 to 1930–39 (averages of selected periods)

						1900–13 = 100				
	1900–13	1915–18	1919–24	1925–29	1930–39	1900–13	1915–18	1919–24	1925–29	1930–39
Argentina	21.58	12.44	13.40	17.38	22.92	100	57.65	62.09	80.54	106.21
Australia	16.86	17.23	17.67	19.63	31.73	100	102.19	104.80	116.43	188.20
Austria	6.04	–	–	7.91	15.36	100	–	–	130.96	254.30
Belgium	1.51	–	1.91	3.27	7.49	100	–	126.49	216.56	496.03
Brazil	39.61	21.27	18.54	23.85	27.40	100	53.70	46.81	60.21	69.17
Bulgaria	15.79	–	21.30	19.04	22.79	100	–	134.90	120.58	144.33
Canada	16.33	16.56	14.30	14.38	14.03	100	101.41	87.57	88.06	85.92
Czechoslovakia (*)	6.04	–	4.94	6.84	9.69	100	–	81.79	113.25	160.43
Denmark	6.78	3.14	3.65	5.38	7.33	100	46.31	53.83	79.35	108.11
Finland	12.99	4.92	16.37	18.99	26.64	100	37.88	126.02	146.19	205.08
France	8.63	6.36	5.80	7.56	21.31	100	73.70	67.21	87.60	246.93
Germany	8.09	–	–	7.83	25.92	100	–	–	96.79	320.40
Greece	–	–	9.02	14.14	30.23	100	–	–	–	–
Hungary (*)	6.04	–	–	10.65	8.75	100	–	–	176.32	144.87
Eire (***)	5.38	–	–	11.44	22.48	100	–	–	212.64	417.84
India	5.87	7.97	13.95	19.52	32.54	100	135.78	237.65	332.54	554.34
Italy	8.83	3.09	2.98	5.14	17.60	100	34.99	33.75	58.21	199.32
Japan	7.66	4.13	3.94	4.87	4.81	100	53.92	51.44	63.58	62.79
Netherlands	0.45	1.14	1.70	2.14	6.38	100	253.33	377.78	475.56	1417.78
New Zealand	18.29	15.59	15.06	17.19	21.68	100	85.24	82.34	93.99	118.53

Norway	11.34	4.56	5.01	10.41	12.84	100	40.21	44.18	91.80	113.23
Poland (**)	31.48	–	9.57	14.04	11.04	100	–	30.40	44.60	35.07
Portugal	25.59	17.00	4.81	14.42	37.91	100	66.43	18.80	56.35	148.14
Romania	10.59	–	20.28	23.27	13.50	100	–	191.50	219.74	127.48
Russia	31.48	–	–	–	–	100	–	–	–	–
Spain	16.74	13.09	18.60	20.96	47.37	100	78.20	111.11	125.21	282.97
Sweden	9.61	4.69	6.94	8.78	9.40	100	48.80	72.22	91.36	97.81
Switzerland	4.45	2.45	5.57	9.02	17.74	100	55.06	125.17	202.70	398.65
UK	5.38	7.26	9.84	9.09	22.90	100	134.94	182.90	168.96	425.65
USA	23.27	8.61	10.53	13.42	16.97	100	37.00	45.25	57.67	72.93

Notes:
* 1900–13 average based on figure for Austria.
** 1900–13 average based on figure for Russia.
*** 1900–13 average based on figure for UK.

Sources: B.R. Mitchell, *European Historical Statistics: 1750–1975*, Macmillan Press, London, 2nd edn, 1978; B.R. Mitchell, *International Historical Statistics: The Americas and Australasia*, Macmillan Press, London, 1983; B.R. Mitchell, *International Historical Statistics: Africa, Asia and Oceania, 1750–1988*, Macmillan Press, 2nd edn, London, 1995.

high as the CRIV ratio throughout the period covered by this study. Table 6.3 reproduces average CRIVs for the periods 1900–13 through to 1930–39.

Sophisticated modern econometric studies seek to discover static GNP loss due to tariff barriers (the 'trade intensity' ratio), or how much trade is deterred by trade barriers (the degree of 'openness'), by comparing actual trade flows with estimates of what trade would have been based on the different resource endowments of different countries.[16] This approach cannot be followed here: we will concentrate more on changes in tariff levels than on their effect on trade volumes. The latter is notoriously difficult to calculate, and would also take us into a general history of inter-war international trade which is beyond the scope of this chapter. Where comment is made here on the effects of tariffs on trade, it is much more intuitive.

TARIFFS IN WARTIME

A nation's tariff policy can be seen as the outcome of a complex matrix of factors, not all of which exercise the same influence in different countries or at different times. The nation's economic strength, its economic structure, the completeness of its parliamentary democracy, the degree of organization and influence of its various business lobbies, say much about its predisposition towards liberal or nationalist economic policies. Changes in any of these factors will operate to alter the general stance towards liberalism or restrictionism in the international economy. Yet no tight and direct determinism is involved – structural changes in the economy will only be mirrored in trade policy through political agency. Policy change will thus attract opponents as well as supporters, and will be complex, drawn-out and uncertain.

In 1914–18, the contingencies of war and the imperatives of national survival provided circumstances in which the scope for 'executive action' increased as governments were given greater and less-questioned latitude on policy.[17] At a time when the increased strength of organized business and organized labour pushed in the direction of 'corporatist' institutions and policies, this might have circumvented the normal checks and balances preventing sudden and dramatic changes in trade policy. But external relations with Allies and neutrals now became vital. Thus, statist impulses were mostly towards direct controls on external trade. Attempts to control imports by tariff manipulation became a minor consideration for most belligerents. In areas remote from the conflict, reduced competition from the great exporting economies of North-west Europe made it, temporarily at least, unnecessary to act on pre-war ambitions for fostering infant industry.

As imperfect as it is, the CRIV ratio probably gives a reasonable picture of the movement of tariff levels during the war itself. Even Canada, which used tariff increases as a principal source of war revenue (augmenting customs receipts by nearly 40 per cent), did not exhibit a large increase in her CRIV ratio.[18] As Table 6.3 shows, only in three cases in the countries shown did the ratio rise appreciably above the pre-war average – the UK, India and the Netherlands. In the case of the Netherlands, the change was of little significance, merely representing a slight rise in revenue duties in what remained essentially a free-trade country. More complex reasons underlie the changes in the UK and India.

In Britain, there was a small rise in the ratio consequent on the imposition of the McKenna duties and the raising of revenue duties.[19] The McKenna duties of 33.3 per cent on luxuries such as pianos and motor cars were justified by the Asquith coalition on grounds of providing revenue, protecting the exchanges and conserving shipping space.[20] However, they added little to revenue, and the other objectives could surely have been achieved more effectively by an extension of the system of licensing being erected for other imports. It is therefore likely that the duties were seen by the Liberal members of the coalition as a gesture which would both mollify their Unionist colleagues Bonar Law and Austen Chamberlain, enthusiastic supporters of Joseph Chamberlain's pre-war tariff reform campaign, and provide a response to the public clamour for a more active war policy. While Asquith and Lloyd George regarded them as temporary wartime measures, they gave encouragement to the Conservative tariff reformers, and were heralded long after as the first historic breach in Britain's established free-trade policy.[21]

Before the war, against a background of growing nationalism, the India Office in Whitehall had discouraged attempts by some more zealous officials in the Government of India in Delhi to foster Indian industry. War brought a new enthusiasm for war products, and in some quarters there was also an appreciation of the defencelessness of an unindustrialized India and the need to prevent India being the dumping ground for foreign goods after war. But nationalist considerations of industrialization were not for the moment the impetus behind a rise in tariffs. Protection came about more directly in response to financial and political factors. War saw a big increase in Indian government expenditure, and in March 1917 a large gift of £100 million was made to reduce Britain's war debt. With revenue considerations paramount, but with a wary eye on the reaction in Lancashire, duties on cotton were soon raised from 3.5 to 7.5 per cent, with the prevailing excise of 3.5 per cent on home production left unchanged.[22]

In the main, however, the essential task of trade policy during war was to secure and finance adequate foreign supply, not to restrict it. For the Central Powers, the need was to maintain imports of food and strategic raw materials as the Allies sought to extend the blockade by enforcing export prohibitions on neutral traders. A contemporary *Reichsbank* estimate put German wartime imports at only 40 per cent of their pre-war level, exports even below this.[23] Serious food shortages developed, pre-war protection of agriculture proving no guarantee of wartime self-sufficiency.[24] For Britain, with her dependence on foreign foodstuffs and her desire for American armaments, and for France, with her agricultural capacity reduced by hostilities and many of her coal and iron regions occupied by Germany, the need for food, materials and munitions was pressing.[25] For their neutral neighbours, Netherlands, Denmark, Norway, Sweden and Switzerland, there was a reluctance to lose either domestic imports or transit trade by complying fully with the Allied blockade.[26]

Thus, import controls for protection were at best unimportant and at worst harmful. If rising import surpluses and inflationary war financing meant a weakening of the exchanges of all the European belligerents which at its ultimate might jeopardize the ability to pay for foreign supplies, they could be more accurately remedied by targeted direct controls than by relying on the price effect of a tariff. If, as in Italy, tariff revision was in process at the outbreak of war, it was postponed.[27] If, as in Britain, France and the US, war revealed deficiencies in domestic supply of critical war products, these could best be met by direct government assistance and not by restrictive protective duties, even though the case for fostering 'strategic' industries *after* the war might be strengthened. The British experience is well known. War revealed a dependence on Germany for important products such as synthetic dyestuffs and fine chemicals, magnetos for automobiles and aeroplanes, optical and chemical glass, shell fuses, etc.[28]

France is a good example of how a belligerent country, historically protectionist, extended her control of external trade through a network of administrative controls and government–industry co-operation. In the process, 'the ordinary questions of commercial policy, applicable to a *laissez-faire* economy, lost all relevance'.[29] Early in the war many import duties on food and war-related manufactures and raw materials were suspended or reduced to facilitate foreign supply, although in some cases duties were left on to encourage home production. In 1916–17 import regulation was intensified as the foreign debt increased and the exchange rate with neutral countries declined. In May 1916 the government was given direct powers to increase duties or introduce prohibitions. Mostly, it used the latter. In March 1917 the system was tightened even further. Imports of all foreign articles except those bought on behalf of the state itself were prohibited. A complete system of regulation previously applied only to exports was now applied to imports. A committee of representatives of various ministries, of industry, agriculture and chambers of commerce, was set up to determine what imports would be allowed by establishing priorities based on wartime need, availability of transport and financial considerations. Purchases were concentrated in countries where the French exchanges were firm, or French credit good. This system of control formed the domestic basis for French participation in inter-Allied joint economic action on supplies, which was extended after the Allied conference in December 1917.[30]

It should be noticed that the wartime reduction in the US CRIV ratio is due to changes which actually *preceded* the war, as the Underwood Tariff (1913) replaced the increasingly unpopular Dingley (1897) and Payne–Aldrich (1909) Tariffs. Given rising discontent against the level of the tariff during the Progressive period among export-orientated manufacturers and public alike,[31] it was no surprise that the Democrats would make reductions, although it took Wilson's unusual efforts to secure party loyalty in the House and an astute manipulation of public opinion to keep the highly protectionist Senate in line.[32] After Underwood, the degree of protection still averaged around 30 per cent *ad valorem* on dutiable imports.[33] Frequently prohibitive, these duties yielded little revenue. Thus, even the USA relied during the war primarily on import and export controls and internal revenues rather than customs revenues.[34]

Most would now accept that Wilson's liberalizing moves were a systemic reaction to changing international economic hegemony, as the US rose to manufacturing ascendancy and the proportion of her industry dependent on export markets increased. David Lake takes the argument further. As tariff reform and imperial preference gained support in the British Conservative Party, the US became less certain of her ability to continue to 'free-ride' on British cosmopolitanism by protecting her own industry with no fear of British retaliation. In consequence, Wilsonian liberalism was part of a permanent and continuing shift towards moderacy, flexibility and the unconditional rather than the conditional form of the MFN treaty.[35] It is still possible, however, to agree with early authorities who regarded the Wilson interlude as an aberration, sustained by war and reversed under the Republican Fordney–McCumber Tariff (1922), 'a tariff with rates higher than any in the long series of protective measures'.[36]

PLANS FOR TRADE WAR AFTER THE WAR

In Germany, the war and the Allied blockade gave a new impetus to discussions about a post-war customs union between Germany and the Austro-Hungarian empire.[37] In Britain and France, those supporting trade war after the war believed that Germany had been practising an acutely belligerent trade policy since the 1880s, in which protection and cartelization were designed to achieve systematic and predatory dumping. Reports of the Dresden conference of November 1915 seemed to confirm the belief that Germany would resume such practices after the peace, fanned Germanophobia, and provoked right-wing groups into preparing responses in kind. In truth, such beliefs exaggerated the monolithic structure of the German export sector, the unilinear direction of German economic policy, and indeed the extent to which the German business community was the willing agent of that policy. They also ignored differing political views within Germany and her allies and neighbours on the desirability of a post-war union with Austria-Hungary. Nevertheless, in a time of uncertainty, they gained wide currency.

In Britain, backbenchers from the pre-war tariff reform faction of the Unionist Party, organized into the Unionist Business Committee, agitated for more active prosecution of the war, full economic mobilization, and the construction of a post-war alliance to meet the threat from a greater Germany.[38] Their sentiments echoed those held by French politicians, especially Minister of Commerce, Etienne Clémentel, and were applauded by chambers of commerce in both countries.[39]

Asquith and the President of the Board of Trade, Walter Runciman, were wary of getting pulled into Allied entanglements, but public opinion and pressure from the Unionist backbenches forced them to respond, albeit cautiously, to French overtures for an economic conference of the Allies. The conference, held on 14–17 June 1916 in Paris, passed a series of resolutions intended by the participants to 'facilitate the organization on a permanent basis of their economic alliance'. Former enemy countries would be denied MFN status and their exports subjected to prohibitions or other penal restrictions for an unspecified period after the war, during which the Allies would collaborate in the sharing of the raw materials that 'reconstruction' would require. Longer-term arrangements, though more vaguely stated, were ominous: the Allies should 'render themselves independent of the enemy countries' in respect of the raw materials, manufactures and services 'essential to the normal development of their economic activities'.[40]

Disappointing to full-blooded 'trade warriors', and in particular containing no explicit reference to a customs union of the Allies, these resolutions nevertheless attracted the wrath of free traders.[41] Rather than cause friction with the French authorities, Asquith and Runciman supported the Paris Resolutions, partly because they regarded them as permissive rather than binding, but also because they allowed them to diffuse the threat posed by the largely-Conservative 'trade warriors' to the wartime coalition. The price they paid was that after Paris British tariff reform appeared to make progress. In a series of reports in 1917 and 1918, the Balfour of Burleigh Committee on Trade Policy after the war endorsed a policy incorporating imperial preference (though it shied away from recommending the introduction of food duties, without which preference would be effectively useless to the Empire), and supported the wide-ranging introduction of protective duties on 'key' industries central to national economic welfare. Shortly after the Armistice, certain import controls were left untouched as others were dismantled, thus retaining the basis for the limited protectionist measures of the 1920s and signalling a distinct change in British policy.[42]

In reality, a formal Allied trading block after the war would have met insuperable obstacles and caused large welfare losses. Germany was too important a trade partner for too many of the Allies. Furthermore, a four-tier scheme – the Allies, the British Empire, former neutrals and the former enemy countries – would have necessitated a wholesale abandonment of the treaty system and caused difficulties with neutrals and non-European countries. An Allied customs union was never practical international politics. Indeed, many French opponents of an Allied union probably feared the USA more than Germany.[43] Belgium and Italy backed away from endorsing the resolutions, and the USA, even when an Ally, remained hostile to a scheme which might cement European and Empire relationships to her own disadvantage.[44]

The views of the more extreme 'trade warriors' lost their influence within the establishment (though less so with the public) as the extent to which war had exhausted German economic strength and diminished the German 'threat' became evident in the West.[45] 'During the summer of 1918 it became clear that the economic solidarity of the Allies would not long survive the demobilization of their armed forces'.[46] This did not mean, however, a total abstinence from short-term measures aimed penally, indeed vindictively, against Germany, and it did not mean that post-war Europe was untroubled by deeply-held feelings of national insecurity and anxiety.

ECONOMIC NATIONALISM IN THE POST-WAR PERIOD 1919–24

From a national standpoint, commercial policy can be seen as an arm of foreign policy, or as a tool of domestic economic policy. The two interact upon each other. They also sometimes conflict, although in that event there is a reasonable presumption that politicians will perceive domestic considerations as more immediate and more important – to ignore them would increase vulnerability to pressure from electors and interest groups. Under pressure from both foreign policy and domestic considerations, post-war commercial policy demonstrated two discontinuities from pre-war patterns. The first was a marked tendency towards greater trade restrictions, either through direct controls or higher tariffs. The second was a large-scale breakdown of the pre-war treaty system which exacerbated the effect of those greater restrictions.

The background to national commercial policy formulation was one of immense fracture in economic, political and social structures. Demobilization, serious food and raw material shortages in parts of Europe, and capital scarcity often dictated the immediate continuation of high, wartime levels of government expenditure, sustaining the inflationary tendencies of the wartime years. In Europe, the process of redirecting production back from war-related industries to civilian supply, and the attempt to stabilize currencies by returning to pre-war international links by a reborn gold or gold exchange standard, occurred against a background of differential inflation and uneven industrial performance and productivity advance between European and non-European countries.

Profoundly different foreign policy objectives did not help. French objectives have been seen variously by historians as based on a vindictive design to keep Germany prostrate, or, more recently and more charitably, on a reasonable desire to find security against German resurgence and make Germany meet the cost of reconstructing the war zones while retaining France's status as an equal power with Germany and the UK.[47] In either case, French strategy towards a prostrate Germany resulted in large transfers of economic capacity, blighted Franco-German relations, exacerbated friction between the Allies, and increased the linkage between reparations and inter-Allied war debts. US desires to lighten the German burden were not furthered by her own reluctance to write off the debts of her former Allies, while her satisfaction at the weakening of Britain's financial strength was not matched by an equal enthusiasm for taking upon herself the management of a reconstituted international gold standard, especially one designed to meet the needs of countries with weaker external accounts. Her objective of restoring stability and harmony in Europe sat uncomfortably with a trade policy dominated by protectionist domestic politics, in which the goal was an expanding export sector coupled with continued isolationism at home.[48]

In Europe, the war and consequent peace left a legacy of chronic territorial insecurity. The peace treaties increased the number of nation-states in Europe from 26 to 38.[49] This alone meant increased barriers to trade, but it also exacerbated the nationalist and racial frictions ignited by the war, frictions which were reflected in tariff policy. Russia's virtual disappearance from the world economy was probably a minor factor, given the high level of her tariffs before 1914, but such considerations particularly affected the central European states formed out of the dismembered Austro-Hungarian Empire.[50] Further west, even the politics of larger states with greater territorial stability were unsettled. Against the background of the Bolshevik Revolution, governments faced increased trade union membership and reflected upon promises for social reform made during the war. The strengthened position of organized labour was paralleled by the greater prominence of employer and trade associations in industries where firm size and organization had been substantially increased during the war, often with government encouragement. Corporatist tendencies were in evidence, wage and price flexibility lessened.

Inflation threatened large payments imbalances, and the response was frequently to increase tariff rates to compensate, sometimes (as in France, Italy, Spain and Czechoslovakia) by use of a 'co-efficient' system which automatically linked tariff increases to price increases,[51] or sometimes simply by continuing the quantitative restrictions introduced in the war. Stabilization of currencies remained a serious problem until the mid-1920s, in France until 1926. Furthermore, European nations returned to gold at very different relations to their respective pre-war parities, some achieving their 1914 parity with gold and others returning at less than 10 per cent of it.[52] Here indeed was a 'ladder' effect. In the early 1920s France could complain at 'exchange dumping' from Germany at the same time as her exports benefited from the depreciation of the franc in the UK market.[53]

There were also other, more structural factors in operation. War and post-war scarcity in Europe led to a substantial expansion of primary production in the New World that was a factor in the worldwide weakness of agricultural and raw materials prices during the 1920s, though this translated surprisingly little into tariff policy before the late 1920s. More important, in disrupting manufactured imports from the industrial powers of the Old World, the war encouraged nationalist aspirations for industrial development in extra-European countries and the predominantly agrarian small states of Eastern and South-eastern Europe alike. At the same time, US industrial products started to appear on international markets to an extent unknown before 1914. In the Italian tariff of 1921, the introduction of the co-efficient system was buttressed by an increase in industrial protection and the requirement that duties were paid in gold or gold equivalent. At the same time, the industrial tariff was 'modernized' – that is, extended to include articles newly important in international trade, such as vehicles and chemicals. Italy was an example of the common trend where such 'modernization' resulted in closer specification of goods and a multiplication of tariff heads (953 compared to 472), lamented by the League of Nations since it limited the spread of treaty concessions to third parties under the MFN clause.[54] In Britain and France, though less so in Germany, there was increasing apprehension of US economic strength and the vigorous attempts of Herbert Hoover's Department of Commerce to expand exports. Coupled with the strong rise of Hollywood, this led in some sectors of European society to a hostility towards American cultural imperialism, reflected in Aristide Briand's fitful support for Franco-German *rapprochement* and European union and in the British Cinematograph Films Act of 1927.[55] A less immediate threat, but one applicable also to embryonic industry in the lesser and would-be industrial powers of Europe, was the rise of Japanese competition in cotton textiles.

In stronger countries, there were early indications of a rapid return to normalcy.[56] By the close of 1919, wartime exchange controls, prohibitions and import licensing had largely been dismantled outside Europe, and in the UK, Scandinavia, Netherlands and Belgium. Elsewhere in Europe, they remained much more common. They were retained alongside an increase in tariff levels in Italy in 1921 and Spain in 1922, while in France direct controls were being increased as late as 1922. In 1927 exchange controls still operated in France, Italy, Spain, Poland, Czechoslovakia, Yugoslavia, Bulgaria and Greece.[57]

Coupled with this was the new instability in tariff relations. If the Paris resolutions had presaged a wholesale reordering of commercial relations along an axis of Allies–friendly neutrals–unfriendly neutrals–enemies,[58] their foundering might have left the way open to a restoration of normalcy. However, the pre-1914 treaty system remained in tatters, in spite of strenuous League of Nations' efforts to reconstitute it. Even where treaty provisions were negotiated, they were so on the basis of higher general and conventional tariff levels than before the war. They were also, overwhelmingly, of shorter duration than the ten-year treaties typically concluded before 1914, often as short as one year.[59]

Let us begin by examining the tariff policies of the three major European trading powers – France, the UK and Germany. In France, tariff increases were prompted by rising prices but in the long run failed to keep up with them. The government sought to increase protection to safeguard the balance of payments, to direct imports for purposes of reconstruction, and to encourage manufacturing. Finding direct prohibitions unpopular with the public, it attempted to offset rising prices first by augmenting the prevailing (1910) specific tariff with surtaxes, then by introducing a 'co-efficient' system whereby the specific rates of the pre-war tariff were subject to a multiplier equal to the increase of prices between 1913 and 1918. This was at best a blunt tool (tracking French inflation, but not foreign currency dumping)[60] and was meant to be temporary, pending the stable price regime necessary for a general revision of the specific tariff. But from July 1920 the coefficient system was continually extended and revised upwards. At first this resulted in a rise in protection, but especially after December 1922, when the executive lost the power to issue changes by decree and control reverted to parliament, tariff increases failed to keep up with inflation. In 1926 the serious financial situation led to the regaining of executive power. An investigating committee considered real tariff levels to be less than half those in 1913, given price inflation and exchange rate depreciation.[61] This led to further sharp tariff increases in May and September 1926, and an upward movement in the minimum tariff in September 1927, only one month after the conclusion of an important MFN treaty with Germany.[62] These rises were made more enduring by the *de facto* stabilization of November–December 1926.

To a large extent, post-war British protectionism was built upon the work of the wartime Balfour of Burleigh Committee. In his 1919 budget speech,

Austen Chamberlain introduced imperial preference on existing duties, foreseeing 'almost limitless expansion'.[63] When put alongside existing dominion preferences on British goods, this seemed to foreshadow a united Empire trading block. This raised American hackles, but they were unable to mount an effective campaign against it because of discriminatory practices within their own tariff.[64] The McKenna duties were extended beyond the Armistice, and the Dyestuffs (Import Regulation) Act of 1920 and the Safeguarding of Industries Act (SIA) (1921) introduced, covering strategic industries whose vulnerability was felt to have been exposed by the war. The 'key industry' schedule of the SIA imposed 33 per cent duties, largely on dyestuffs, fine chemicals and electrical products, many of which had been imported from Germany. Provisions in the Act designed to protect British industry from dumping and foreign exchange depreciation were largely inoperable, since accusations of the first were difficult to prove and action against the second stood in danger of breaching Britain's commercial treaties. They did afford an avenue for penalizing Germany, with whom there was no commercial treaty until 1925, but duties to counter the depreciated currencies of France and Belgium were vetoed because of the treaty consideration.[65]

Thus, although wartime schemes for an Allied customs union did not survive the peace, there was still scope for discrimination against Germany, even though less severe than wartime 'trade warriors' would have hoped. From Germany's own point of view, a major struggle was to gain re-acceptance into the international community, while her pre-war importance to European trade made her recovery vital to the restoration of Europe. Yet Versailles deprived Germany of 90 per cent of her merchant fleet and almost all her iron ore, zinc, lead, potash and petrol, as well as resulting in the short-term paralysis of her coal production. At the same time, she was forced to accord the allies MFN treatment on what was effectively her 1902 tariff for five years, while Alsace-Lorraine and Luxemburg were given free access to the German market for five years (Poland for three) without reciprocity.

'While [Germany] was obliged to accord to the Allies her lowest tariffs, they reserved for themselves the right to apply to German imports their most discriminatory tariffs, which all of them actually did'.[66] This was at a time when heavy depreciation of the mark would have otherwise provided ample opportunity for 'exchange dumping'. The British 'key industry' and 'safeguarding' duties of 1921 were inordinately imposed on German products,[67] while a Reparation (Recovery) Act of 1921 subjected all German goods to a levy of 26 per cent (5 per cent under Labour in 1924) beyond any duty. Although this latter was mostly paid by the German government, exporters were at first not fully compensated since the reimbursement was paid in arrears in a currency devalued by rapid inflation.[68] A similar French reparations duty was not enforced until September 1924 (and one in Belgium never enforced), but France denied Germany access to her minimum tariff at a time when she was hugely increasing the differential between her minimum and maximum tariff rates to increase her strength in treaty negotiations.[69] Such discrimination only made it harder to see how Germany was supposed to pay reparations.[70]

Because Germany was deprived of tariff autonomy, continuation of wartime direct controls was the only means she had to protect home production and maintain the exchanges, although it is doubtful that the freedom to impose swingeing tariffs and widespread prohibitions would have contributed significantly to the stabilization of the mark.[71] To the end of 1925 German foreign trade operated under a licensing system controlled by a Reich Commission for Import and Export Licenses. There were export prohibitions and export duties on raw materials and semi-manufactures from 1920 to 1923, mostly imposed to maintain Germany's capacity to export finished manufactures in difficult circumstances. In addition, exporters had to surrender 30 per cent of export earnings to the Reichsbank in exchange for marks or gold-based credits.[72]

Before 1925, high tariffs would have been unpopular with businessmen and would have conflicted with a government strategy of concluding trade treaties and using Germany's ability to absorb primary products to improve her international relations. Import licenses were used carefully, and priority given to raw materials. The strategy was partly successful: treaties were signed with Czechoslovakia (1920), the USA (1923) and Britain (1924), although there was no accommodation with France until 1927.[73] Nevertheless, with the recovery of tariff autonomy in 1925 there was a partial revision of the 1902 tariff, affecting 400 of the 946 tariff heads. There were big increases on cattle and livestock, flour, vegetable oils, sugar, chemicals and textiles. Increases on raw materials were less heavy. Further revision was made difficult by the continued instability of European currencies, but the remaining direct trade controls were almost completely abolished as the new tariff came into effect.[74]

Dislocation was most severe in Central and South-eastern Europe, where trade was at a standstill after the war, and only gradually resumed, first on the basis of government barter, then against a background of prohibitions, government import and export monopolies, severe currency restrictions, and export duties on farm products. The new boundaries of Versailles frequently trampled upon underlying economic structures. The nationalist aspirations that were realized at Versailles pushed in the direction of economic autarky, and trade restrictions were used as an offensive weapon in the pursuit of both. Efforts by the Supreme Economic Council of the League of Nations in 1919 and resolutions at the Brussels Financial Conference of 1920 urged that the Central European states should resume more normal trading with each other.

At the Portorose Conference in 1921, the Succession States of the Austro-Hungarian Empire signed a protocol agreeing to abolish prohibitions, moderate tariffs and negotiate MFN treaties with each other. However, the protocol was not ratified by any of its signatories, and no substantial progress made for several years. In Central Europe the breakdown of the pre-war treaty system was particularly acute. The application of maximum tariff rates was the rule rather than the exception it had been before 1914.[75] Much less appreciated at the time, however, were the widespread cartel agreements that in many industries may have diminished or negated the effects of these formal trade barriers.[76]

According to contemporaries and many historians since, Austria's difficulties were acute.[77] Her manufacturing industry had previously supplied an Empire of 52 million, but now faced trade barriers erected by former provinces with a long-standing antipathy towards control from Vienna. Spinning enterprises found the weaving firms they had previously supplied now situated in Hungary, and the Hungarian authorities determined to erect tariffs in order to foster an infant spinning industry of their own.[78] At the same time, Austria depended on food imports subjected to export controls by the agrarian successor states. She suffered high food prices, heavy unemployment, a large import surplus and chronic inflation. Under League of Nations' control from 1922, currency stabilization was quite quickly effected, but trade normalization was more difficult.

Some recent scholars argue that this exaggerates the new Austria's difficulties. Her relative strengths in manufacturing and services, and the need of the agrarian successor states to find outlets for raw materials, gave her a strong position in the region. 'Once the immediate chaos was surmounted, the exchange of goods quickly re-established itself', often facilitated by industrial reorganization through multinational holding companies and cartel agreements.[79] It is not clear however that this was a full solution to Austria's predicament. Her particular need to export about 50–80 per cent of her industrial production favoured a regional free-trade stance: hence she sought trade treaties and MFN status, but her former provinces were slow to negotiate.[80] Between 1923 and 1925 the League attempted to encourage the negotiation of commercial treaties in Central Europe. Negotiations between Austria and Czechoslovakia in 1925 under League auspices broke down when Italy insisted on being included. On their failure, Austria sharply increased its tariff in 1926.[81] There might have been difficulties too in freer trade with the advanced industrial economies, where Austria's relative productivity was less impressive.[82] In any case, at Versailles the Western Allies had secured *unilateral* MFN treatment from Austria until 1923, and therefore initially had little incentive to reciprocate.

War had diverted European industry's attention from exports, thus allowing the USA and Japan to capture market share in the periphery. Also, in increasing the opportunities for import substitution in countries such as in Canada, Australia, India and South America, it intensified what were sometimes long-standing pressures for a nationalist policy on manufactures. Even so, the post-war trend beyond Europe was on the whole less acute (Table 6.4). Even US protectionism in the 1920s can be portrayed as moderate compared with 1900–13, though less so in relation to Underwood, especially if account is taken of increasing US superiority in manufacturing productivity.

Canada's revenue surtaxes were abolished shortly after the war, and the reaction to the US tariff increases of 1921–2 on agricultural goods, probably hitting Canada above all others, was restrained partly on account of the growing strength of the Western agrarians in Canadian politics. Minor tariff reductions were made in 1922–3 and British preference was increased at the Imperial Conference of 1923, although Baldwin's defeat in the British election that November left the British government unable to reciprocate. Thereafter, Canadian commercial policy up to 1929 consisted of minor juggling of tariffs, drawbacks and subsidies.[83] In Australia, however, politicians and public alike felt that peace threatened wartime industrial development as powerful overseas economies returned to normal trading. Employment, revenue and the need to correct a large post-war trade deficit were offered as additional considerations. The Greene Tariff of 1920–21 extended protection to 71 per cent of all imports, compared with 57 per cent before 1914, although increased rates were partially offset by increased preference on British goods, 40–50 per cent of total imports. An unashamedly protectionist Tariff Board encouraged lobbying from industry. There was little opposition from a public which accepted arguments giving high priority to the development of the steel, chemicals, electrical and vehicles industries, and claims by government economists that industrial protection would do little further damage to agricultural exports, given the general depression of world trade in primaries.[84]

Given her need for large imports of raw materials and her structural tendency to chronic trade deficit, Japan's external trade policy was directed more at increasing exports than at constraining imports. Japanese business groups observed, and indeed exaggerated the importance of, tentative experiments by foreign governments to facilitate exports, notably the British Trade Facilities Act (1921) and the US Webb–Pomerene Act (1918). Partly in consequence, Japanese trade policy during the 1920s laid emphasis on industrial and commercial rationalization, and particularly the cartelization of the export sector.[85]

Discussion of the Government of India Bill in 1919 brought to the fore the question of Indian fiscal autonomy left unsettled during the war, and a Fiscal Autonomy Convention was established. Although this did not formally bind the Government of India to accommodating Indian nationalist opinion, it

Table 6.4 Customs revenue as % of import values: 1900–13 to 1925–9 (averages of selected periods)

	1900–13	1915–18	1919–24	1925–9	1919/24 cf. 1900/13 (absolute rise)	1925/9 cf. 1900/13 (absolute rise)	1919/24 cf .1900/13 (1913 = 100)	1925/9 cf .1900/13 (1913 = 100)
India	5.87	7.97	13.95	19.52	8.08	13.65	237.65	332.54
Australia	16.86	17.23	17.67	19.63	0.81	2.77	104.80	116.43
New Zealand	18.29	15.59	15.06	17.19	–3.23	–1.10	82.34	93.99
Canada	16.33	16.56	14.30	14.38	–2.03	–1.95	87.57	88.06
Japan	7.66	4.13	3.94	4.87	–3.72	–2.79	51.44	63.58
Argentina	21.58	12.44	13.40	17.38	–8.18	–4.20	62.09	80.54
USA	23.27	8.61	10.53	13.42	–12.74	–9.85	45.25	57.67
Brazil	39.61	21.27	18.54	23.85	–21.07	–15.76	46.81	60.21

Sources: As Table 6.3.

became less and less realistic to ignore it as demands for protection grew more insistent, and in 1921 the cotton duties were raised to 11 per cent. Agitation continued, especially in areas such as iron and steel where severe post-war dumping was alleged. After fighting a rearguard action, Viceroy Lord Reading admitted in 1924 that protection was now 'quite inevitable' and a Steel Protection Act was passed. Even so, in 1927 an element of imperial preference was built into the scheme (justified by quality differences in imports from Britain and elsewhere) against the wishes of Indian nationalists. 'Discriminating protection' was extended to cotton goods in 1930 when the duty was increased to 15 per cent on British cottons and 20 per cent on foreign cottons.[86]

Britain, and especially her cotton masters, might anguish at the new-found though limited tariff freedom of India, but on a wider screen it was the US tariff increases of 1921–2 which were of particular concern in setting the tenor of the post-war world trade order. It may well be that that these increases were redundant, that retaining Underwood would have done little to stimulate US imports in view of the US's comparative advantage in many primaries and the rapid advances in her manufacturing sector.[87] Nevertheless, the US, emerging from the war as the only country strong enough in terms of its productive efficiency, its financial strength, and its balance of payments, to lead the world economy in the way that Britain had done before 1914, was hegemon-in-waiting. On this ground, at least, a liberal stance was vital.

If the Wilson interlude had given grounds for optimism, that optimism was dashed by the post-war resurgence of traditional Republican protectionism. In the US, the dichotomy between internal and external policy considerations was particularly acute. Growing export potential in manufactures and an enhanced desire to adopt a new role in promoting European stability suggested the need for more liberal trade policies, but American instincts for high protectionism were too strong. The resulting attempt to pursue an interventionist foreign policy and trade expansion while retaining many of the features of pre-war tariff isolation had at best mixed results.

The sweeping Republican victory in 1920 made higher protection inevitable, even though the tariff had not figured prominently in the elections. Even in the USA, there were tremors of national insecurity after the war, outbursts of 'nativism', the introduction of immigration controls, and demands from politicians for self-sufficiency and from 'war baby' industries for protection. Another decisive factor behind the Emergency Tariff Act (1921) and the Fordney–McCumber Tariff (1922) was the collapse of agricultural prices in 1921–2. Tariff rises on many agricultural products were superfluous and did nothing to stem falling prices, but the wool growers regained the protection enjoyed under Payne–Aldrich (1909), and the beet sugar producers got a large tariff hike against Cuban competition. The free list was reduced and the average rate on dutiable imports was raised from Underwood's historic low of 26.8 per cent to 38.2 per cent under Fordney–McCumber.[88]

For industry, the 1922 Act also attempted to 'equalize' costs of production between America and the exporting country, giving the president power to alter duties to secure this after investigation by a Tariff Commission. This was not only undesirable but unachievable, since determining costs at home and especially abroad was impossible. Indeed, many US rates were so high that the logic would have been hugely to reduce the US tariff, which may possibly have been what the architects of the Act intended. Nevertheless, this power was more frequently used to raise rates than reduce them,[89] perhaps partly because of foreign currency depreciation. With exceptions such as steel and agricultural machinery, where duties were in any case superfluous, many industries regained or nearly regained the degree of protection prevailing before Underwood. The rates on lace (90 per cent), some razors and small arms (up to 400 per cent), dyestuffs (60–90 per cent) and coal-tar intermediates (57–172 per cent) were little short of preposterous.[90]

There was increasing awareness in the USA of her changed world economic position, her new international creditor status and her need to import more in order to fuel export expansion. Under the influence of William S. Culbertson of the Tariff Commission, there was a growing executive acceptance of the unconditional MFN arrangement and the need for tariff 'flexibility'.[91] However, the only imports the US was prepared to tolerate were non-competitive raw materials: Fordney–McCumber essentially 'stacked benefits heavily on the American side',[92] and, as before 1914, policy-makers intent on removing 'discrimination' against US exports objected to two-tier tariffs, or at least considered US products had the automatic right to the lowest tariff enacted by a foreign country. This was because their own tariff was single-tier and discriminated against nobody! Of course, the reason the US was 'discriminated' against in a two-tier tariff system was because her single-tier tariff was unusually high, irreducible even if she was granted access to lower foreign 'conventional' or 'minimum' tariffs. Europeans, who had used a two-tier system to lower the tariffs facing their exports, had been reasonably content with the 'unconditional' MFN clause before 1914, but now there was increasing exasperation that US practice left no room for bargaining. Hence, some in Europe, especially in France, gravitated towards the 'conditional' MFN clause just as the US was moving towards the 'unconditional'! As British rubber producers cartelized to force high prices on American importers under the state-encouraged Stevenson plan, Austen Chamberlain made amelioration conditional on US tariff changes.[93]

At a time when the League of Nations was attempting to re-establish the unconditional MFN principle and the European treaty network, US practice was unhelpful. Indeed, it could also be inconsistent even in its own terms, as when under Fordney–McCumber the president was given the power to impose penalty duties against 'offending' countries.[94] Whereas Payne–Aldrich had intended the 'maximum–minimum' system as offering US reductions as an *inducement* to foreign tariff reduction, Section 317 of Fordney–McCumber essentially resurrected the system under McKinley and Dingley which threatened US increases if foreign countries did not accept the already high US tariff. The US justified her own practice by equating it with those who had a single-tier but much lower tariff. The League thought differently. The policy of countries with non-negotiable but moderate tariffs (e.g., the Netherlands and the UK) was 'clearly unobjectionable', but not so that of countries such as the US, which, 'having established tariffs intolerable for other countries, refuse to contemplate their reduction'.[95] Between 1923 and 1929 the US was able to force such one-sided 'unconditional' MFN treaties with 22 countries, the most important of which were Germany, Spain, Poland, Hungary and Brazil, but was unsuccessful with Britain and France.[96] In 1927, France's decision to subject many US goods to its maximum rather than intermediate tariff caused the US to threaten retaliatory penalty rates, although both sides stepped back from a major tariff war.[97] Only with the Reciprocal Trade Agreements Act of 1934 did the US move somewhat towards an internationally acceptable interpretation of unconditionality.[98]

Given universal contemporary opinion that trade barriers increased sharply after the war, what is surprising is the number of tariff reductions discovered in the British Balfour Committee on Industry and Trade's 1924 examination of the tariffs facing Britain's major exports. For each of 33 product groups, details were gathered on the tariffs imposed by those countries (different in each case) which took from 70–90 per cent of total exports. Out of 528 country/product 'instances', there were 248 instances of increase in tariff rate, 176 of no change, 76 of reduction and 28 ambiguous instances. Even in itself, this suggests that more duties were unchanged or reduced than were increased. However, the Committee's published tables mix *ad valorem* duties indiscriminately with specific duties. Where *ad valorem* duties rose between 1914 and 1924, there was clearly an increase in real terms, but the Committee did not deflate the increase in specific duties by price increases. Thus, the 248 recorded increases are undoubtedly an exaggeration, most probably a significant one.[99]

Similarly, the crude CRIV ratio gives only mixed support to the idea of a marked upward movement in tariffs in the immediate post-war period (Table 6.3). Between 1900–13 and 1919–24 the ratio rose for 10 out of 24 countries for which data is available, whereas it fell for 14, although it is noticeable that, among those countries in which the ratio had risen by more than 10 per cent, Europe was heavily represented. As might be expected, the trend is stronger if 1919–24 is compared with the low ratios prevailing in 1915–18

(Table 6.5), a rise occurring in 12 out of 19 cases. Even so, there is a fall in seven.

Such measures sit oddly with the more or less universal contemporary belief that trade barriers were more prominent than during the Edwardian period. Especially when put alongside the French experience, they suggest that contemporaries may not have fully deflated nominal tariff rises by the price rises that underlay them, or that they accorded trade policy too important a role in the stagnating trade of the 1920s. However, the trend of the CRIV is likely to understate the real situation: indeed, the years 1919–24 may be ones when ratio is a particularly poor indicator of trade barriers. We might note the need to correct for the anomaly caused by the heavy reduction in US tariff levels in 1913. Even the Fordney–McCumber tariff hike of 1922 still left tariff levels low compared with 1900–13. More globally important in those factors not reflected in the CRIV, however, was the post-war persistence of quotas, prohibitions and exchange controls, and perhaps the tendency of high tariffs to alter trade patterns and reduce trade volumes. The CRIV, it should be stressed, only measures the average level of duty paid on *realized* imports. Hence, those imports which are discouraged by high tariffs or other trade controls do not figure in it.

This would in turn suggest the predominance of direct controls over higher tariffs in the conduct of 1920s' trade policy. Certainly, this would explain the League of Nations' strategy. Although the suppression of commercial warfare, the stabilization of tariff rates and classifications, and the conclusion of long-term treaties with unconditional MFN arrangements, occupied much attention, the League directed most of its efforts towards abolishing direct controls. Indeed, one enduring plank in its strategy was a broad attempt to *replace* prohibitions and quantitative restrictions by *stable tariffs*. Since it was far from successful in this, it followed that *actual tariff reduction* could seldom be at the centre of the League's attention – it simply never got as far as that. Indeed, those countries which *did* agree to replace direct controls by tariffs usually did so by introducing tariffs at considerably higher than pre-1913 levels.

The League's task was indeed vexing, and direct controls still remained in the second half of the decade, in spite of some tendency towards their replacement by tariffs. In 1925 Poland reintroduced import prohibitions abolished earlier because of currency instability and lack of reciprocity by her trading partners. There remained a hard core of prohibitions and quantitative restrictions in many countries which it was hard to eradicate. After prolonged study by the League's Economic Committee, a conference was summoned at Geneva in October 1927. Twenty-nine states, including the USA, the UK, France, Germany, Italy and Japan, agreed to get rid of all import and export prohibitions and restrictions within six months. Only 17 states had ratified by

Table 6.5 Customs revenue as % of import values: 1915–18 to 1930–39 (averages of selected periods)

	1915–18	1919–24	1925–9	1930–39	1919–24 (1915–18 = 100)	1925–9 (1915–18 = 100)	1930–39 (1915–18 = 100)
Argentina	12.44	13.40	17.38	22.92	107.72	139.71	184.24
Australia	17.23	17.67	19.63	31.73	102.55	113.93	184.16
Austria	–	–	7.91	15.36	–	–	–
Belgium	–	1.91	3.27	7.49	–	–	–
Brazil	21.27	18.54	23.85	27.40	87.17	112.13	128.82
Bulgaria	–	21.30	19.04	22.79	–	–	–
Canada	16.56	14.30	14.38	14.03	86.35	86.84	84.72
Czechoslovakia (*)	–	4.94	6.84	9.69	–	–	–
Denmark	3.14	3.65	5.38	7.33	116.24	171.34	233.44
Finland	4.92	16.37	18.99	26.64	332.72	385.98	541.46
France	6.36	5.80	7.56	21.31	91.19	118.87	335.06
Germany	–	–	7.83	25.92	–	–	–
Greece	–	9.02	14.14	30.23	–	–	–
Hungary (*)	–	–	10.65	8.75	–	–	–
Eire (***)	–	–	11.44	22.48	–	–	–
India	7.97	13.95	19.52	32.54	175.03	244.92	408.28
Italy	3.09	2.98	5.14	17.60	96.44	166.34	569.58
Japan	4.13	3.94	4.87	4.81	95.40	117.92	116.46
Netherlands	1.14	1.70	2.14	6.38	149.12	187.72	559.65
New Zealand	15.59	15.06	17.19	21.68	96.60	110.26	139.06
Norway	4.56	5.01	10.41	12.84	109.87	228.29	281.58

Poland (**)	–	9.57	14.04	11.04	–	–	–
Portugal	17.00	4.81	14.42	37.91	28.29	84.82	223.00
Romania	–	20.28	23.27	13.50	–	–	–
Russia	–	–	–	–	–	–	–
Spain	13.09	18.60	20.96	47.37	142.09	160.12	361.88
Sweden	4.69	6.94	8.78	9.40	147.97	187.21	200.43
Switzerland	2.45	5.57	9.02	17.74	227.35	368.16	724.08
UK	7.26	9.84	9.09	22.90	135.54	125.21	315.43
USA	8.61	10.53	13.42	16.97	122.30	155.87	197.10

Notes:
* 1900–13 average based on figure for Austria.
** 1900–13 average based on figure for Russia.
*** 1900–13 average based on figure for UK.

Sources: As Table 6.3.

September 1929, however, and some of those were conditional on Poland and Czechoslovakia ratifying. Czechoslovakia finally agreed in December, but Poland refused because of a dispute with Germany. All that happened was that a few states which anyway had only exceptional prohibitions ratified – Denmark, the UK, Japan, the Netherlands, Norway, Portugal and the USA. Even these had denounced the convention by 1934, as the world slump saw the problem of quantitative restrictions reappear in a new and alarming form.[100]

TARIFF LEVELS 1925–9

For 1925–9 as for 1918–24, the CRIV ratio continues to be a poor estimator of tariff levels. It is no surprise to find that between 1915–18 and 1925–9 CRIV ratios rose for 17 out of 19 countries and fell for only two (Table 6.5), since the 1915–18 ratio was unusually low. However, in 1925–9 only 14 out of 28 countries took a distinctly higher proportion of import values in the form of revenue duties than they had done in 1900–13 (India and Australia being the only non-European countries in this group), 14 taking a distinctly smaller proportion (Table 6.6a). In no less than 12 of the 14 showing increases, the absolute rise in the CRIV ratio was 6 per cent or less, and in six of them the CRIV ratio stood at 10 per cent or less in 1925–9 (Table 6.7).

This does not sound a dramatic rise above 1913 levels, and might again be taken to suggest that the contrast between tariff barriers in the later 1920s and those prevailing before 1914 was not as stark as was perceived by contemporaries, and that contemporaries placed undue emphasis on commercial policy when seeking to understand and explain the depressed world trading conditions of the 1920s. However, comparison of CRIV ratios for 1925–9 with Liepmann's less ambiguous measure of *ex ante* or 'potential' tariff levels for 1927 (see pp. 154–9) shows a very poor correlation between the two (Table 6.8). Again, we must conclude that direct controls, other non-tariff barriers, and sometimes very high tariffs were reducing trade volumes, and therefore serving to distort *ex post* CRIV ratios.

It is perhaps more significant that 22 out of 25 countries collected a higher proportion of import values in the form of revenue duties in 1925–9 than they did in 1919–24, and only one a distinctly lower proportion (Table 6.6b). Since, in terms of the incidence of direct controls in the world economy, 1918–24 and 1924–9 were more comparable than either period was with 1900–13, it therefore seems likely that the movement in the crude ratio is significant in this case. If this is so, it might suggest that, as prohibitions, quantitative controls and exchange restrictions were replaced by higher tariffs, CRIV ratios rose, but that the new tariffs were sufficiently high to have a volume effect large enough to dampen the rise.

Table 6.6(a) Customs revenue as % of import values: 1900–13 to 1925–9

	1900–13	1925–9	1925–9 (1900–13 = 100)
Netherlands	0.45	2.14	475.56
India	5.87	19.52	332.54
Romania	10.59	23.27	219.74
Belgium	1.51	3.27	216.56
Eire (***)	5.38	11.44	212.64
Switzerland	4.45	9.02	202.70
Hungary (*)	6.04	10.65	176.32
UK	5.38	9.09	168.96
Finland	12.99	18.99	146.19
Austria	6.04	7.91	130.96
Spain	16.74	20.96	125.21
Bulgaria	15.79	19.04	120.58
Australia	16.86	19.63	116.43
Czechoslovakia (*)	6.04	6.84	113.25
Germany	8.09	7.83	96.79
New Zealand	18.29	17.19	93.99
Norway	11.34	10.41	91.80
Sweden	9.61	8.78	91.36
Canada	16.33	14.38	88.06
France	8.63	7.56	87.60
Argentina	21.58	17.38	80.54
Denmark	6.78	5.38	79.35
Japan	7.66	4.87	63.58
Brazil	39.61	23.85	60.21
Italy	8.83	5.14	58.21
USA	23.27	13.42	57.57
Portugal	25.59	14.42	56.35
Poland (**)	31.48	14.04	44.50

Table 6.6(b) Customs revenue as % of import values: 1919–24 to 1925–9

	1919–24	1925–9	1925–9 (1919–24 = 100)
Portugal	4.81	14.42	299.79
Norway	5.01	10.41	207.78
Italy	2.98	5.14	172.48
Belgium	1.91	3.27	171.20
Switzerland	5.57	9.02	161.94
Greece	9.02	14.14	156.76
Denmark	3.65	5.38	147.40
Poland (**)	9.57	14.04	146.71
India	13.95	19.52	139.93
Czechoslovakia (*)	4.94	6.84	138.46
France	5.80	7.56	130.34
Argentina	13.40	17.38	129.70
Brazil	18.54	23.85	128.64
USA	10.53	13.42	127.45
Sweden	6.94	8.78	126.51
Netherlands	1.70	2.14	125.88
Japan	3.94	4.87	123.60
Romania	20.28	23.27	114.74
New Zealand	15.06	17.19	114.14
Spain	18.60	20.96	112.69
Australia	17.67	19.63	111.09
Canada	14.30	14.38	100.56
UK	9.84	9.09	92.38
Bulgaria	21.30	19.04	89.39

Notes:
* 1900–13 average based on figure for Austria.
** 1900–13 average based on figure for Russia.
*** 1900–13 average based on figure for UK.
(1) Ranked by rate of increase (high to low).
(2) Unavailability of base or end year figure leads to exclusion of Eire, Hungary, Austria, Germany and Greece from either Table 6(a) or 6(b).

Sources: As Table 6.3.

Table 6.7 Customs revenue as % of import values: 1900–13 to 1930–39 (averages of selected periods)

	1900–13	1915–18	1919–24	1925–9	1925/9 cf. 1900/13 (absolute rise)	1925/9 cf. 1900/13 (1913 = 100)
India	5.87	7.97	13.95	19.52	13.65	332.54
Romania	10.59	–	20.28	23.27	12.68	219.74
Eire (***)	5.38	–	–	11.44	6.06	212.64
Finland	12.99	4.92	16.37	18.99	6.00	146.19
Hungary (*)	6.04	–	–	10.65	4.61	176.32
Switzerland	4.45	2.45	5.57	9.02	4.57	202.70
Spain	16.74	13.09	18.60	20.96	4.22	125.21
UK	5.38	7.26	9.84	9.09	3.71	168.96
Bulgaria	15.79	–	21.30	19.04	3.25	120.58
Australia	16.86	17.23	17.67	19.63	2.77	116.43
Austria	6.04	–	–	7.91	1.87	130.96
Belgium	1.51	–	1.91	3.27	1.76	216.56
Netherlands	0.45	1.14	1.70	2.14	1.69	475.56
Czechoslovakia (*)	6.04	–	4.94	6.84	0.80	113.25
Germany	8.09	–	–	7.83	–0.26	96.79
Sweden	9.61	4.69	6.94	8.78	–0.83	91.36
Norway	11.34	4.56	5.01	10.41	–0.93	91.80
France	8.63	6.36	5.80	7.56	–1.07	87.60
New Zealand	18.29	15.59	15.06	17.19	–1.10	93.99
Denmark	6.78	3.14	3.65	5.38	–1.40	79.35
Canada	16.33	16.56	14.30	14.38	–1.95	88.06

Japan	7.66	4.13	3.94	4.87	–2.79	63.58
Italy	8.83	3.09	2.98	5.14	–3.69	58.21
Argentina	21.58	12.44	13.40	17.38	–4.20	80.54
USA	23.27	8.61	10.53	13.42	–9.85	57.67
Portugal	25.59	17.00	4.81	14.42	–11.17	56.35
Brazil	39.61	21.27	18.54	23.85	–15.76	60.21
Poland (**)	31.48	–	9.57	14.04	–17.44	44.60
Russia	31.48	–	–	–	–	–

Notes:
* 1900–13 average based on figure for Austria.
** 1900–13 average based on figure for Russia.
*** 1900–13 average based on figure for UK.

Sources: As Table 6.3.

Table 6.8 Europe: potential tariff levels, 1927 versus CRIV ratio 1925–9

	Potential tariff level 1927 (1900–13 = 100)				CRIV 1925–9 (1900–13 = 100)
	Foodstuffs	Semis	Mfgs	U/W AVG	All goods
Yugoslavia	138.29	143.60	155.56	145.82	–
Romania	131.41	108.67	190.20	143.43	219.74
Belgium	46.27	138.16	122.11	102.18	216.56
Switzerland	146.26	157.53	189.25	164.35	202.70
Hungary	108.25	132.50	164.77	135.17	176.32
Finland	117.35	107.45	47.34	90.71	146.19
Austria	56.70	76.00	108.81	80.50	130.96
Spain	108.92	150.77	147.53	135.74	125.21
Bulgaria	319.84	204.55	384.62	303.00	120.58
Czechoslovakia	124.74	108.50	185.49	139.58	113.25
Germany	125.69	94.77	190.00	136.82	96.79
Sweden	88.84	71.15	84.90	81.63	91.36
France	65.41	96.05	158.28	106.58	87.60
Italy	111.36	114.40	193.84	139.87	58.21
Poland	103.75	52.28	65.41	73.81	44.60

Sources: H. Liepmann, *Tariff Levels and the Economic Unity of Europe*, George Allen and Unwin, London, 1938; B.R. Mitchell, *European Historical Statistics: 1750–1975*, Macmillan Press, London, 2nd edn, 1978.

Trends set by world leaders in international trade are always important in providing highly visible examples of good or bad practice. In terms of specific rises, the US did not offer further provocations after Fordney–McCumber. Britain did not consolidate strongly the protectionist direction taken under McKenna and the SIA in 1916–21, and in particular did not respond to the Fordney–McCumber rises. Decisive defeat in the election of 1923 made the Conservative leaders wary of extending the protectionist net, an effective Cabinet veto ensuring that no industry of significant size was granted the Board of Trade enquiry necessary to obtain safeguarding.[101] The best-known example was steel. There was widespread support for protecting the industry within the Conservative Party, but Winston Churchill insisted that protection would lead to a deluge of knock-on claims from a wide range of steel-using industries[102] and other leading Conservatives feared that a tariff would allow the industry to avoid much-needed modernization.[103] The real rather than potential impact of changing British attitudes was, for the present, small. The

McKenna duties remained, their most important impact being on motor cars, where protection contributed to the economies of scale being realized by emerging large-scale producers such as Morris and Austin.[104] But safeguarding was not significantly extended. Britain's new protective devices covered only 2–3 per cent of imports and, despite minor extensions under Colonial Secretary Leo Amery in 1925, the imperial preference introduced in 1919 was effectively inoperable, since it remained almost unthinkable in Britain to impose duties on cereals and meat, the products which most interested colonial negotiators.

Seen from abroad, however, it could appear differently. We have already seen that what US politicians and tariff officials regarded as their new 'open door', and 'flexibility' was regarded very differently in a Europe watching with mixed admiration and horror the progress of American mass-production industry and the growing US penetration of European markets. The US reluctance to engage positively in international negotiations such as the World Economic Conference (WEC) of 1927 confirmed their fears. Existing British safeguarding and revenue duties were a source of irritation on the continent,[105] and foreigners could have been forgiven for thinking that in Britain a full-scale movement towards protection and imperial preference was at least on the agenda, particularly when the safeguarding legislation was revised in 1925, and as protectionist business groups such as the National Union of Manufacturers and Empire Industries Association grew in confidence and influence with Conservative MPs, and their free-trade opponents dwindled or lost heart.[106]

Optimists discerned some easing of world trade barriers just after the German and French tariff hikes of 1925 and 1926.[107] Although the WEC of 1927 was internally riven by disputes over European integration and cartelization, and hobbled by governments' unwillingness to tie themselves to its recommendations,[108] it nevertheless seemed to happen in auspicious circumstances. The Dawes Plan had calmed the reparations issue, the Locarno Treaty had improved Franco-German relations and Germany had been admitted to the League. Foreign loans to Germany and financial reconstruction schemes in Austria and Hungary were apparently working. With the gold exchange standard also working over most of Europe, currency stability was largely re-established, although not in Italy, France and Belgium. Trade was also more buoyant. As the organizers of the WEC recognized, however, the retreat from quantitative restrictions and exchange controls to protective tariffs resulted nevertheless in tariff levels high beyond historical precedent:

> Europe remains to-day with its tariffs higher and more complicated, less stable and more numerous than in 1913. Moreover, Europe has failed to restore its former system of commercial treaties, and the habit has developed of putting tariffs designed for purposes of negotiation [*ie.* tariffs with a large margin between autonomous and conventional rates] into force before those negotiations

> take place. If, as has often happened, these tariffs have failed to result in agreement, the obstruction remains higher than before. The tendency of the last three years has continued to be in an upward direction … [109]

In the League, there was optimism after the WEC, especially when the International Chambers of Commerce at Stockholm (July 1927) and 29 countries endorsed its recommendations, and when the important Franco-German agreement (August 1927) was signed in the favourable atmosphere created by the WEC. The number of tariff revisions in Europe fell from 16 in each of 1925 and 1926 to ten in 1927, five in 1928, and two in 1929, while tariff treaties concluded rose from 30 in 1927 to 42 in 1928. In May 1928 the Economic Consultative Committee (ECC) of the League thought the WEC had 'already substantially checked the upward movement of tariffs which was in full swing in May 1927'. France and Norway had moderated planned upward tariff increases, there had been some reductions (Czechoslovakia and Canada) through autonomous action, and in Denmark, Netherlands, and Australia demands for increased protection had been refused. Although little happened in the following year, in May 1929 the ECC still harboured hopes of stabilization.[110]

In retrospect, this was wishful thinking. If there was such a pause, the diffused lens of the unweighted average CRIV ratio for 24 countries (Table 6.9) showed no sign of it. Tariff increases soon resumed (France, Germany and Poland), and the League admitted that the general level of tariffs appeared to be rising again. During 1929 the general level of duties was raised in Bulgaria, China, Chile and Persia, and elsewhere rises were being prepared against a domestic background of increased protectionist sentiment. Most worrying for Europeans was the commencement of the US congressional hearings early in 1929, to result 18 months later in the infamous Hawley–Smoot Tariff.[111] Against these ominous signals, the German industrial tariff was moderated slightly, but there were no other significant bilateral or autonomous reductions.

Up to about 1925–7 tariff increases on manufactures outstripped those on agricultural products – indeed, lower agricultural duties could be commensurate with a raising of overall tariff levels. After mid-decade, however, this process was reversed. Although this was recognized by informed contemporaries,[112] it was most forcibly demonstrated by Liepmann. Liepmann produced the most detailed and sophisticated analysis of inter-war tariff levels, although his analysis was confined to 15 European countries and to the benchmark years 1913, 1927 and 1931. He used two measures, the potential (and average potential) tariff level, which assessed the height of the *ex ante* tariff imposed by the legislature, and the actual tariff level, a measure of the height of protection after trade flows had adjusted to barriers imposed (see p. 122).

Table 6.9 CRIV ratio, 1919–24 and 1925–9 (crude average, 24 countries, unweighted by country size)

	1919–24	1925	1926	1927	1928	1929
Argentina	13.40	17.56	16.27	16.08	18.82	18.17
Australia	17.67	17.83	21.05	18.18	20.27	20.83
Belgium	1.91	3.08	3.07	3.09	3.42	3.70
Brazil	18.54	21.38	21.36	24.81	25.41	26.30
Bulgaria	21.30	19.25	18.95	20.61	19.51	16.90
Canada	14.30	14.27	14.09	14.44	15.30	13.78
Czechoslovakia (*)	4.94	4.81	6.61	7.79	7.82	7.15
Denmark	3.65	4.13	18.95	5.58	19.51	5.95
Finland	16.37	21.29	18.01	19.21	17.35	19.10
France	5.80	4.79	4.86	7.49	8.72	11.95
India	13.95	20.25	19.68	18.43	18.72	20.54
Italy	2.98	3.48	2.56	3.17	6.65	9.83
Japan	3.94	3.57	5.17	5.20	5.50	4.92
Netherlands	1.70	1.83	2.21	2.27	2.12	2.24
New Zealand	15.06	15.84	16.43	17.63	17.86	18.20
Norway	5.01	9.14	10.16	11.36	11.53	9.88
Poland (**)	9.57	17.11	14.91	12.86	12.64	12.70
Portugal	4.81	5.35	11.96	13.15	16.61	25.03
Romania	20.28	24.34	23.58	27.34	21.78	19.33
Spain	18.60	25.73	12.12	22.27	20.77	23.93
Sweden	6.94	9.68	8.39	8.90	8.31	8.61
Switzerland	5.57	8.09	9.19	8.78	9.27	9.78
UK	9.84	7.80	8.70	9.20	9.95	9.83
USA	10.53	12.77	12.86	14.29	13.68	13.49
Crude average	10.28	12.22	12.55	13.01	13.81	13.84
(1919–24 = 100)	100.00	118.94	122.10	126.54	134.41	134.67

Notes:
* 1900–13 average based on figure for Austria.
** 1900–13 average based on figure for Russia.
Countries included are those for which a complete run of CRIV ratios are available for each of the years 1919–29.

Sources: As Table 6.3.

Liepmann found a marked distinction between duties on foodstuffs and semi-manufactures on the one hand, and on finished manufactures on the other. Before the war, rates of 30 per cent *ad valorem* (or their equivalent) on

Table 6.10 Europe: potential tariff levels, 1913–31 (ranked by increase 1913–27)

	1913	1927	1931	1927 1913 = 100	1931 1913 = 100
(a) Foodstuffs					
Bulgaria	24.70	79.00	133.00	319.84	538.46
Switzerland	14.70	21.50	42.20	146.26	287.07
Yugoslavia	31.60	43.70	75.00	138.29	237.34
Romania	34.70	45.60	87.50	131.41	252.16
Germany	21.80	27.40	82.50	125.69	378.44
Czechoslovakia	29.10	36.30	84.00	124.74	288.66
Finland	49.00	57.50	102.00	117.35	208.16
Italy	22.00	24.50	66.00	111.36	300.00
Spain	41.50	45.20	80.50	108.92	193.98
Hungary	29.10	31.50	60.00	108.25	206.19
Poland	69.40	72.00	110.00	103.75	158.50
Sweden	24.20	21.50	39.00	88.84	161.16
France	29.20	19.10	53.00	65.41	181.51
Austria	29.10	16.50	59.50	56.70	204.47
Belgium	25.50	11.80	23.70	46.27	92.94
Crude average				119.54	245.94
(b) Semi-manufactures					
Bulgaria	24.20	49.50	65.00	204.55	268.60
Switzerland	7.30	11.50	15.20	157.53	208.22
Spain	26.00	39.20	49.50	150.77	190.38
Yugoslavia	17.20	24.70	30.50	143.60	177.33
Belgium	7.60	10.50	15.50	138.16	203.95
Hungary	20.00	26.50	32.50	132.50	162.50
Italy	25.00	28.60	49.50	114.40	198.00
Romania	30.00	32.60	46.30	108.67	154.33
Czechoslovakia	20.00	21.70	29.50	108.50	147.50
Finland	18.80	20.20	20.00	107.45	106.38
France	25.30	24.30	31.80	96.05	125.69
Germany	15.30	14.50	23.40	94.77	152.94
Austria	20.00	15.20	20.70	76.00	103.50
Sweden	25.30	18.00	18.00	71.15	71.15
Poland	63.50	33.20	40.00	52.28	62.99
Crude average				117.09	155.56

Table 6.10 continued

	1913	1927	1931	1927 1913 = 100	1931 1913 = 100
(c) Manufactures					
Bulgaria	19.50	75.00	90.00	384.62	461.54
Italy	14.60	28.30	41.80	193.84	286.30
Romania	25.50	48.50	55.00	190.20	215.69
Germany	10.00	19.00	18.30	190.00	183.00
Switzerland	9.30	17.60	22.00	189.25	236.56
Czechoslovakia	19.30	35.80	36.50	185.49	189.12
Hungary	19.30	31.80	42.60	164.77	220.73
France	16.30	25.80	29.00	158.28	177.91
Yugoslavia	18.00	28.00	32.80	155.56	182.22
Spain	42.50	62.70	75.50	147.53	177.65
Belgium	9.50	11.60	13.00	122.11	136.84
Austria	19.30	21.00	27.70	108.81	143.52
Sweden	24.50	20.80	23.50	84.90	95.92
Poland	85.00	55.60	52.00	65.41	61.18
Finland	37.60	17.80	22.70	47.34	60.37
Crude average				159.21	188.57

Source: H. Liepmann, *Tariff Levels and the Economic Unity of Europe*, George Allen and Unwin, London, 1938.

food were unusual, and confined to countries which imported little agricultural produce anyway. During the war, duty rates were suspended or considerably reduced, and this persisted after 1918 as European agriculture was slow to recover. During these first post-war years, there was a big increase in cereal cultivation in the Americas and Australia to make up the deficit.

Tariff *rates* on food were generally higher in 1927 than 1913 (except in Belgium, Austria and Sweden). The rises were larger for agricultural countries, but these imported little, so the significance was limited. More importantly, *rates adjusted for a 30 per cent price rise* between 1913 and 1927 (Table 6.10(a)) show a real fall for France, and mitigate the increase for other countries. The increase in Poland, Hungary and Spain falls to less than 10 per cent. This is supported by Tracy, who shows the main European countries reimposing agricultural duties as shortages subsided after the war, but at fairly moderate levels comparable with those prevailing before 1914.[113]

Almost without exception, 1927 saw a rise in tariff *rates* compared with 1913 for both semis and manufactures. The only exceptions were Sweden and Poland for semis and Finland for manufactures. However, a marked increase in semi prices (42.2 per cent, 1913–27) had the effect of reducing the real increase on semis to a figure little different from those on agricultural products, and only Switzerland, Spain and the ubiquitous Bulgaria increased their general level of protection by more than 50 per cent (Table 6.10(b)).

Increases on manufactures, whether imposed by industrial or by agrarian countries, were generally considerably greater than those on semis. Given the lower price increase for manufactures (20.8 per cent, 1913–27), the level of protection (Table 6.10(c)) rose more sharply, both in industrial Europe (especially Germany) and in agrarian Europe (except in Poland and Finland, where the comparison is with the extreme Russian figure of 1913, and in Sweden). In Bulgaria, Spain and Romania tariffs on manufactures rose to unprecedented levels.

Particularly important was the universal rise in protection of the textile trades. On the other hand, increases in tariffs on motor cars were common only to industrial and not agrarian Europe. For machinery, increases in duties were less widespread even in the industrial countries (except France and Italy), while agrarian Europe generally imposed relatively small increases.

Liepmann thus discerned a pattern. Throughout agrarian Europe, especially high duties were concentrated more on consumer goods than on capital goods, and on labour-intensive rather than capital-intensive goods. Exemplified by the textile trades, protection was used offensively to promote industrialization. In industrial Europe also, extreme protection was in consumer goods rather than capital goods, although automobiles received special consideration. Here defensive motives were more prominent, as was shown at its most extreme in textiles. The threat to old industrial Europe was less from Southern and Eastern Europe than from Asia and from the losses of non-European export markets for textiles. This caused keener competition in Europe itself and led to the defensive protection of national home markets.[114]

Between 1927 and 1931 these trends were reversed. Commercial treaties saw some stabilization of industrial duties in 1927–9, lasting generally until 1931, but there was an extreme agrarian protectionist reaction in 1929–31. Agricultural tariffs rose to enormous heights in industrial Europe, although more slowly in agrarian Europe, perhaps because they were already higher.[115] Moreover, in a situation where exporters would tolerate slaughterhouse prices, there was an increasing use of direct controls, particularly the use of the home: foreign 'milling ratio' in wheat, first introduced by Norway in 1927.[116] Industrial tariffs in industrial Europe rose more slowly, due rather to falling prices than to increasing rates. Industrial tariff levels in agrarian Europe, already high in 1927, rose higher, but this was largely although not entirely due to their higher starting point, coupled again with declining prices. Until 1931, the intra-European trade in agricultural produce was the harder hit but, as the use of quantitative restrictions spread widely in 1932, the industrial exports of industrial Europe shrank heavily.[117]

CONCLUSION

As Augé-Laribé wrote in 1925, 'Protectionism is not a policy for wartime'.[118] The need for foreign supply and the need to target it were best met by direct controls, which were all but ubiquitous. Such interventions were largely intended to be temporary. However, the war also stoked up animosities among the Western belligerents that were later reflected in penal policies against Germany, and was the catalyst for hostility and nationalist rivalries in Eastern Europe. Perhaps because of the uncertainties and instabilities it bequeathed to the post-war period, and because of the demonstration effect of the importance of industry in war, it also intensified the desire for accelerated industrial development in the major European powers, the agrarian states of Eastern Europe, and the primary producers of the periphery alike.

Even so, the early 1920s were in one sense a 'loaded pause'. Although tariffs were quickly re-established at levels higher than those obtaining in the war period itself, increases above the 1913 level were not always large when adjusted for price inflation. What was new in peacetime was the extent of direct controls on imports or foreign exchange. Dismantled quickly by stronger states, these persisted in weaker ones. Even here, they were often seen as temporary measures, waiting upon the restoration of world currency stability. In a decade of suspicion and bad feeling, few were willing to make the first steps towards marked liberalization. Nations waited for others to act. Even Britain seemed to threaten a historic retreat from her long-standing policy of free trade. America alone seemed prepared to preach the virtues of liberalism, but her manufacturing superiority and the one-sided nature of the MFN bargain she offered held little attraction for Europeans. A treaty system which had worked reasonably well before 1914 was only slowly being reconstituted by the second half of the 1920s.

Trade barriers, specifically *other people's* trade barriers, were seen as a major obstacle to restoring pre-war stability. In fact, trade barriers, and especially tariff barriers, were probably something of a scapegoat in a period when more structural factors were largely responsible for preventing the recovery of world trade. Despite some optimism about a return to normalcy around mid-decade, a rise in agricultural tariffs from 1927 onwards testified to the continued instability of international economic relations. Even without Hawley–Smoot, this fragility would have been blown apart by the world slump. Acting together, they ushered in a decade of trade barriers unparalleled in modern world history.

NOTES AND REFERENCES

1. M. Tracy, *Agriculture in Western Europe: Crisis and Adaptation since 1880*, Jonathan Cape, London, 1964, Pt. 1.
2. J.A.C. Conybeare, *Trade Wars: The Theory and Practice of International Commercial Rivalry*, Columbia University Press, New York, 1987.
3. P. Ashley, *Modern Tariff History: Germany–United States–France*, John Murray, London, 1904.
4. F. Capie, *Depression and Protectionism: Britain between the Wars*, George Allen and Unwin, London, 1983; F. Capie, *Tariffs and Growth: Some Insights from the World Economy, 1850–1940*, Manchester University Press, Manchester, 1994.
5. G. Toniolo, 'Effective Protection and Industrial Growth: The Case of Italian Engineering, 1898–1913', *Journal of European Economic History*, **6**, 1977; G.R. Hawke, 'The United States Tariff and Industrial Protection in the Late Nineteenth Century', *Economic History Review*, **28**, 1975; S.B. Webb, 'Tariff Protection [for] the Iron Industry, Cotton Textiles and Agriculture in Germany, 1879–1914', *Jahrbuch für Nationalökonomie und Statistik*, 183, 1977.
6. W.H. Becker, *The Dynamics of Business–Government Relations: Industry and Exports, 1893–1921*, University of Chicago Press, Chicago, 1982.
7. D.A. Lake, *Power, Protection, and Free Trade: International Sources of U.S. Commercial Strategy, 1887–1939*, Cornell University Press, Ithaca, New York, 1988, pp. 131–6, 148–59.
8. A. Marrison, 'Insular Free Trade, Retaliation, and the Most-Favoured-Nation Treaty, 1880–1914', in A. Marrison (ed.), *Free Trade and its Reception, 1815–1960*, Routledge, London, 1998, pp. 229–30.
9. A. Sykes, *Tariff Reform in British Politics, 1903–1913*, Clarendon Press, Oxford, 1979; A.L. Friedberg, *The Weary Titan: Britain and the Experience of Relative Decline, 1895–1905*, Princeton University Press, Princeton NJ, 1988; E.H.H. Green, *The Crisis of Conservatism: The Politics, Economics and Ideology of the British Conservative Party, 1880–1914*, Routledge, London, 1995.
10. A. Plummer, *International Combines in Modern Industry*, Sir Isaac Pitman and Sons, London, 1934.
11. A. Loveday, 'The Measurement of Tariff Levels', *Journal of the Royal Statistical Society*, **92**, 1929.
12. League of Nations, *Tariff Level Indices*, Geneva, 1927.
13. H. Liepmann, *Tariff Levels and the Economic Unity of Europe: An Examination of Tariff Policy, Export Movements and the Economic Integration of Europe, 1913–1931*, George Allen and Unwin, London, 1938.
14. Ibid., pt. 111.
15. For other difficulties inherent in the use of CRIV ratios (in the pre-1914 context) see D.A. Irwin, 'Free Trade and Protection in Nineteenth-Century Britain and France: A Comment on Nye', *Journal of Economic History*, **53**, 1993, pp. 146–58.
16. E.g., for 1913, see A. Estevadeordal, 'Measuring Protection in the Early Twentieth Century', *European Review of Economic History*, **I**, 1997, pp. 89–125.
17. D. Verdier, *Democracy and International Trade: Britain, France, and the United States, 1860–1990*, Princeton University Press, Princeton, 1994, pp. 150–155.
18. O.J. McDiarmid, *Commercial Policy in the Canadian Economy*, Harvard University Press, Cambridge, MA, 1946, pp. 257–9.
19. C. Mallet and C.O. George, *British Budgets: Second Series: 1913–14 to 1920–21*, Macmillan and Co., London, 1929, pp. 73–4, 98, 125–6, 157–60.

20. J. Turner, *British Politics and the Great War: Coalition and Conflict, 1915–1918*, Yale University Press, New Haven, 1992, p. 84.
21. F.W. Hirst and J.E. Allen, *British War Budgets*, Clarendon Press, for Carnegie Endowment for International Peace, Oxford, 1926, p. 73.
22. B. Chatterji, *Trade, Tariffs, and Empire: Lancashire and British Policy in India, 1919–1939*, Oxford University Press, Delhi, 1992; C. Dewey, 'The End of the Imperialism of Free Trade: The Eclipse of the Lancashire Lobby and the Concession of Fiscal Autonomy to India', in C. Dewey and A.G. Hopkins (eds), *The Imperial Impact: Studies in the Economic History of Africa and India*, Athlone Press, London, 1978.
23. G. Hardach, *The First World War*, English edn, Allen Lane, London, 1977, pp. 32, 32n.
24. A. Offer, *The First World War: An Agrarian Interpretation*, Clarendon Press, Oxford, 1989, pp. 23–78.
25. M. Olson, *The Economics of the Wartime Shortage: A History of British Food Supplies in the Napoleonic War and in World Wars I and II*, Duke University Press, Durham, NC, 1963, pp. 81–95; M. Urofsky, *Big Steel and the Wilson Administration: A Study in Business–Government Relations*, Ohio State University Press, Columbus, 1969, pp. 84–116.
26. Hardach, *First World War*, pp. 28–9.
27. O. Delle Donne, *European Tariff Policies Since the World War*, Adelphi, New York, 1928, p. 224.
28. E.g. R. and K. MacLeod, 'War and Economic Development: Government and the Optical Industry in Britain, 1914–18', in J.M. Winter (ed.), *War and Economic Development: Essays in Memory of David Joslin*, Cambridge University Press, Cambridge, 1975, pp. 165–203.
29. F.A. Haight, *A History of French Commercial Policies*, Macmillan, New York, 1941, p. 76.
30. Ibid., pp. 78–90.
31. Becker, *Dynamics of Business–Government Relations*; F. Pierce, *The Tariff and the Trusts*, Macmillan, New York, 1907; J.M. Tarbell, *The Tariff in Our Times*, Macmillan, New York, 1912.
32. Lake, *Power, Protection, and Free Trade*, pp. 159–62.
33. G.M. Fisk and P.S. Peirce, *International Commercial Policies with Special Reference to the United States*, Macmillan Company, New York, 1925, p. 43; cf. Lake, *Power, Protection, and Free Trade*, p. 167.
34. Fisk and Peirce, *International Commercial Policies*, p. 44; F.W. Taussig, *Tariff History of the United States*, 8th edn, New York, 1931, pp. 450–451.
35. Lake, *Power, Protection, and Free Trade*.
36. Taussig, *Tariff History of the United States*, p. 453.
37. F. Naumann, *Central Europe*, trans. C.M. Meredith, P.S. King and Son, London, 1916.
38. W.A.S. Hewins, *The Apologia of an Imperialist: Forty Years of Empire Policy*, Constable and Co., London, 1929, II, pp. 1–77.
39 M. Trachtenberg, '"A New Economic Order": Etienne Clémentel and French Economic Diplomacy during the First World War', *French Historical Studies*, **10**, 1977–8; A. Marrison, *British Business and Protection, 1903–1932*, Clarendon Press, Oxford, 1996, pp. 222–41.
40. Cited in J.A. Hobson, *The New Protectionism*, T. Fisher, Unwin, London, 1916, pp. 143, 149.
41. Hobson, *The New Protectionism*, pp. vii–xx.
42. Marrison, *British Business and Protection*, pp. 241–59.
43. Haight, *History of French Commercial Policies*, pp. 93–5.
44. C.P. Parrini, *Heir to Empire: United States Economic Diplomacy, 1916–1923*, University of Pittsburgh Press, Pittsburgh, 1969, pp. 31–9.
45. P. Cline, 'Winding Down the War Economy: British Plans for Peacetime Recovery, 1916–19', in K. Burk (ed.), *War and the State: The Transformation of British Government, 1914–1919*, George Allen and Unwin, London, 1982, pp. 172–8.
46. Haight, *History of French Commercial Policies*, p. 98.

47. J. Jacobson, 'Strategies of French Foreign Policy after World War I', *Journal of Modern History*, **55**, 1983, pp. 78–95.
48. M.P. Leffler, *The Elusive Quest: America's Pursuit of European Stability and French Security, 1919–1933*, University of North Carolina Press, Chapel Hill, NC, 1979, pp. 362–5: F. Costigliola, 'Anglo-American Financial Rivalry in the 1920s', *Journal of Economic History*, **37**, 1977, pp. 911–34; B. Eichengreen, *Golden Fetters: The Gold Standard and the Great Depression, 1919–1939*, Oxford University Press, New York, 1992, esp. pp. 187–257.
49. C.H. Feinstein, P. Temin and G. Toniolo, *The European Economy between the Wars*, Oxford University Press, Oxford, 1997, p. 30.
50. J. Foreman-Peck, *A History of the International Economy since 1850: International Economic Relations since 1850*, Harvester Press, Brighton, 1983, pp. 188–9.
51. Donne, *European Tariff Policies*, pp. 228–9.
52. Feinstein, Temin and Toniolo, *European Economy between the Wars*, Table 3.2, p. 46.
53. Haight, *History of French Commercial Policies*, p. 113.
54. Donne, *European Tariff Policies*, pp. 229–30, 233–4; League of Nations, *Commercial Policy in the Interwar Period: International Proposals and National Policies*, Series of League of Nations Publications, II. Economic and Financial, 1942 II.A6, Geneva, 1942, p. 47.
55. R.W.D. Boyce, *British Capitalism at the Crossroads, 1919–1932: A Study in Politics, Economics, and International Relations*, Cambridge University Press, Cambridge, 1987, pp. 108–9; D. Abel, *A History of British Tariffs, 1923–1942*, Heath Cranton, London, 1945, pp. 39–41.
56. S.M.H. Armitage, *The Politics of Decontrol of Industry: Britain and the United States*, L.S.E. Research Monographs, **4**, Weidenfeld and Nicolson, London, 1969; R. Lowe, 'The Erosion of State Intervention in Britain, 1917–1924', *Economic History Review*, **31**, 1978; Cline, 'Winding Down the War Economy'.
57. League of Nations, *Commercial Policy in the Interwar Period*, pp. 17–18, 32n.
58. J. Viner, 'The Most-Favoured-Nation Clause', *Index*, **VI**, 61, 1931, pp. 2–3.
59. A. Loveday, 'Postwar Economic Tendencies from the Armistice to 1925', *Nineteenth Century and After*, April–May 1927.
60. Haight, *History of French Commercial Policies*, pp. 108–19.
61. Donne, *European Tariff Policies*, p. 152.
62. Lake, *Power, Protection, and Free Trade*, p. 172.
63. Sir K. Hancock, *Survey of British Commonwealth Affairs, II, Problems of Economic Policy, 1918–1939*, Oxford University Press, London, 1940–42, I, pp. 139–40.
64. Parrini, *Heir to Empire*, pp. 220–247.
65. Marrison, *British Business and Protection*, pp. 259–65.
66. Donne, *European Tariff Policies*, p. 198.
67. Marrison, *British Business and Protection*, pp. 258–65.
68. T. Balderston, *The Origins and Course of the German Economic Crisis, 1923–1932*, Haude und Spener, Berlin, 1993, p. 91.
69. League of Nations, *Commercial Policy in the Interwar Period*, p. 37.
70. Eichengreen, *Golden Fetters*, p. 133.
71. Balderston, *Origins and Course of the German Economic Crisis*, pp. 129–31.
72. Donne, *European Tariff Policies*, pp. 206–11; F.D. Graham, *Exchange, Prices, and Production in Hyper-Inflation: Germany, 1920–1923*, Princeton University Press, Princeton, 1930, pp. 79–83.
73. H.-J. Schröder, 'Zur politischen Bedeutung der deutschen Handelspolitik nach dem Ersten Weltkrieg', in G.D. Feldman *et al.* (eds), *Die Deutsche Inflation: Eine Zwischenbilanz*, Walter de Gruyter, Berlin, 1982, p. 250; Balderston, *Origins and Course of the German Economic Crisis*, p. 131.
74. Donne, *European Tariff Policies*, pp. 213–18.
75. League of Nations, *Commercial Policy in the Interwar Period*, p. 20.
76. A. Teichova and P.L. Cottrell (eds), *International Business and Central Europe, 1918–1939*, Leicester University Press, Leicester, 1983.

77. L. Pasvolsky, *Economic Nationalism of the Danubian States*, George Allen and Unwin, London, 1928, pp. 175–99.
78. Foreman-Peck, *History of the International Economy since 1850*, p. 189.
79. H. Matis, 'Disintegration and Multi-National Enterprises in Central Europe during the Post-War Years (1918–23)', in Teichova and Cottrell, *International Business and Central Europe*, pp. 73–96.
80. Pasvolsky, *Economic Nationalism of the Danubian States*, pp. 175–99.
81. League of Nations, *Commercial Policy in the Interwar Period*, pp. 37–8.
82. E.g. P.G. Fischer, 'The Österreichisch-Alpine Montangesellschaft, 1918–38', in Teichova and Cottrell, *International Business and Central Europe*, pp. 257–8.
83. McDiarmid, *Commercial Policy in the Canadian Economy*, pp. 259–68.
84. B. Dyster and D. Meredith, *Australia in the International Economy in the Twentieth Century*, Cambridge University Press, Cambridge, 1990, pp. 96–101.
85. W.M. Fletcher, *The Japanese Business Community and National Trade Policy, 1920–1942*, University of North Carolina Press, Chapel Hill, 1989, pp. 28–38, 43–52.
86. D.M. Wagle, 'Imperial Preference and the Indian Steel Industry, 1924–39', *Economic History Review*, 2nd Series, **34**, 1981, pp. 120–131; L.G. Sandberg, *Lancashire in Decline: A Study in Entrepreneurship, Technology and International Trade*, Ohio State University Press, Columbus, Ohio, 1974, pp. 185–7.
87. M.E. Falkus, 'United States Economic Policy and the "Dollar Gap" of the 1920s', *Economic History Review*, **24**, 1971 (also comment by Glynn and Lougheed, *Economic History Review*, **26**, 1973); Foreman-Peck, *History of the International Economy since 1850*, p. 193.
88. Lake, *Power, Protection, and Free Trade*, p. 167.
89. Ibid., p. 169.
90. Taussig, *Tariff History of the United States*, pp. 447–88.
91. Leffler, *Elusive Quest*, pp. 43–53.
92. F. Costigliola, *Awkward Dominion: American Political, Economic, and Cultural Relations with Europe, 1919–1933*, Cornell University Press, Ithaca, NY, 1984, p. 66.
93. Ibid., p. 145.
94. W. McClure, *A New American Commercial Policy: As Evidenced by Section 317 of the Tariff Act of 1922*, Columbia University, New York, 1924, p. 44.
95. League of Nations, *Commercial Policy in the Interwar Period*, pp. 47–8.
96. Lake, *Power, Protection, and Free Trade*, pp. 171–2.
97. Leffler, *Elusive Quest*, pp. 43–53, 165–73; Lake, *Power, Protection, and Free Trade*, p. 172n.
98. P. Bidwell, *Our Trade with Britain: Bases for a Reciprocal Tariff Agreement*, Council on Foreign Relations, New York, 1938, pp. 27–37; T. Rooth, *British Protectionism and the International Economy: Overseas Commercial Policy in the 1930s*, Cambridge University Press, Cambridge, 1993, pp. 283–305.
99. Board of Trade, Committee on Industry and Trade, *Survey of Overseas Markets*, HMS0, London, 1926, pp. 538–85.
100. League of Nations, *Commercial Policy in the Interwar Period*, pp. 32–5.
101. Marrison, *British Business and Protection*, pp. 279, 286–7.
102. K. Middlemas and J. Barnes, *Baldwin: A Biography*, George Allen and Unwin, London, 1969, p. 311.
103. S. Tolliday, 'Tariffs and Steel, 1916–1934: The Politics of Industrial Decline', in J. Turner (ed.), *Businessmen and Politics: Studies of Business Activity in British Politics, 1900–1945*, Heinemann Educational Books, London, 1984, pp. 55–9.
104. J. Foreman-Peck, 'Tariff Protection and Economies of Scale: The British Motor Industry before 1939', *Oxford Economic Papers*, **31**, 1979, pp. 237–57.
105. Boyce, *British Capitalism at the Crossroads*, pp. 126–30.
106. Marrison, *British Business and Protection*, pp. 324–86; Capie, *Depression and Protectionism*, pp. 61–76.
107. Loveday, 'Postwar Economic Tendencies from the Armistice to 1925'.
108. Boyce, *British Capitalism at the Crossroads*, pp. 110–122.

109. League of Nations, *Commercial Policy in the Interwar Period*, p. 37.
110. Ibid., pp. 42–3.
111. F.W. Taussig, 'The Tariff Bill and Our Friends Abroad', *Foreign Affairs*, **8** (1), October 1929, pp. 1–12; A. Siegfried, 'European Reactions to American Tariff Proposals', *Foreign Affairs*, **8** (1), October 1929, pp. 13–19; J.M. Jones, *Tariff Retaliation: Repercussions of the Hawley–Smoot Bill*, University of Pennsylvania Press, Philadelphia, 1934, pp. 5, 9–10.
112. League of Nations, *Commercial Policy in the Interwar Period*, p. 114; Loveday, 'Post-war Economic Tendencies from the Armistice to 1925'.
113. Liepmann, *Tariff Levels and the Economic Unity of Europe*, pp. 102–5; Tracy, *Agriculture in Western Europe*, pp. 120–122.
114. Liepmann, *Tariff Levels and the Economic Unity of Europe*, pp. 178–82.
115. Ibid., pp. 105–9, 184.
116. Tracy, *Agriculture in Western Europe*, p. 122.
117. Liepmann, *Tariff Levels and the Economic Unity of Europe*, p. 184.
118. Quoted in Tracy, *Agriculture in Western Europe*, p. 170.

7. German banking and the impact of the First World War

Hans-Joachim Voth

When the failure of the Darmstädter- und Nationalbank sparked a banking panic in July 1931, the stage was set for the final chapter of Germany's descent into its deepest depression in recorded history. Exactly 17 years earlier, in July 1914, German support for the Habsburg Empire's policy in the Balkans led to the Austrian ultimatum to Serbia and Russia's mobilization: the outbreak of war had become a certainty.[1] This chapter examines the relationship between these two events, or, more accurately, the historical processes for which they stand *pars pro toto*. I begin with an overview of the existing literature that argues that the German banking system emerged fatally weakened from the ashes of war and inflation. Inter-war developments are then placed in a long-term perspective and compared with international evidence. The conclusion argues that the impact of the First World War on the banking system, while pronounced, has been overstated, and that it is not one of the main causes of German slump's severity. The main consequences of the war are to be found in an environment for which the bank's specific role and abilities was particularly well suited, and consequently in the banking sector's much expanded contribution to Germany's financial system and to the economy as a whole.

FROM WAR TO DEPRESSION: THE ROLE OF THE BANKS

That the slump was more severe in Weimar Germany than in virtually any other country has often been noted. Industrial output fell by almost 40 per cent, as compared to 11 per cent in Britain and 29 per cent in France.[2] In most accounts of the Great Depression in Germany, the banking system plays a prominent role. The banking crisis of 1931 immediately preceded the final downturn of the economy, ushering in the depressed conditions of 1932. Even if the role of monetary factors in causing the Depression has sometimes been called into question (Temin, 1971, 1976), there is little debate that the banking crises in Germany, the US and 11 other countries aggravated the downturn considerably (Bernanke and James, 1991). Both scholars and contemporaries at the time have argued that the collapse of numerous German banks can also indirectly be regarded as a repercussion of the First World War and the inflation that followed in its wake.

For the purposes of this chapter, we will not attempt to distinguish between the effects of the First World War and the inflation of 1918–23. While some have argued that harbingers of the monetary mayhem that was to come could already be detected in the rising price level in Germany before 1914 (Ferguson, 1995), the dominant view is clearly that the inflation would not have run its course without the outbreak of war in 1914 and the way in which the unprecedented military expenditures were financed (Holtfrerich, 1980). We will therefore treat inflation as one of the main channels through which the First World War's impact was communicated to the banking sector.[3] The impact of the Great War on the German banking system can therefore only be studied at one remove.[4]

The crisis of the banks was a result both of their structural weaknesses and of the economic environment in which they had to operate. The structural vulnerability of the banking system during the crisis was caused by the dual impact of war and inflation. In addition, the poor economic conditions in Germany during the second half of the 1920s can also be attributed to the banks' weakened position after the end of inflation in 1923. Since the rapid descent into a downward economic spiral was caused by structural imbalances and weak performance before the outbreak of the crisis, the banking system is immediately responsible for the severity of the crisis. These are the two main features of the dominant interpretation of linkages between the war and the instability of the banking system. The first one emphasizes the connection between structural changes and the deepening of economic crisis in 1931–2, and the second emphasizes the link between the Depression's severity and misguided lending prior to 1929. I shall briefly describe these two views in turn.

Five developments undermined the resilience of Weimar's banking system, according to the dominant view as described by Balderston and others:

1. The demands of reconstruction after war and inflation, as well as the large-scale destruction of the German rentier class left the Reich dependent on a massive inflow of foreign capital. Interest rates were high, and foreigners were ready and willing to increase their exposure to German assets. Companies and municipalities – much to the chagrin of the Reichsbank's president, Hjalmar Schacht – often tapped overseas capital markets directly (James, 1986, p. 138). Lending through the banking sector was also very strong, with as much as 39 per cent of all deposits at

German banks coming from abroad (Balderston, 1991, Table 5.7, p. 144). Since the proportion of balances for transaction purposes (relative to speculative balances) tends to be lower for foreign nationals, the high share of deposits coming from abroad – it is argued – meant that banks' balance sheets had been built on quicksand.

2. The memory of inflation and currency depreciation was very much on the minds of German banking customers and foreign investors. Both had lost billions during the early 1920s with hyperinflation and the fall of the exchange rate. Thus, even small events that undermined trust in the (internal or external) value of the Reichsmark led to rapid deposit withdrawals, as happened in the run-up to the banking crisis in July 1931. Similar tendencies were on display in 1929 when, in the aftermath of fiscal crisis, the mark began to weaken against the Dutch guilder and Swiss franc, and bank deposits stopped growing, as well as in the summer and autumn of 1930, when the political crisis and the election results left their mark on the exchange rate and banks' deposits. When in early June 1931 the Brüning government announced that Germany had reached the limits of her economic abilities with respect to the payment of reparations the Reichsbank began to lose gold and foreign exchange on a massive scale (Hardach, 1995, pp. 127f.). Bank deposits began to fall, and when the collapse of the textile firm *Nordwolle* wrought havoc on the Darmstädter- und Nationalbank, a general bank panic ensued. While many earlier historians had linked the deposit withdrawals and the difficulties in the German banking sector to foreign investors, Harold James has convincingly demonstrated that domestic holders of Reichsmark balances were largely to blame for the rapid reduction in the banks' deposit base, at least during the earlier stage of deposit withdrawals in 1931 (James, 1985a, pp. 182ff.; James, 1985b, p. 222).
3. The experience of inflation did not only render depositors highly sensitive to changes in the Reichsmark's and the banks' perceived solidity at any one point in time; it also led to a shortening of the maturity of deposits made (cf. Table 7.3). Interpreted literally, the evidence in Table 7.3 (p. 174) implies that during the 1920s, the majority of depositors only felt comfortable holding money on call with less than three months' notice. This contrasts sharply with the pre-war pattern, when numerous banking customers deposited their savings for a minimum of three months. Uncertainty can also be discerned in the bond market, where securities with long maturities yielded unusually high premia. Investors therefore preferred short-dated instruments, and to such an extent that they demanded yields-to-maturity that were often double the pre-war figures to be compensated for the risk they perceived *ex ante*. To lend long and borrow short is part of normal banking practice. The

unusually steep incline of the yield curve meant that interest rate 'gapping' was particularly profitable – and risky – for the German banks during the inter-war period. Yet the banks proved to be unprepared for the level of risk that they were taking on to their balance sheets.

4. Liquidity and capital ratios during the inter-war years were also markedly lower than they had been prior to 1914. Whereas the average Great Berlin bank had shown a capital + reserves ratio of 19 per cent in 1913 (expressed as a percentage of the balance sheet), this value had dropped to 11 per cent by 1925 and 7 per cent by 1929.[5] Liquidity ratios showed much the same trend – while the great Berlin banks had held cash and bills equivalent to 27 per cent of the balance sheet total, this figure had declined to 22 per cent by 1929 and 16 per cent in 1931. Both trends were the result of war and inflation – the reduction in capital ratios more directly than the fall in the banks' liquidity. After the stabilization of the currency in 1924, balance-sheet growth outstripped the rate of increase of the banks' equity base, thus further reducing the capital ratio (cf. Holtfrerich, 1985, Table 3, p. 200; Balderston 1991, p. 579). The liquidity ratios of the great banks suffered for a closely related reason. Competition with both foreign banks and other domestic institutions such as the 'Sparkassen' (savings banks) was heating up – especially after the latter had received the right to conduct the full range of payments operations and also to engage in securities transactions on behalf of their clients (Holtfrerich, 1985, p. 187; Hardach, 1995, p. 272). The large credit banks in Berlin had to compete harder for the business of their corporate clients which had once been awarded according to the 'Hausbank' principle — the more fiercely competitive environment transformed banking from a largely traditional, relationship-based business into a transactions-based one. That the large credit banks responded with aggressive lending policies was, however, not inevitable. A wide range of possible responses was available, and individual banks such as the Berliner Handelsgesellschaft (BHG) pursued markedly more cautious policies (Balderston, 1993, p. 164). The vulnerability of the banks, as signalled by their low liquidity and capital ratios, was ultimately a matter of choice (Balderston, 1991, p. 580).

5. Finally, there was one more change in the banking regime of the inter-war years that was to have dangerous consequences in the dark days of July 1931 – the dwindling willingness of the Reichsbank to act as lenders of last resort. Prior to the First World War, it had – as matter of policy – made liquidity available to the banking sector, if for a price (the so-called 'real bills doctrine'). This meant that banks were comfortable holding comparatively large bill portfolios, as these could readily be discounted at the central bank should some unforeseen liquidity need arise. The unhappy experience with unlimited discounting of bills during the period

of inflation as well as pressure from the Allies meant that the Reichsbank abandoned the real bills doctrines (James, 1985b, pp. 217ff.). Occasionally, the Reichsbank even used the threat of halting discounting operations to influence the banking sector's lending behaviour (i.e., during Schacht's 1927 attempt to engineer a 'soft landing' of the stock market), thus giving further cause to doubt the resilience of the banking sector as a whole in the event of a major shock.

The second main argument linking war and depression via the banking sector holds that Weimar's banks, because of their lending policies, also weakened the economy as a whole. The most vocal proponent of this view is Harold James (1986, p. 141). As the commissions of enquiry (Enquete-Kommissionen) during the early 1930s were to show, much of the banks' lending had been concentrated in stagnant industries of peripheral importance, whereas new sectors with quickly growing markets and a large number of innovations received disproportionately small credits. Textiles and the food industry obtained 23 per cent of overall bank lending; coal mining and iron and steel received only 8.7 per cent of credits, and the innovative chemical industry accounted for a mere 3.6 per cent of the total. The figures for engineering and automobile construction as well as the electro-technical industry were even lower (James, 1986, p. 141). By investing in the sunset sectors of the German economy, the banks failed to perform their pivotal function as co-ordinators of industrial development – a role that they had occupied before the First World War. This in turn continued to reduce the dynamism of the economy as a whole. These findings stand in contrast to the banks' role in the Wilhelmine Empire, where their lending policies had contributed significantly to balanced yet rapid growth.[6]

The banks' credit allocation can be explained as part of a general flight towards safety during the inter-war years as a result of inflation and war. The general tendency, however, was aggravated by changes in the sociological composition and general outlook of bank managers. James has pointed out that the entrepreneurial bankers of the nineteenth century had largely been replaced by sedate lawyers: 'The Directors of the Great Banks of the Weimar Republic were, with a few exceptions, solid and decent men who lacked any sense of exploring risks. They looked for safe bets: brewing and textiles' (James, 1986, p. 143). In addition, bankers sought to lend more to industries that had strong political support, i.e., textiles in Saxony or industries of strategic value (James, 1985b, p. 229). The bankers' admissions of mistakes before the committee in 1933 may have reinforced this view, though it is obviously strongly coloured both by the aftermath of the banking crisis and the particular circumstances in which Schacht was conducting the hearings (Feldman, 1992).

Considered in combination, these two views suggest that no other industry was as responsible for the dramatic downturn in Germany's economy as the banking sector. Balderston argues that ' ... only at this late stage [1931] were the risky liquidity policies of the banks in the later 1920s a material cause of the crisis. The illiquidity of advances was a product of the macro-financial environment ... ' (Balderston, 1991, p. 585). This, according to James, can partly be explained by the 'mental ossification' of bank management – as documented in their lending policies. The thread that links all these disparate aspects and undermined the banks' resilience during the early 1930s as well as their contribution to the economy's growth during the 1920s is the impact of war and inflation: aggressive lending policies were instigated by the increased competition from the savings banks and from abroad. Also, the new role of the 'Sparkassen' was inevitable as they took on an ever more important role in financing the war effort. Similarly, the large-scale reduction in invisible overseas earnings and much weaker exports were directly linked to the war as German patents and overseas assets were expropriated; the inflow of capital was thus necessary to compensate for the trade deficit.

LONG-TERM TRENDS IN THE GERMAN BANKING SECTOR AND THE IMPACT OF THE FIRST WORLD WAR

Assessing the impact of war and inflation on the German banking sector poses formidable methodological challenges. Comparisons between 1913 and 1924–9, say, are largely static in nature. They are also often overshadowed by the banking crisis of 1931. Yet many of the developments that became apparent in the inter-war years were already under way well before the outbreak of the First World War. To attribute changes to the impact of war therefore requires that we show not only how 1924–9 differed from 1913, but that developments after the stabilization in 1924 constituted a clear break with pre-war trends.[7]

Capital ratios were under pressure even before 1914, as Figure 7.1 demonstrates. A powerful long-run trend seems to have reduced capital ratios even before the First World War (Holtfrerich, 1985). Higher leverage of balance sheets increases profitability, of course; as size itself becomes an advantage in competing for business, growing the absolute size of bank assets base through a higher leverage ratio may be an economically rational strategy.[8] As Figure 7.1 demonstrates, capital ratios in Weimar Germany for the joint stock and publicly held banks never fell below the values inferred by extrapolating the pre-war trend.[9]

Of course, leverage cannot be increased beyond reasonable limits before the risk of collapse grows exponentially. However, by any absolute standard,

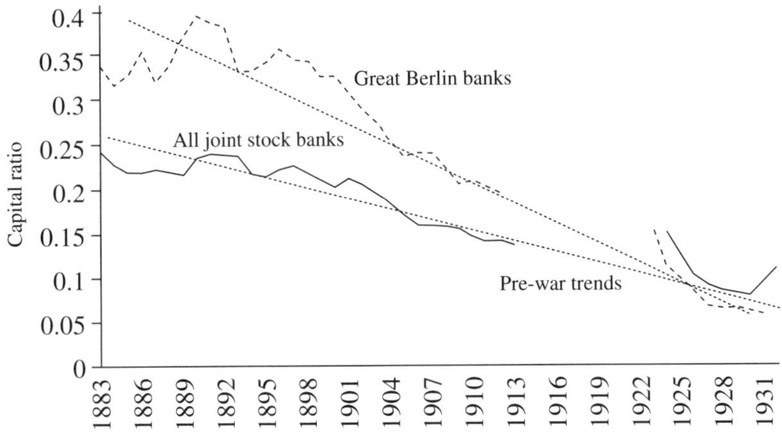

Figure 7.1 Capital ratios of joint stock banks and the great Berlin banks, 1884–1932

Weimar's banks were not even close to levels which, at other times or in other countries, proved sufficient to underpin a stable banking system. In West Germany in 1965, for example, the banking sector as a whole held capital and reserves (plus loan-loss provisions) of 6.2 per cent of total assets; in Weimar Germany during the 1920s, when ruthless competition and excessive lending practices particularly among the big banks are said to have prevailed, capital ratios never dipped below the 8 per cent level (Deutsche Bundesbank, 1976, D. IV, Table 1.01, pp. 136–7). Even the great Berlin banks which are often seen as synonymous with easy credit registered an absolute low of only 6.7 per cent in 1929. In the US in 1987, for example, the aggregate balance sheet for all commercial banks showed a capital ratio of 7 per cent (Mishkin, 1989).

Bank lending was indeed unusually strong in the inter-war years; the banks' contribution to the financing of investment in the German economy rose dramatically (Table 7.1).[10] In real terms, bank lending contributed almost twice as much in 1925–9 to the expansion of German industry as it had in 1908–13.[11] The banks succeeded in making funds on this scale available partly by letting capital ratios slip below their 1913 values, but this is not a departure from the long-term pre-war trend.

It is also hard to charge bank managers with reckless lending. The claim that excessively competitive practices underpinned the lending boom has often been made. It is difficult to see evidence of this in the banks' pricing. Table 7.2 shows the gross spread earned by the banks on deposits and credits (Deutsche Bundesbank, 1976, Section F, Table 2.01, p. 278). The average

Table 7.1 Banks' contribution to net investment, 1907–29

	Banks' contribution (in mn marks)	Price index of investment goods (1913 = 100)	Banks' contribution (in contrast 1913 mn marks)
1907	2367	98.7	2398
1908	1342	92.3	1454
1909	3319	91.2	3639
1910	3300	92.7	3560
1911	2338	92.3	2533
1912	3299	99.8	3306
1913	782	100	782
Average 1907–13	2392	95	2525
1925	6113	159.9	3823
1926	7698	129.7	5935
1927	8903	151.5	5877
1928	9844	159.6	6168
1929	5951	162.5	3662
Average 1925–9	7702	153	5093

spread in 1913 had been 5.4 per cent. Immediately after stabilization, the banks captured much higher spreads, and even at the nadir in 1927, they were higher than they had been before the war. Table 7.2 also decomposes the overall gross spread into the deposit-taking and the lending side of the operation, using the money market rate to decompose the total. If excessive competition was driving banks into irresponsible lending practices, the credit spreads should have been under severe pressure. In 1925 and 1926, this is clearly not true, with credit spreads being approximately 1 per cent higher than before the war. From 1927 onwards, the credit spreads drop, but hardly in a dramatic fashion. Profits in the banking sector also show little evidence of dramatic competition – for the years 1925–9, banks earned an average of 9.1 per cent return on equity (Sweezy, 1940, Table 1, p. 390). Only one other industry could boast an even higher level of profitability – chemicals, where both the existence of patents and of powerful trusts such as I.G. Farben boosted the return on equity.[12]

Table 7.2 also provides an alternative interpretation of the term structure of deposits. While Balderston and others have argued that the shifting of deposits from longer maturities (greater than 3 months) to shorter ones was driven

Table 7.2 *Spreads earned in banking, 1913–29*

	Interest rate on overdrafts (%)	Interest earned on balances, daily availability (%)	Gross spread (%)	Index	Money market rate (%)	Spread on credits (%)	Spread on deposits (%)
1913	7.9	2.5*	5.4	100	4.12	3.78	1.62
1925	14.11	5.05	9.06	167.8	9.18	4.93	4.13
1926	10.18	3.28	6.9	127.8	5.43	4.75	2.15
1927	8.83	3.19	5.64	104.4	6.11	2.72	2.92
1928	10	4	6	111.1	6.72	3.28	2.72
1929	10.2	4.19	6.01	111.3	7.69	2.51	3.5

Note: * Deutsche Bundesbank (1976, Section F, Table 2.01, p. 278) gives a range of 2–3.

by fear of price increases, the deposit spreads suggest that investors' responses to interest rate differentials may have been at least as important as inflationary expectations. As Table 7.3 shows, deposits at maturities between 7 days and 3 months grew by 24 percentage points between 1913 and 1929; the decline in deposits with more than 3 months notice of withdrawal accounted for 9 percentage points, while the reduction in deposits with notices of less than 7 days saw a 16 per cent reduction.[13] Instead of foregoing the substantial interest rates offered even for short-term deposits, investors shifted some of their cash balances into interest-bearing accounts with maturities of between 7 days and 3 months, thus capturing some of the potential 'gapping profits' that would otherwise have been earned by the banks.[14] That deposits with long notices (greater than 3 months) fell markedly may also not be a sign of nervousness – the much more developed market for deposits with medium maturities in the inter-war years as well as the attractive returns offered simply changed the risk/return profile of such long-dated investments. A change in investor psychology, however, does not necessarily follow. This is also borne out by the overall maturity profile of deposits. We do not exactly know what the average minimum notice for withdrawals was in each category. However, using a wide range of likely values, it can be shown that the maturity of the average deposit actually increased between 1913 and 1929 as more and more clients held balances with maturities between 7 days and 3 months (Table 7.3).[15]

Table 7.3 Distribution of deposits by maturity

Scenario	A			B		
	Average maturity (days)	Percentage of deposits 1913	1929	Average maturity (days)	Percentage of deposits 1913	1929
< 7 days	3	59	43	3	59	43
7 days to 3 months	80	29	53	70	29	53
> 3 months	180	12	3	120	12	3
Average maturity (days)		46.6	49.1		36.5	42.0

That excessive competition existed is hard to argue given the spreads and profits that banks could earn in the German inter-war economy, yet the allegedly over-intense battle for business is also said to have led to unnecessary mergers that undermined the stability of the banking system further. That larger banks should be weaker banks appears counterintuitive – larger branch networks and a wider deposit base should enhance regional and industry-sector diversification. It is also not supported by the empirical evidence. Grossman (1994) recently explored the connection between banking stability during the early 1930s and the environment in which banks were operating, including their competitive positions. He uses a sample of 25 countries across Europe and North America, and analyses the factors that distinguished those banking systems that saw major crises and those that did not. He finds that the degree of concentration in the banking industry is an important predictor of banking stability – the higher the average number of branches per bank, and the more banking customers per branch, the higher the degree of stability. Figure 7.2 presents his data on the connection between branch network density and banking crises. Countries that experienced a banking crises are highlighted in black. The probability of undergoing a crisis is clearly inversely related to the size of the branch network in the country relative to population. In Grossman's study, Germany is noteworthy for having both few branches per bank and for being

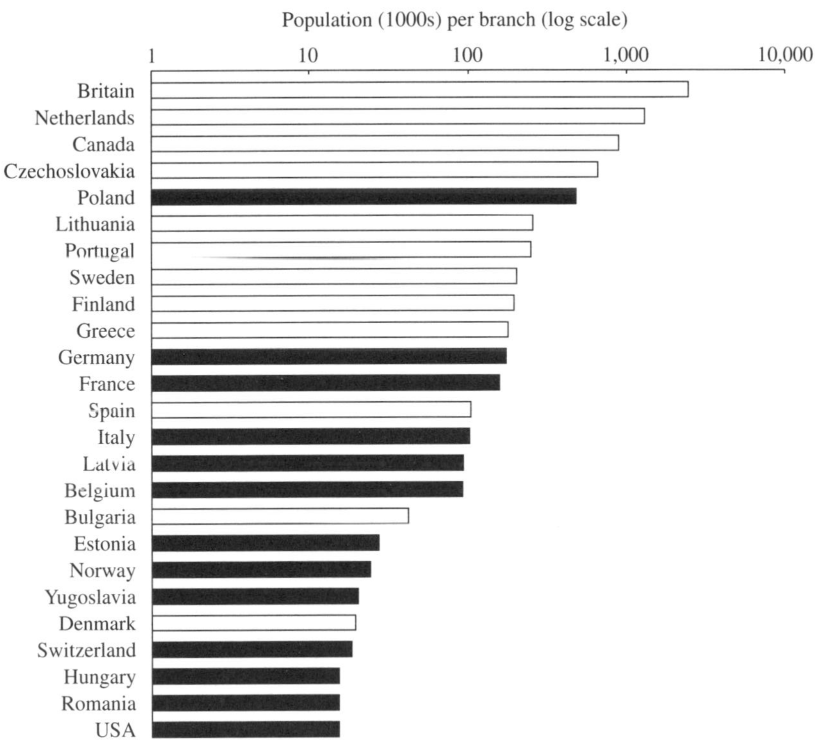

Figure 7.2 Branch network density and banking crises

'overbanked', i.e., having many more branches relative to population than countries that did not experience a crisis (Grossman, 1994, Table 1, p. 659; Table 5, p. 676). The average country without a banking crisis had 454,000 inhabitants per bank, whereas crisis countries had a mere 90,000. Germany is only slightly above the average of this group (176,000/bank). It therefore seems more convincing to argue that additional mergers would have strengthened the German banking sector, not weakened it.

The Grossman study also puts paid to the myth that the altered policy of the Reichsbank – and its more restrictive approach to discounting bills in particular – was central in bringing about the crisis of 1931. Central bank discounts have low explanatory power in Grossman's sample – differences in central bank policy are not a good predictor of whether countries underwent 'runs' or not (Grossman, 1994, Table 5, p. 676). Countries that were spared a crisis on the German or US model saw bill discounting by their central bank rise rapidly during the early 1930s, and more so than in countries with a banking crisis, but the difference is small and not statistically significant. What matters most in Grossman's cross-country study (apart from the variables that have already been mentioned, such as branches per bank and population per bank) is currency value – the countries that left gold early could quickly institute expansionary monetary policies (cf. Eichengreen and Sachs, 1985, pp. 925ff.), whereas those countries that tried to defend parities experienced severe deflationary contractions. German prices fell by 21.9 per cent between 1928 and 1932 (James, 1986, Table XIV, p. 160). Since deflation implies high real interest rates, both the economy at large and the banking sector in particular are hard hit.

The available evidence therefore suggests that the vulnerability of the German banking system on the eve of the Great Depression has been overstated. The pressure on capital ratios was part of a long-run trend and does not distinguish the inter-war years from the developments in the Wilhelmine Empire. Evidence of excess competition is also hard to find, since the banks' margins were large and stable and overall returns were more than healthy. Viewed from an international comparative perspective, the merger activity that took place was probably beneficial overall, as it increased the diversification of loan portfolios. The crisis of the banks in 1931, then, is perhaps better explained not by their inherent weaknesses as a result of misguided business strategies, but – as Grossman's results suggest – by the size of the macroeconomic shock to which they were exposed.

James's finding that the banks channelled most of their credits into stagnant industries suggests that the weakness of the economic environment in which the German banks found themselves was not entirely independent of their own policies. Yet the evidence speaks against the hypothesis that unimaginative lending created a drag on industrial development. The innovative and dynamic sectors in Weimar's economy such as chemicals that received a low share in the banks' total lending also showed high rates of profit (Sweezy, 1940, Table 1, p. 390). If expansion could be financed out of profits instead of turning to the banks, it is hard to fault the banks for a lack of risk-taking in the more dynamic sectors. Also, the available evidence suggests that lending to the more conventional industries made good business sense. This can be demonstrated by comparing the overall volatility of a portfolio of 'sunset' industries, such as textiles, food processing and clothing. We follow the approach pioneered by Kennedy and Britton (1985), who use the macro-performance (as measured by growth rates) of individual sectors as proxies for the return and risk of investing in companies in these sectors. Instead of employing growth rates, however, we use the profit rates calculated by Sweezy (1940). It is not unreasonable to suppose that the rate and volatility of profits in an industry are a good proxy for the level of risk that a creditor takes when lending. If we compare the risk inherent in this portfolio to that in new, innovative industries such as chemicals, electrical goods, fine mechanics and optics we find that for the years 1926–38, it is markedly higher – volatility (as measured by the coefficient of variation) in the new industries was 213 per cent, markedly higher than the 99 per cent for mature industries (cf. Table 7.4). The same result holds for the other periods: in 1926–31, for example,

Table 7.4 Rates of return by industrial group, 1926–9

	Portfolio A (Electrical, chemical, fine mechanics and optics)	Portfolio B (Textiles, food processing, clothing)	Average	Difference
1926	4.7	5.6	5.1	–0.9
1927	6.4	9.2	7.8	–2.8
1928	6.7	6.8	6.7	–0.1
1929	5.2	2.0	3.6	3.2
1930	0.6	1.6	1.1	–0.9
1931	–11.8	–5.3	–8.6	–6.5
1932	–6.1	–1.3	–3.7	–4.8
1933	1.3	3.5	2.4	–2.1
1934	4.9	5.5	5.2	–0.6
1935	5.0	5.2	5.1	–0.2
1936	7.3	5.9	6.6	1.3
1937	5.3	5.0	5.2	0.3
1938	4.6	7.1	5.9	–2.5

Portfolio A shows a volatility of 361 per cent, as compared to 156 per cent for the more 'stagnant' industries (Portfolio B). Note that average rate of profit in the backward sectors are also higher 3.9 per cent per year (1926–38) versus 2.6 per cent.[16] The allocation of credit during the 1920s was therefore strikingly prescient – we have used information on profits that were still in the future for the protagonists when lending decisions were made. Since the probability of default on a loan will normally be inversely related to the profit rate of the company that received the loan, any portfolio constructed with risk reduction in mind would have increased the mature industries' relative proportion in overall lending – which is precisely what Weimar's banks did.[17]

Neither frivolous lending practices, uneconomical empire building nor an economy fatally weakened by cheap credit were primarily responsible for the banking collapse in 1931, but Brüning's questionable policies of deflation and budgetary austerity.[18]

CONCLUSION

Gerald D. Feldman (1992) recently argued that the banks' policies in inter-war Germany have been treated too generously by later historians. The case arguing for a stronger link between the performance of the banking sector and the depth of the depression has been made more strongly in recent years (Balderston, 1993, 1991; James, 1986). This chapter has sought to demonstrate that the reverse is likely to be more accurate – that the banking sector in inter-war Germany has been compared more unfavourably with the days of the Empire than it deserves.[19] This is particularly true of the lending policies of the banks, which merely continued an existing pre-war trend towards lower liquidity ratios and higher leverage of capital employed. As the previous section sought to demonstrate, capital ratios were not unusually low either compared to pre-war trend or to the standards of post-war Germany and the US. It was not so much the fragility of the system that was exposed by the dramatic events in the summer of 1931, but rather the sheer size of the shock that came from staying on gold and the pursuit of consciously deflationary policies. Consequently, the connection between banking practices and the slide into depression is also much more tenuous than has often been argued. In this sense, the impact of war and inflation on the German banking sector has been overstated.

Also, banks continued and expanded their role in providing funds for industrial development, and did so in an economically rational fashion.[20] The sectors that they favoured appear in retrospect less dynamic than some alternatives, but then they were judged to be sensible choices given the trade-off between risk and reward. That the economic health of the Weimar republic in the 1920s was undermined by the banking sector's follies is hard to argue.

This is not to deny that the First World War – largely through inflation after 1918 – exerted a powerful influence on the banking sector. Much has been written about competition between different forms of banks within Germany, and the expanded role of foreign banks. Yet one of the most important discontinuities brought about by the First World War was the expanded role of the banking sector as a whole *vis-à-vis* the domestic bond and equity markets.[21] Figure 7.3 compares the relative (domestic) contributions to net investment by the bond market the equity market and by the banking sector.

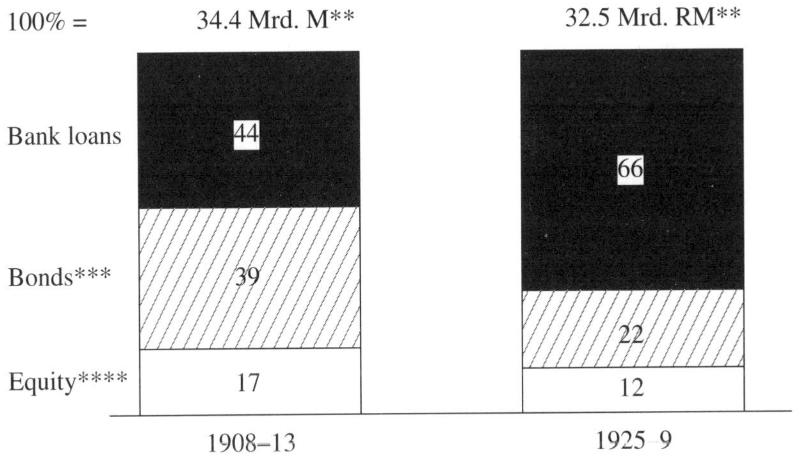

Notes:
* Bank loans, bonds and equity issuance only; net investment in the case of bank loans.
** Adjusted for changes in the price of investment goods using Hoffmann's series (Hoffmann, 1965, Table 148, p. 601).
*** Nominal value.
**** Market value.

Source: Deutsche Geld- und Bankstatistik, 1976, Table 1.07; Hoffmann, 1965, Table 239, p. 813.

*Figure 7.3 Domestic sources of finance for investment 1907–13 and 1925–9**

In contrast to the process of disintermediation that has occurred in many OECD countries over the past 20 years, the reverse appears to be true for the inter-war years. If internal sources of finance had been included, the increase in the relative importance of bank credit would probably have been even greater (James, 1986, p. 132).[22] It could be argued that, since bondholders –

despite a partial revaluation of their assets – had suffered dramatic losses as a result of inflation, the bond market was left permanently impaired. Note, however, that shareholders, who fared much better during the inflation since they held claims to real assets (rather than promises of nominal payments), were apparently also reluctant to provide funds – even if the change is much less dramatic than in the case of bonds. That the banks' service of intermediation became relatively more valuable is largely explained by their two primary functions: (i) risk management and (ii) aggregation of savings. Domestic saving had been hard hit by the massive reduction in the number and wealth of rentiers (Balderston, 1993). That banks rather than the markets should provide the outlet for savers with much lower average wealth (and much smaller portfolios) is not surprising: the fees for investing in bonds and equities are normally high, and the investments required are 'lumpy' – prior to the invention of mutual funds, the average denomination of bonds may have been too high for many investors in the Weimar Republic, particularly if transactions costs are taken into account. That those who still invested in bonds were unusually wealthy can be demonstrated by the different yields of gold bonds. Prices of bonds with different coupons can vary for a variety of reasons. If the yield curve is upward-sloping, bonds with lower coupons will have higher current yields, since they are (even for the same maturity) effectively 'longer' bonds – their Macaulay duration will be higher since the money is returned to the investor later.[23] Thus, the interest rate risk that he bears will also be higher. Strikingly, the yields of gold bonds in the Weimar Republic show the opposite kind of behaviour.[24] The reason is that interest payments were taxed as income, whereas capital gains were tax-free (cf. Balderston, 1993, p. 185, fn. 5). Given sensible assumptions about the average maturity of the bonds, we can calculate the tax rate that equalizes the yields on both types of bond. Using data for 1925 (and assuming an average of 20 years to maturity for the gold bonds), the average tax rate faced by investors must have equalled 30 per cent; assuming 15 years, the implied tax rate is 40 per cent. Since the top rate of 40 per cent was only applied to incomes above 80,000 RM per annum, those that held bonds must have belonged to the thinned ranks of Germany's propertied classes.[25] For the rest, investment opportunities were provided largely by the banking sector, which aggregated the savings of larger groups of society so that they could be used effectively by debtors.[26]

In addition, the risk-management component became relatively more important. Both bonds and equity are typically long-term investments; short-term returns for both of these instruments can easily be significantly negative. The amount of risk an individual can take should depend, among other things, on the time horizon of the investment and the individual's wealth. Only relatively wealthy investors can accept high volatility in exchange for higher long-term returns – the danger that they will have to cash in their investments at short notice is much smaller than in the case of those who manage to save smaller amounts from their weekly pay cheques. If the average wealth of investors fell, as every account of war and inflation suggests, then instruments with lower risks had to become more important *vis-à-vis* the traditional outlets of investment, and these were overwhelmingly provided by the banking sector – hence the advertising campaigns of the banks for savings books, their expansion of branch networks and the offering of savings accounts by the Berlin great banks (Feldman, 1995; Hardach, 1995, p. 280). The banks were thus able to capitalize on the huge demands for funding in inter-war Germany by offering aggregation of savings and management of the maturity mismatch of the funds required by borrowers and those deposited by lenders.

The impact of the Great War was therefore transmitted through a shift in the structure of domestic saving, which tended to enhance the competitive role of the banks *vis-à-vis* other sources of finance. The means to expand their business had to come from abroad, given the destruction of capital during the inflation and the decline of the rentier class which – prior to the First World War – had provided an important part of total savings. Neither the wave of bank mergers, misallocation of credit, nor the banks' tendency to lend long and borrow short can be described as the main causes of the 1931 banking crisis. The chief implication of these findings is that, while the First World War's role in undermining the stability of Weimar's banking system has been overstated, it did have a profound impact by increasing the banks' business opportunities. The volatility of the environment in which the banks had to operate was largely caused by Weimar politics and dislocations in the way the gold standard operated in the inter-war period (Eichengreen, 1992) – sources of instability that were themselves direct results of the First World War.

NOTES

1. Ironically, the coincidence is even more precise – it was on 13 July that the banking panic began, and it was 17 years earlier to the day that the German ambassador to Vienna, Count Heinrich von Tschirschky informed the Empire's Chancellor Bethman-Hollweg that, following the *carte blanche* for the Habsburg Empire, the Austrian ultimatum to Serbia would be making demands so harsh that they could not be accepted; the outbreak of the First World War had become only a matter of time.
2. Only in the United States was the contraction more severe. Cf. James, 1986, p. 6.
3. This is not to deny the monetary stabilization might well have been possible before the hyperinflation of 1923 (Paddags, 1997).
4. Holtfrerich (1985, pp. 187–9) argues for a similar approach.
5. The figure for 1931 was also 7 per cent. Cf. Deutsche Bundesbanke, 1976, Section D II, Table 1.03, pp. 78f.

6. Kennedy and Britton (1985) demonstrate that the banks' portfolio of loans to different industries was close to the capital market line, implying that the sectoral composition of bank lending was highly efficient.
7. This is the methodology employed by Holtfrerich (1985, p. 188).
8. The mechanism could take two forms – either by growing the equity base directly through the 'ploughing-back' of profits, or by issuing new shares. For the latter operation to succeed, the bank would have to show healthy profits (and overall solidity) – which was again easier to achieve by leveraging bank capital further.
9. Data come from Deutsche Bundesbank, 1976, Section D 11, Table 1.02, Table 1.03, pp. 76–9 and Section D I, Table 1.01, pp. 56–9. Figures for the Great Berlin banks are taken directly from Deutsche Bundesbank. The series for all joint stock banks uses the inter-war figures for all joint stock banks plus publicly held institutes; the series is then spliced to match the pre-war series for joint stock banks.
10. Data are from Hoffmann (1965, Table 239, pp. 812f.; Table 148, p. 601).
11. Even if the unusually weak figure for 1913 is excluded from the pre-war average, the rise is still larger than 75 per cent.
12. Recently, Spoerer (1996) has presented revised estimates of profitability in inter-war Germany. For our purposes, however, we prefer Sweezy's study from the 1940s, as it is less affected by problems of changes in tax laws etc.
13. Does not sum to 24 because totals in Table 7.3 (from Balderston, 1993, Table 6.7, p. 198) do not sum to 100.
14. This possibility is also mentioned by Balderston, 1993, p. 198.
15. If extreme values are used (i.e. 3/50/210), there is a shortening of the average maturity from 41 to 34 days – hardly a dramatic change.
16. Again, the same result also holds for 1926–31: 3.3 versus 2.0 per cent. Note also that the highly profitable chemicals sector is included in the set of 'new' industries; nonetheless, average profitability is low.
17. We have not demonstrated that the portfolio of the banks was efficient, but that the features which have been interpreted as signs of irrationality increased the risk/return profile of a two-industry portfolio. Assuming that only two kinds of industries are present in the portfolio is admittedly a heroic assumption; these results are part of a larger research project into the efficiency of bank lending during the 1920s, and an extension to all German industries will be completed as part of this exercise.
18. On these, cf. Holtfrerich, 1984; Borchardt, 1991; Voth, 1993. Alternative interpretations of Weimar's pre-crisis investment performance are explored in Voth, 1995.
19. A similar note is struck by Borchardt (1987), pp. 270ff.
20. It is nonetheless possible that rationality at the firm level – i.e. profit maximization – was socially suboptimal, and that individual banks should have taken larger risks in lending to the more innovative sectors of the Weimar economy. Such an argument, however, is rather different from the one advanced by James.
21. Note that, if the sum of long-term capital imports until 1929 (6.6 billion RM in current prices, or 4.3 billion in 1913 prices, cf. Balderston, 1993, Table 5.1, p. 133) was added to the bond total, the proportion of the bond market overall would only rise to 31 per cent – still markedly less than its pre-war share.
22. Rates of internal financing fell rapidly. Note, however, that rules for the depreciation of capital equipment etc. had been changed so dramatically during the inter-war period that it is hard to compare the volume of self-finance before WWI and after inflation. Cf. the seminal work by Schröder (1996).
23. Cf. Mishkin, 1989, p. 187.
24. The maturity of the different bonds is not given; everything that follows is based on the assumption that the maturity distributions of 10 per cent and 5 per cent gold bonds is similar.
25. Even if all the bonds had remaining maturities of 25 years (mortgage bonds are typically issued with a maturity of 25 years), the implied tax rate would be 23 per cent.
26. Also, the banking sector provided a convenient form of investment for foreigners, as evidenced by their high share in total deposits. Cf. Balderston, 1993, Table 5.7, p. 144.

REFERENCES

Balderston, T. (1991), 'German Banking Between the Wars: The Crisis of the Credit banks', *Business History Review*, **65**, 554–605.

Balderston, T. (1993), *The Origins and Course of the German Economic Crisis*, Haude & Spener: Berlin.

Bernanke, B. and H. James (1991), 'The Gold Standard, Deflation and Financial Crisis in the Great Depression: An International Comparison', in R.G. Hubbard (ed.), *Financial Markets and Financial Crises*, Chicago: University of Chicago Press.

Borchardt, K. (1987), '"Das hat historische Gründe" Zu Determinanten der Struktur des deutschen Kreditwesens unter besonderer Berücksichtigung der Rolle der Sparkassen', in H. Henning *et al.* (eds), *Wirtschafts- und sozialgeschichtliche Forschungen und Probleme*, Sankt Katharinen.

Borchardt, K. (1991), 'Economic Causes of the Weimar Republic', in K. Borchardt (ed.), *Perspectives on Modern German Economic History and Policy*, Cambridge: Cambridge University Press.

Deutsche Bundesbank (1976), *Deutsches Geld- und Bankwesen in Zahlen 1876–1975*, Frankfurt am Main: Knapp.

Eichengreen, B. (1992), *Golden Fetters. The Gold Standard and the Great Depression*, Oxford: Oxford University Press.

Eichengreen, B. and J. Sachs (1985), 'Exchange Rates and Economic Recovery in the 1930s', *Journal of Economic History*, **45**, pp. 925–46.

Feinstein, C.H., P. Temin and G. Toniolo (1995), 'International Economic Organization: Banking, Finance and Trade in Europe Between the Wars', in C.H. Feinstein (ed.), *Banking, Currency and Finance in Europe between the Wars*, Oxford: Oxford University Press.

Feldman, G. (1992), 'Banks and Banking in Germany after the First World War: Strategies of Defence', in Y. Cassis (ed.), *Finance and Financiers in European History, 1880 1960*, Cambridge: Cambridge University Press, pp. 243–62.

Feldman, G. (1995), 'The Deutsche Bank from World War to World Economics Crisis 1914–1933', in L. Gall (ed.), *The Deutsche Bank 1870–1995*, London: Weidenfeld & Nicholson.

Ferguson, N. (1995), *Paper and Iron. Hamburg Business and German Politics in the Era of Inflation, 1897–1927*, Oxford: Oxford University Press.

Grossman, R.S. (1994), 'The Shoe that Didn't Drop: Explaining Banking Stability During the Great Depression', *Journal of Economic History*, **54** (3), 654–82.

Hardach, G. [1941] (1976), *Weltmarkorientierung und relative Stagnation: Währungspolitik in Deutschland, 1924–1931*, Berlin: Duncker and Humblot.

Hardach, G. (1995), 'Banking in Germany 1918–1939', in C.H. Feinstein, *Banking, Currency and Finance in Europe between the Wars*, Oxford: Oxford University Press.

Hoffmann, W.G. (1965), *Das Wachstum der deutschen Wirtschaft seit der Mitte des 19. Jahrhunderts*, Berlin/Heidelberg: Springer.

Holtfrerich, C.-L. (1980), *Die deutsche Inflation 1914–1923. Ursachen und Folgen in internationaler Perspektive*, Berlin/New York: De Gruyter.

Holtfrerich, C.-L. (1984), 'Zu hohe Löhne in der Weimarer Republik? Bemerkungen zur Borchardt-These', *Geschichte und Gesellschaft* (10), 122–45.

Holtfrerich, C.-L. (1985), 'Auswirkungen der Inflation auf die Struktur des deutschen

Kreditgewerbes', in G.D. Feldman (ed.), *Nachwirkungen der Inflation auf die deutsche Geschichte 1924–1933*, München: Oldenbourg.
James, H. (1985a), *The Reichsbank and Public Finance in Germany 1924–1933*, Frankfurt: Knapp.
James, H. (1985b), 'Did the Reichsbank Draw the Right Conclusions from the Great Inflation?', in G.D. Feldman (ed.), *Nachwirkungen der Inflation auf die deutsche Geschichte 1924–1933*, München: Oldenbourg.
James, H. (1986), *The German Slump*, Oxford: Oxford University Press.
James, H. (1992), 'Banks and Bankers in the German Interwar Depression', in Y. Cassis (ed.), *Finance and Financiers in European History, 1880–1960*, Cambridge: Cambridge University Press, 263–82.
Kennedy, W.P. and R. Britton (1985), 'Portfolioverhalten und wirtschaftliche Entwicklung im späten 19. Jahrhundert. Ein Vergleich zwischen Großbritannien und Deutschland', in R. Tilly (ed.), *Beiträge zur quantitativen vergleichenden Unternehmensgeschichte*, Stuttgart: Klett-Cotta.
Mishkin, F.S. (1989), *The Economics of Money, Banking and Financial Markets*, Glenview, IL: Scott, Foresman and Co.
Paddags, N. (1997), 'The German Railways – the economics and Political Feasibility of Fiscal Reforms During the Inflation of the Early 1920s', *University of Oxford Discussion Papers in Economic and Social History* (13).
Schröder, S. (1996), *Steuerlast der Aktiengesellschaften und Veranlagung zur Körperschaftssteuer im Deutschen Reich und den USA von 1918 bis 1936*, Berlin: Duncker & Humblodt.
Spoerer, M. (1996), *Von Scheingewinnen zum Rüstungsboom. Die Eigenkapitalrentabilität der deutschen Industrieaktiengesellschaften 1925–1941*, Stuttgart: Steiner.
Sweezy, M. (1940), 'German Corporate Profits: 1926–1938', *Quarterly Journal of Economics*, **54** (3).
Temin, P. (1976), *Did Monetary Forces Cause the Great Depression?*, New York: Norton.
Temin, P. (1971), 'The Beginning of the Great Depression in Germany', *Economic History Review*, (24), 240–248.
Voth, H.-J. (1993), 'Wages, Investment and the Fate of the Weimar Republic: A Long-term Perspective', *German History*, **11**, 265–92.
Voth, H.-J. (1995), 'Did High Wages or High Interest Rates Bring Down the Weimar Republic?', *Journal of Economic History*, **55** (4), 801–21.

APPENDIX TECHNICAL TERMS

balance sheet	A statement summarizing the financial condition of a company, listing all liabilities and assets at a given point in time.
disintermediation	The process by which the role of middlemen is reduced. Examples include the growth of direct sales via mail or the Internet, or growth of mutual funds in the US over the past 25 years.

'gapping'	The extent to which a bank lends long and borrows short; a good proxy for exposure to changes in the term structure of interest rates.
leverage	Generally measured as a multiple of an institution's capital. Indicates the extent to which borrowed funds are used to enhance returns.
liquidity ratio	The ratio of liquid assets – i.e., cash and other assets than can readily be exchanged for cash – to the total size of the *balance sheet* (see above). Higher liquidity ratios provide a hedge against payment difficulties in case of sudden deposit withdrawals.
Macaulay duration	In contrast to a bond's *maturity* (see below), the Macaulay duration incorporates information both about the timing of coupon payments and the repayment of principal. For zero-bonds (which do not carry a coupon), the duration and the maturity will be identical.
maturity	The maturity of a bond measures the number of years until the bond's principal will be repaid. The maturity of loans and deposits measures the number of years until loans need to be repaid and deposits can be withdrawn (without penalty).
spread	The margin earned on financial transactions. In the trading of financial instruments, spreads are equivalent to the difference between bid and offer price. In bank transactions, the difference of interest rates charged for loans and those paid for deposits (adjusted for maturity mismatch) is equivalent to the spread.
yield curve	Plots the yield on bonds against their maturity, thus summarizing the term structure of interest rates. Upward-sloping yield curves thus imply that interest rates on bonds with longer maturities are higher than on bonds with short maturitics.

8. Women and the First World War

Sarah Palmer

I

Among the enduring social changes commonly assumed to have been hastened by the First World War, the emancipation of women is usually at the forefront. Whether emancipation is thought of in terms of gaining political rights, as with the granting of the vote to women which occurred in a number of countries shortly after the coming of peace, or in the sense of women's status more generally, the claim is, first, that there was improvement and, second, that such improvement was a direct consequence of the war itself. In particular, the wartime movement of women into types of work formerly undertaken only by men is seen as a prime instigator of change, challenging traditional attitudes and opening the way for future progress.

An accurate assessment of the short-term and longer-term impact of the First World War on women requires a more sceptical approach to the issue of emancipation than might be suggested by this conventionally accepted account. It also needs a broader interpretation of the area of interest than one focused primarily on employment, or indeed on a search for signs of discontinuity, for indications of a break with the past. From an international perspective account must obviously be taken of national differences in the degree to which the claims of women to equality had been recognized before the war, but it is equally important even when dealing with the experience of one nation to recognize the variety of individual female experience masked by every generalization. The conflation of middle-class, bourgeois encounters with war work together with that of working-class or peasant women is one recognizable trap, but even within a clear frame of reference, there is a limit to which prominent witnesses like Vera Brittain can serve to testify for thousands of other women.[1]

One effect of the large amount of recent research has been to make the task of re-evaluation in some respects easier than was the case in the past, although also perhaps more difficult because of the complexity it has exposed. In the British context, for example, reaction against Arthur Marwick's influential study, *The Deluge: British Society and the First World War* (1st edn, 1965), with its emphasis on 1914–18 as a watershed in British social history, has inspired several studies of which the most extreme recent example in terms of a counter-argument for continuity and stability is Gerard J. DeGroot's *Blighty: British Society in the Era of the Great War* (1996). This follows Gail Braybon's earlier *Women Workers in the First World War* (1981) in challenging the significance of wartime employment in changing attitudes to, and prospects for, women.[2] Similar questioning studies in respect of other belligerent powers have also altered perceptions of war as an automatic force for social change elsewhere. These new approaches, emphasizing continuity as they do, have been dubbed 'revisionist'.[3]

As important, however, for the advance of understanding have been the results of painstaking quantitative research into twentieth-century European health, population and employment trends. This has provided a longer-term context into which the experience of war can be set, so helping to distinguish developments which can be put down to the conflict from those which feature as part of the general drift. Differences in national experiences of the home front have been highlighted and some counterintuitive conclusions have resulted, of which the most noteworthy in the present context has been to reveal that in Britain, and even to some extent in France, which had even heavier proportionate losses of life, the killing of marriageable young men in large numbers did not create a generation of women destined not to marry and therefore by implication more likely to participate in the post-war labour force.[4]

To identify 'the lost generation' as a myth is not, however, to rule it out of discussion as a historical question. Rather, it requires the focus to shift to finding an explanation for the creation and pervasiveness of the myth. Here too the tenor of recent scholarship, informed in this case by insights coming from feminist, literary, cultural and psychological perspectives, makes a contribution. If, as will be discussed below, there is a strong case for concluding that the First World War had only a temporary effect on the status of women, why has so much more been claimed – not just by historians but by contemporary observers as well? How are we to account for the gap between reality and perception? Posing these questions is an acknowledgement that there is more to discovering how great was the impact of the First World War on women than merely establishing whether there was, or was not, an objective change in their economic, political or social standing, compared with the last years of peace; the position of women has to be set against a background which was itself changing.[5]

II

There is no dispute that with the recruitment of millions of men into the armed forces, and the expansion of war-related industries, war created new employment opportunities, particularly for women. War, however, also closed off opportunities. In Britain, for instance, an initial effect of the outbreak of war was a rise in unemployment as industries, ranging from confectionery to fish gutting, which were dominated by women workers laid off workers; in Paris cut-backs in the production of luxury goods raised female unemployment. The production of textiles was particularly affected by wartime raw material shortages and loss of markets; in Germany by 1918 the textile industry employed fewer than a quarter of the number of men, and three-fifths of the number of women who had worked in the industry in 1914. A similar shrinkage occurred in Britain and France.[6]

Within the total picture, however, the shortage of some types of work was more than compensated for by openings elsewhere. In Britain the total female workforce, roughly a third of the entire labour force in 1911, increased by just over a quarter during the war years, rising from 4,934,000 in July 1914 to 6,193,000 four years later; in Germany employment of females in industrial enterprises with more than ten workers increased from 1,593,000 in 1913 to 2,320,000 in 1918 – a rise approaching 50 per cent; in France women made up a quarter of the war factory workforce; in Russia the proportion of women in industrial employment soared from 26.6 per cent in 1914 to 43.4 per cent in 1917; in Italy 'tens of thousands of working-class women were thrust into factory jobs'.[7]

Female involvement in the production of armaments attracted attention in the press and was the subject of much government propaganda, but by no means all the work undertaken by women in wartime was industrial. As many as 5,000 Russian women fought alongside men as combatants at the front, while here as also in other countries many served as drivers or as nurses for the military. In Britain numerically the greatest impact was on white-collar, clerical and secretarial jobs in banking, finance and commerce, where the numbers of women workers grew by approaching half a million. A similar expansion of female work in the service sector, which also included 'blue-collar' jobs such as transport (where in Britain the numbers of women jumped from 18,000 in 1914 to 117,000 in 1918) was also evident in other countries.

In assessing the significance of the greater numbers of women in the wartime workforce a number of aspects deserve attention. It sometimes seems to be carelessly assumed, for example, that the First World War was responsible for bringing a female workforce into being. In fact, most of the women who had jobs during the war were not fresh recruits to the labour force, although the type of work they had familiarity with or would have expected to undertake in peacetime might be different. In Britain working-class women had always worked, although the range of opportunities for full-time paid work was limited, with domestic service by far the commonest occupation and textiles accounting for most female factory employment. Once married, and taking on family commitments, it was customary to cease working: the 1911 England and Wales Census records 13.7 per cent of married women in full-time employment compared with 54.5 per cent unmarried. (The census statistics took no account of women working part-time, and certainly understate the prevalence of paid work among married women before the war.) The effect of the war was to draw British married women back into full-time jobs and to encourage girls to start work earlier than they might otherwise have done.[8]

A similar pattern of returning, rather than new, female workers can be detected elsewhere. In Germany, as Bessel has written, 'generally the women who took advantage of the new employment possibilities created by the War came from the working class; the majority were in their thirties and forties; most had worked previously; and often women took up the places that their men had vacated'.[9] In France, war industries took on numbers of women who had lost their normal peacetime jobs as a result of the conflict.[10] For peasant women who remained on the land, here (as also in France, Italy and Russia) substituting for absent males in the running of farms which were worked as family enterprises, the war added one more pressure in a life of unremitting daily toil, but did not present any fundamental challenge to conventional norms of female behaviour.

Other norms remained intact. Although women joined trade unions in greater numbers than before the war, they failed to penetrate the inner reaches of a male-dominated type of institution. In the United States, those black women who joined other racial groups in moving out of domestic service into manufacturing jobs found patterns of segregation reproduced in the lowest levels of work and pay, as also commonly in separate eating, locker and washroom facilities. Even so, the exodus of African-Americans from the rural South to the North attracted by wartime job opportunities offered the possibility of a better existence to women as well as men.[11]

For these First World War women workers, the mere fact of working was not a transforming or emancipating experience, although the jobs on offer and the level of possible earnings differed from peacetime. In Britain, despite impressions to the contrary, relatively few middle- or upper-class women appear to have joined the workforce. Typically, those who did moved into white-collar or supervisory jobs, where educational level and class status were assets. Some were able to apply their driving skills, but few took on factory work at shop-floor level, although the small Women's Land Army proved a greater attraction.[12] Here, as in other countries, for educated women war provided an outlet for philanthropy and charity, with the common effect of endorsing rather than narrowing the gap between women of different social classes. Even in Russia, where some radical intellectual feminists looked to war to reduce differences between women, there appears to have been little appreciation of the problems women workers faced in their daily lives.[13]

Second, most wartime female work was regarded by governments, employers, trade unions and, it appears, by women themselves as temporary; an emergency response. In Britain such an understanding was built into formal agreements with trade unions, but in any case it was to be anticipated that with peace would come demobilization, the return of men to their jobs, and an end to the massive demand for munitions. Furthermore, despite the emphasis of national propaganda on patriotic service to 'Country', 'Patrie', 'Fatherland', for many women, perhaps the majority, the motivation for war work was economic necessity produced by the war itself. Government allowances to the wives of those in the armed forces were scant compensation for the absence of a breadwinner, even more so once prices began to rise as shortages developed, and excluded other dependants such as mothers, sisters and typically those not in married relationships. One historian's comment on the importance of economic motives underlying industrial mobilization in France can be applied to women more generally: 'when the opportunity arose to take up jobs in the war factories and elsewhere, housewives, domestic servants and unemployed female workers seized the chance to provide for their families'.[14] It is worth noting that not all war-related paid work took women out of the house; in Germany female homeworkers produced uniforms, shoes, gas masks, and even containers for grenades and shells.[15]

Another reason for women to see the jobs they took on in wartime as temporary, to be abandoned as soon as possible, was that their presence was at best accepted with extreme reluctance by the male workforce and at worst evoked outright hostility. The attitude of skilled workers towards the entry of women into industries which had previously been almost the exclusive preserve of men was not based purely on social prejudice, although there were plenty of examples of this. Given that women were invariably paid less than men, skilled men feared if women took on men's jobs this would drive down their wages. In Britain, in an effort to shore up the status of skilled male workers, unions campaigned for equal pay for men and women under the assumption that with pay the same for men and women, a man would always be preferred by an employer, but in practice the danger they perceived was averted by the fact that women were rarely used as direct substitutes. Rather, under 'dilution' schemes, many industrial processes were reorganized to enable them to be performed by less-skilled workers, male or female. As a result, women took on lower-level work, or performed parts of skilled tasks, roles which offered little challenge to assumptions of female inferiority as workers.[16]

The tough, repetitive and unhealthy nature of much war-related work (in Germany for instance some women laboured for 12-hour shifts) no doubt further encouraged women to see their involvement as a temporary expedient. In France, indeed, there is evidence of a swift turnover of women factory workers, some able to stand the work for less than a week, and everywhere the dangers of war work on the home front were reflected in increased numbers of industrial accidents and evidence of chemical poisoning.[17]

Nevertheless, the degree to which war work was seen as exceptional hardship can only be understood in the wider context of the impact of war on living standards. One benefit everywhere of the opening up of a wider range of employment opportunities for women was a rise in earnings over peacetime norms, and a narrowing of pay differentials between men and women.[18] But the extent to which this appeared as gain varied. For Britain, there is considerable direct and indirect evidence that working-class living standards actually rose during the First World War; the impact of higher earnings for lower-paid workers, including women, was not substantially eroded by shortages or inflation. Crucially, nutritional standards were maintained or even improved; people did not go short of essential foods, and, in fact, those on lower incomes were able to spend more on food than before the war, although queues were common and caused unrest among munitions workers in some towns.[19]

In stark contrast, the experience of the majority of Germans was one of a steep decline in real incomes, little to buy in the shops, deprivation and a struggle to survive. By early 1916 what a woman might be able to earn in a day would not buy even a dozen eggs.[20] Similarly, in Russia's northern cities women who had come off long shifts in factories faced as many hours waiting outside bakeries and food shops for pathetically inadequate supplies. The daily struggle for survival facing many women was arguably as much a factor in developing the potential for revolution as the experience of work itself.[21] Small wonder, then, that there was little echo in Germany or Russia of the undeniable enjoyment of working during the war which comes through some of the British accounts of women's experiences.

Such accounts suggest that this enjoyment was not just a reflection of good wages and regular earnings. For young British women living and working away from home alongside others of much the same age offered possibilities for fun, fellowship and independence which would not have been open to them in the ordinary course of events. To their social superiors, female as well as male, the exercise of freedom by working-class women, even if this amounted to little more than wearing showy clothes, was suspect, raising issues of propriety and morality. The appointment of factory welfare supervisors and the duty of women's police patrols to check on women found out on the streets in the evening reflected concerns that, once free of the surveillance of fathers and husbands, women would fall prey to the temptations of drink and carnal desire. A number of charges of sexual licence, dismissed as myths by a 1918 Commission of Enquiry, in particular attached themselves to those women most directly engaged with the military who joined the Women's

Auxiliary Army Corps.[22] Similar fears of moral decline – in effect, that women who took on male roles might also take on male standards of sexual conduct, were also voiced in other countries, although, as with Britain (where the number of illegitimate births declined, although to a lesser degree than legitimate births) actual evidence of greater permissiveness was in short supply.

In other respects, too, the appearance of change obscured the continued force of convention. The references above to the involvement of women in shopping is a reminder that, whether doing paid work or not, women remained responsible for the domestic burdens of home and family, and war did little or nothing to change this or to make it easier for married women to cope with the multiple roles of wife, mother and war worker. After the introduction of conscription in Britain some assistance was provided by sponsored crèches in government munitions factories, but the 108 nurseries existing in 1917 provided a mere 4,000 places, open to the children of these workers alone. A survey done in Leeds in 1916 of how 129 pre-school children of munitions workers were being looked after suggests that little had changed in the way in which women who worked and had families managed to cope; most of these infants were being minded by other women – grandmothers, near relatives or neighbours.[23] The lack of official provision for childcare other than in munitions factories reflected a fundamental concern that, if things were made too easy, women might not be content to leave their jobs when the war ended. In fact, even the gains in factory conditions associated with the employment of girls and women, such as provision of protective clothing, canteens and lavatories, were defended in terms of an ultimate female purpose; 'the workers of today are the mothers of tomorrow' said Lloyd George.[24]

Indeed, with her husband absent at the Front, if a married woman's role changed this was in the direction of emphasizing her centrality in the domestic scene. To her fell the task of *keeping the home fire burning*; she exemplified the ideal of *la femme au foyer* (woman by the hearth) . It is difficult for us to retrieve the thinking of women faced with the absence, and in the event often death, of their chosen or hoped-for life partners, but we certainly would not be justified in assuming that the war years undermined the importance of the home. Even if we do not go as far as Gerard DeGroot in contending that 'rather than encouraging [British] women out of the home, war's greatest effect was to draw them back',[25] the possibility that the First World War strengthened, rather than undermined, support for traditional roles, has to be taken seriously, not least because this may help us to explain why some of the changes which might have been expected to be the outcome of such a socially and economically disruptive conflict seemingly failed to materialize.

III

The First World War proved that women could do almost any type of work, but this did not mean that they would be allowed to continue to demonstrate this once war ended. In all the combatant countries in 1918 the return of the soldiers and the demobilization of the economy meant the rapid dismissal of women workers, and consequent higher unemployment rates for women than for men. Although, as has been shown, much war work had been seen as temporary, this did not make the shunting of women out of jobs to make way for men any the easier to bear. Far from melting away, back into the home or domestic service, as the authorities hoped, women signalled their claim to work by registering as unemployed. In May 1919 women accounted for half of those registered as looking for a job in Germany and two-thirds of those unemployed in Britain, and the same year saw unemployed women demonstrating in the streets of France's major cities.[26] A sustained propaganda campaign in the British press against working women, backed by the withdrawal of benefits from unemployed women who would not accept offers of jobs available as laundry or domestic workers, succeeded in forcing women off the unemployment register.[27]

Women in other countries involved in the conflict were similarly left in no doubt as to their reduced peacetime status as workers. (An important exception is post-revolution Russia, by now embroiled in civil war, where the Communists were intent on building a new society. Though in practice gender divisions were to prove resilient, and 1917 was not a watershed in terms of women's work, repudiation of the old order promised a transformed role for women.[28] With the beginning of the slump in Britain in 1920, affecting particularly the traditionally 'feminized' textile and clothing industries, women's job prospects diminished still further, but with unemployment rising for men also it is difficult to judge how far women were specifically excluded from jobs on account of gender. Oral testimony suggests that numbers of women were not happy to surrender skilled, better-paid work and the fact that, despite all the pressures, fewer women were prepared to work as servants after 1918 than before the First World War also suggests a change in attitudes. Whether in the light of greater freedom experienced during the war this was a reaction against the petty tyrannies which went with domestic service or part of a more general working-class rejection of former class relations, is impossible to say. Probably both were factors, but there is evidence here to counter the argument that war did not substantially affect the way in which women perceived themselves or alter their aspirations.

Further support for this contention comes from the German case, where again women who had experienced other types of work during wartime showed themselves unwilling to return to work as servants but, as in Britain, were forced out of jobs considered to be suitable for men. In Germany immediate post-war unemployment was replaced by labour shortage as the German inflationary boom gathered pace in the early 1920s, with the result that women were drawn back into paid employment to the extent that the numbers of women in the workforce again reached the level of the last months of the war. However, although the numbers were comparable, the types of work they took were different and resembled pre-war patterns of employment, with cooking, cleaning and sewing featuring strongly.[29] The French situation closely mirrored that of Britain, with peace leading to an ousting of women from the workplace, but its impact was more intense. Despite the fact that 1.4 million French men had died during the war, the number of working women actually fell to the extent that, by 1926, they actually made up a smaller percentage of all workers than in 1911.[30] In Italy, where the feminization of the workforce had not been as extensive as in Britain or Germany, the elimination of women from the workforce was nevertheless marked, predating the fascist seizure of power.[31]

This is not to say that the 1920s did not see women in both Europe and the United States employed in greater numbers than before the war in the service sector as office workers, shop assistants and teachers and in newer industries such as light engineering, electricity and chemicals. However, this development, as also the slow progress of women into medicine and the law, was part of a process of transformation evident well before 1914. Older-established sectors of feminized employment such as textiles were already declining as a result of technological and market changes and being replaced by newer sectors such as assembly work. In addition the expansion of bureaucracy and a growing concern with provision of mass education, in part associated with increasing state power, offered more white-collar jobs. War accelerated this shift towards tertiary services, and with it the alteration in the sorts of jobs customarily done by women, but certainly did not bring it into being.

When evaluating these changes it is important to note that, if the pattern of women's work changed, the notion that certain types of work were suitable for women and other types of work were suitable for men did not alter. Furthermore, the idea that men were destined to work outside the home as breadwinners and women to work inside the house as homemakers still persisted. Indeed, far from challenging this perception or having a neutral effect, the First World War may have strengthened it. Whether or not, as has been claimed, women, including some feminists, themselves contributed to this separation through emphasis on the need to meet the special social and health needs of women when mothers, rather than by pursuing an egalitarian agenda, the fact remains that after the war, as before, most married women did not do paid work outside the home. In France, indeed, the proportion of married women participating in the workforce (other than in agriculture) which stood at 20 per cent in 1906, was slightly lower (18.79 per cent) in 1936. In 1921 just 9 per cent of British married women were recorded as working and, although ten years later this had risen to 11 per cent, clearly 1914–18 had not altered the pre-war characterization of paid work and marriage as alternatives.[32]

Evidence of the continued importance of marriage as a defining feature of the pattern of a woman's life in the 1920s brings the demographic impact of the First World War to the fore. As already noted, in Britain, far from creating a generation of women who had never married, the effect of war seems in Britain to have worked in precisely the opposite direction, making marriage more probable for both men and women. Strikingly, marriage rates which were already rising prior to the war continued on their upward trend, apparently maintained by a decreased concern about class and a reduction in geographical distinctions in the choice of a marriage partner. Similar adaptive strategies, although involving adjustment in expectations as to the age of a partner, occurred in France, albeit here as also in Belgium and Italy not on a scale sufficient to compensate fully for the impact of war deaths. If, however, it seems reasonable to conclude that the slaughter did not create a generation of potentially independent women, for those women widowed with dependants, and who did not remarry, the longer-term impact of war was inevitably economically as well as personally profound. In Germany, for instance, about a third of those widowed by the war remarried within a few years, leaving about 400,000, many of whom faced a descent into extreme poverty, without the support of a husband.[33]

IV

If the war can be judged to have had only transitory effects on women as workers, and if most of those changes which appear to have been the outcome of the war can be shown in fact to be the continuation of earlier developments, what about those changes in women's political and civil rights which are also frequently identified as consequences of the war? Although some feminist campaigners opposed the war, and until the entry of the United States into the war its suffrage movement was largely pacifist in inclination, national campaigns for women to have the vote were generally put on hold for the duration of the conflict. In both France and Britain many of those who had been involved in pressing for female rights saw women's patriotic contribution to the war effort as an alternative way of furthering their cause: 'Let us show ourselves worthy of citizenship, whether our claim to it be recognized or not'.[34] Once it was seen what women could do, it was argued, the falsity of the case made against women that their female nature made them mentally and morally unfit for political responsibility would be clearly demonstrated. In due course, it was trusted, with the return of peace they would be 'rewarded' for their efforts.

In the event, in the immediate post-war years women did make advances towards full formal political acceptance as citizens in Britain, the United States, Germany and the Soviet Union. In France, however, although the Chamber of Deputies voted overwhelmingly in May 1919 to enfranchize women on the same basis as men, the bill was subsequently thrown out by the Senate. French women did not get the vote until after the Second World War and, according to the historians of the French franchise movement, far from furthering the emancipation of women, the First World War set the cause back, both by creating problems seen by politicians as more urgent, and by setting up a national mood fixated on the past.[35] In Italy, too, the war created an atmosphere which ran counter to feminist political progress. There is, therefore, no automatic connection between participation in the war and feminist advance, and in the cases of Russia and Germany intervening major political developments make direct links difficult to trace.

Surprisingly, in view of the claim frequently made that the war brought votes for women, even the British example is less straightforward than at first sight may appear. Here, ironically, the issue which put the female franchise back into consideration by Parliament was that of votes for men. With the vote based on an occupying residential qualification, the war had deprived thousands of men of the right to vote and, even prior to the war, the complexities of the system had disenfranchized many, so changes in qualifications for the franchise for men were being considered from 1916. This context presented the opportunity for supporters of votes for women to press for the inclusion of women in any constitutional change, but the resulting 1918 Representation of the People Act, which restricted franchise entitlement to women aged 30 or over, was a compromise engineered to minimize opposition, and therefore less than a victory for full equality. Understandably those in favour of women having the vote buttressed their arguments by references to what women had contributed to the war effort, but thanks to the efforts of the suffrage campaigners the argument had largely already been won by 1914. Arguably, it was not women proving themselves which made the difference (if so, why exclude the younger women necessarily most active in the war effort), but the time gap provided by the war which freed politicians from the risk of appearing to respond to suffragette militancy.[36]

V

Freedom to participate fully in politics was not the only area in which women's rights were extended in a number of countries in the period of the

First World War, but, as with the issue of the franchise, the connection between changed roles for women in the war and peacetime advances in legal status is unclear. Total war poses such an extreme challenge to the existing order, sometimes to the extent of furthering revolution, that opportunities arise to introduce changes which otherwise might have had to wait longer. However, war is here the means, the agent, of change, not its origin, and men and women did not benefit equally. Furthermore, as we have seen, faced with the impermanence and limitations of much of what women achieved during the war as workers, the case for emphasizing continuity rather than transformation when considering the longer-term impact of the war on the status of women seems compelling.

There remain to be considered, however, two contrasting counterpoints to the argument for continuity. The first concedes the difficulty of identifying obvious signs of improvement in women's status following on from the war, but suggests that nevertheless wartime experiences raised women's consciousness, their awareness of their potential, and also loosened the forces of convention, the types of conduct expected of respectable women, which still constrained female behaviour in 1914. From this perspective the shorter skirts and bobbed hair of the 1920s, like the greater freedom for women to go out unaccompanied without inviting comment, can be seen as marks of greater female inner confidence and self-identity, which in the longer term provided the basis for more concrete gains for women.

These are difficult claims to evaluate, because they are so reliant on testimonies of internal personal experience which are for the most part inaccessible to others. Even so, we should respect, rather than choose to reject, the reports of those relatively few women who have written about the personal impact of the war or whose comments have been recorded, in which they express their belief that it did make a permanent impression on their inner selves, and that somehow life was 'different' after the war.[37]

In recent years an equal assault on the revisionist rejection of war as a watershed has come from a very different direction. This follows from the attempt to address one question which arises if it is concluded that war changed very little for women. That question is, 'Why?' If, as we have seen, the conduct of the war in its entirety was not wholly a male enterprise but substantially engaged the efforts of women, why did everything apparently revert so quickly to the traditional order?

A part of the answer may be, as we have shown, that the terms under which women participated in the economy during the war years were not those of equality with men. Traditional assumptions were incorporated in the new arrangements. Women were praised for doing a 'man's job'; a job which belonged to him and which he would reclaim. Even when participating directly in warfare, the context was either one of gender separation, as in

Britain's Women's Army Corps, or gender denial, as in Russia's female soldiers who disguised themselves as men.[38]

However, this argument which, far from challenging perceived sexual difference in the First World War, in fact endorsed it, can be taken further. Some scholars suggest that the impact of the conflict on the movement towards greater female emancipation was not neutral but negative. One historian of France, for instance, argues that the war set back the feminist movement, not only by diverting the campaign for equality into patriotic endeavours and so weakening its effectiveness (as also might be said to be the case with Britain) but, when wartime deaths raised the issue of depopulation, led to a new law of July 1920 making even advocating birth control or abortion illegal, thus profoundly affecting women's prospects.[39]

Such an example may be dismissed as very specific, related as it was to a particular country, but there is also a more general, and profound, point to be made in support of the possibly regressive impact of the war. The war meant a public emphasis on 'masculine' values of aggression, heroism and bravery, while the private experiences of the Front linked men together in a community of horror which excluded women. Reflecting this duality, the male literature of the war provides examples of fierce and bitter resentment against women for their incomprehension of the grim realities of combat, tempered by other examples of relief that at least some part of life remained inviolate.[40] Either way, the war deepened the divide between the sexes; the experience of war was not shared. Writing of Germany, Bessel's comment is apposite here: 'The First World War saw the development of two quite different but interdependent societies: the one a male society structured with the military; the other a civil society which consisted disproportionately of women'.[41]

Following on from this approach, one possible psychological consequence of the very success with which women coped, in particular the way in which they took on tasks previously reserved for men, was that at an unconscious level this appeared as a threat to male sexual identity, to which the peacetime response was inevitably a call to a return to a 'normality', in which the subordinate status of women was once again unquestioned. For women, too, the confusion of roles was unsettling and the lessons of the war unexpected. Feminists who, in pursuit of equal rights, had before the war repudiated the idea of fundamental differences between the sexes, in the face of perceived evidence of innate male aggression now found value in the idea of women as mothers and homemakers.[42]

Accordingly, it has been argued, in the same period that political and legal barriers to the advancement of women were being dismantled, the experience of the war ensured that psychological barriers were strengthened. The First World War, then, according to this view, far from bringing equality between men and women nearer, actually made it a more distant prospect.[43]

VI

In conclusion, it must be stressed that tracing the impact of the Great War on women is no simple task, and any account which attempts to reflect the experience of millions of women in many different personal and national circumstances is bound to be inadequate. What should be clear, however, is that this is an area of investigation which continues to produce new insights and perspectives. From a situation where women were treated as almost invisible in accounts of the First World War and then to one where their contribution was seen as both as significant for the war and also very important for their social status, the debate has now moved on, first to a denial of the war's significance as a watershed, and most recently to a reassertion of its importance, but as a source of reaction, and not as the basis for female progress towards equality. However, a convincing interpretation of the impact of war must allow for the possibility of simultaneous advance and setback. To see women as either victims or victors is a false dichotomy, and takes too little account of the complexity of the responses to the experience of war.

NOTES AND REFERENCES

1. Brittain, Vera (1936), *Testament of Youth*, is a widely quoted key text on wartime female experience. For discussion of the variety of responses, see Kent, Susan Kingsley, 'Love and Death: War and Gender in Britain 1914–1918', in Coetzee, Frans and Shevin-Coatzee, Marilyn (eds) (1995), *Authority, Identity and the Social History of the Great War*, Providence and Oxford: Berghahn Books, pp. 165–70; Liddle, Peter, 'British Loyalties: The Evidence of an Archive', in Cecil, Hugh and Liddle, Peter (eds) (1996), *Facing Armageddon: the First World War Experienced*, London: Leo Cooper, pp. 529–36.
2. See Marwick, Arthur (1965), *The Deluge: British Society and the First World War*, London: Macmillan (1974), *War and Social Change in the Twentieth Century: A Comparative Study of Britain, France, Germany, Russia and the United States*, London: Macmillan; (1977) *Women at War*, London: Fontana; DeGroot, Gerard J. (1996), *Blighty: British Society in the Era of the Great War*, Harlow: Addison Wesley Longman; Braybon, Gail (1981), *Women Workers in the First World War*, London: Croom Helm.
3. See Marwick, Arthur (1988) (ed.), *Total War and Social Change*, London: Macmillan, for a collection of 'revisionist' essays.
4. See in particular Winter, J.M. (1985), *The Great War and the British People*, London: Macmillan; Winter, Jay and Robert, Jean-Louis (eds) (1997), *Capital Cities at War: London, Paris, Berlin 1914–1919*, Cambridge: Cambridge University Press.
5. A good introduction to recent feminist scholarship on these themes is Higonnet, Margaret Randolph (ed.) (1987), *Behind the Lines: Gender and the Two World Wars*, New Haven: Yale University Press.
6. DeGroot (1996), pp. 126–7; McMillan, James F. (1988), 'World War I and Women in France', in Marwick (1988), pp. 9–10; Bessell, Richard (1993), *Germany after the First World War*, Oxford: Clarendon, p. 16.
7. DeGroot (1996), p. 128; Bessel (1993), p. 16; McMillan (1988), p. 4; McDermid, Jane and Hillyar, Anna (1998), *Women and Work in Russia 1880–1930: A Study in Continuity through Change*, Harlow: Addison Wesley Longman, pp. 144–5; De Grazia (1992), *How Fascism Ruled Women*, Oxford: University of California Press, pp. 26–7.

8. Roberts, Elizabeth (1988), *Women's Work 1840–1940*, London: Macmillan, p. 45.
9. Bessel (1993), p. 20.
10. Hause, Steven, C. (1987), 'More Minerva than Mars: The French Women's Rights Campaign and the First World War', in Higonnet (1987), p. 105.
11. Rowbotham, Sheila (1997), *A Century of Women: The History of Women in Britain and the United States*, London: Viking, pp. 104–5.
12. DeGroot (1996), pp. 129–30.
13. McDermid and Hillyar (1998), p. 143.
14. McMillan (1988), p. 9.
15. Bessel (1993), p. 21.
16. For the British case, see Braybon, Gail and Summerfield, Penny (1987), *Out of the Cage: Women's Experiences in Two World Wars*, London: Pandora, pp. 47–56.
17. McMillan (1988), p. 9.
18. See Manning, Jonathan (1997), 'Wages and Purchasing Power', in Winter and Robert (1997), pp. 255–85.
19. See the discussion in Winter (1985), pp. 230–237.
20. Bessel (1993), pp. 31–3.
21. McDermid and Hillyar (1998), pp. 149–51.
22. See the discussion in Marwick (1988), pp. 115–31; Braybon and Summerfield (1987), pp. 107–13.
23. Braybon and Summerfield (1987), p. 101; DeGroot (1996), p. 222.
24. Rowbotham (1997), p. 78.
25. DeGroot (1996), p. 225.
26. Bessel (1993), p. 131; McMillan (1988), p. 8.
27. Braybon and Summerfield (1987), pp. 122–4.
28. See McDermid and Hillyar (1998), pp. 174–82.
29. Bessel (1993), pp. 163–4.
30. Hause (1987), pp. 105–6.
31. See De Grazia (1992), pp. 168–72.
32. McMillan (1988), p. 11; Lewis, J. (1989), 'Women and Society: Continuity and Change since 1870', in Digby, Anne and Feinstein, Charles (eds) (1989), *New Directions in Economic and Social History*, London: Macmillan, pp. 135–7.
33. See Hausin, Karin (1987), 'The German Nation's Obligations to the Heroes Widows', in Higonnet (1987), pp. 126–40.
34. Mrs Fawcett, cited in Marwick (1977), p. 27.
35. See Hause (1987), pp. 108–13.
36. For the strongest exposition of this argument, see Pugh, Martin (1978), *Electoral Reform in War and Peace 1906–1918*, London: Routledge and Kegan Paul.
37. For a detailed survey of women's writings about the war, see Tylee, Claire M. (1990), *The Great War and Women's Consciousness: Images of Militarism and Womenhood in Women's Writings, 1914–64*, London: Macmillan.
38. See Gould, Jenny (1987), 'Women's Military Services in Britain in the First World War', in Higonnet (1987), pp. 114–25; Meyer, Alfred G. (1991), 'The Impact of the First World War on Russian Women's Lives', in Clements, Barbara A.P. *et al.* (eds) (1991), Berkeley: University of California Press, pp. 208–24.
39. Hause (1987), pp. 108–13.
40. There is an immense literature on the poetry and other writing associated with the First World War. For an anthology of verse see, for example, Brian Gardner (ed.) (1966), *Up the Line to Death: The War Poets, 1914–18*, London: Methuen.
41. Bessel (1993), p. 10.
42. See DeGroot (1996), pp. 304–7.
43. The contributions in Higonnet (1987) provide a good introduction to these arguments.

9. Organized labour and the international economy

Chris Wrigley

There was a two-way relationship between organized labour and the international economy, even if the impact of the international economy on organized labour was much the greater. These relationships were especially important in times of major wars, perhaps above all during and in the aftermath of the First World War. Some of the most important revisionism in the history of organized labour has focused on two-way relationships, including gender, nationalism and ethnicity.[1] The impact of international economic change still remains another very important area for consideration.

The First World War had a massive impact on the fortunes of organized labour. Trade unionism spread rapidly in the belligerent nations, in spite of the departure of high proportions of male labour to the armed forces. Socialist and Labour Parties also grew and in many countries entered coalition governments or took power during the war or in its aftermath. Organized labour's enhanced strength was accompanied in some cases by changed economic policies, including changes to labour market institutions, and changed employee expectations. However, the stresses of the war also deepened divisions within labour movements, divisions which had been present before 1914 but which had not been so threatening to united action when there had been common causes in opposing systems of varying degrees of repressiveness (as in Russia, Austria-Hungary and Germany).

Labour had a substantial impact in the period immediately after the end of the war. Unlike the period after the Second World War when US economic predominance and a new set of international financial institutions reined in changes, after the First World War there were moves away from financial orthodoxies. Nevertheless, in spite of the much enhanced strength of many countries' labour movements, economic outcomes were largely determined by changes in the international economy. This was at least so where the changes were not suppressed by military intervention, as in Hungary in 1919, or where an economy was substantially segregated from the international economy, as in Bolshevik Russia. As a broad generalization, exceptional demand (1915–20 for most countries, continuing longer for Germany) gave strength to organized labour, while recession and less buoyant international economic conditions (1921 and after) weakened it. Changes in the international economy were major variables, among several, in explaining the fortunes of organized labour.

THE WAR AND LABOUR MARKETS

Organized labour has generally thrived in vigorous upturns in trade cycles and been weakened, and vulnerable to attack, during downturns. The First World War and its immediate aftermath created massive demand in the belligerents' and many other economies, along with a huge withdrawal of men for the armed forces. The full potential effects of this were tempered by new or enhanced state restrictions on labour markets and, especially early on in the war, by patriotic feelings of the need for those at 'the back' to maximize production for those at 'the front'.

The withdrawal of men from the civilian labour force was immense. By the end of the war 11.1 million men had entered the armed forces in Germany, 7.8 million in Austria-Hungary, 8.3 million in France, 5.7 million in Britain, 5.0 million in Italy and 15.3 million in Russia (up to the October 1917 Revolution). In the case of Britain, 2 million men had enlisted under voluntary recruiting by July 1915. Later, with conscription operating, there were 3.5 million men in the armed forces in 1916, 4.25 in 1917 and 4.5 million in 1918. A rough idea of the impact on the British labour market of such a withdrawal of men can be gathered when these figures are related to the total male labour force of 12.6 million at the time of the 1911 census. Thus, in 1916 some 28 per cent of the 1911 size of male labour force had gone (or 20 per cent of the total 1911 labour force) and in 1918 some 36 per cent (or 25 per cent of the total 1911 labour force). While some of these men were replaced with substitute labour (older, unemployed, overseas, partially disabled males or females), there was a fall in the numbers in civil employment of 12.2 per cent between 1914 and 1918. In Russia the overwhelming majority of those mobilized were peasants. There the total workforce in industry rose from 3,114,945 to 3,338,580 between 1913 and the start of 1917.[2]

While the massive withdrawal of labour into the armed forces in the belligerent nations strengthened the economic position of labour as a whole, that in key areas of war work – such as engineering, shipbuilding and coal mining – was made stronger still. In Britain, where the overall numbers of workers in industry fell, those in the metal trades rose by a third. Similarly, in Germany, where there was also a reduction in the number of industrial workers, there was a 44 per cent increase in war industries (metals, chemicals, electrical and petroleum). In Russia, where the industrial workforce grew by 7.2 per cent, the numbers of metal workers nearly doubled (a 93 per cent rise); while in Petrograd, the greatest engineering centre, the increase was even larger: some 135 per cent.[3]

The expansion of the war industries put pressure both on working practices and housing. The shortage of skilled labour resulted in the upgrading of semi- and unskilled labour, including the introduction of large numbers of female workers, often leading to serious friction with the male skilled workers. Such dissent was led in Britain, Germany, Austria and elsewhere by 'unofficial leaders', militant shop stewards. There was also substantial support for socialist criticisms of large private profits being made from armaments produced to save their nation in war. In Britain, for instance, there was a tax explicitly called the Excess Profits Duty (and, in addition, there was a Munitions Levy) and in August 1919 the Profiteering Act, under which profiteering enquiries were launched to the chagrin of Conservatives, the dominant group in the Lloyd George coalition government.[4] With the combination of state control of war industries and the intensification of work, long working hours and the suspension of many safety regulations, the antagonism of workers with grievances was directed at the state and (in the autocracies) at undemocratic systems of government.

The mass increase in workers in war industries was not accompanied by notably greater provision of accommodation for them. In such industrial areas as those of the west of Scotland there was already substantial dissatisfaction over housing shortages before the outbreak of war. The influx of workers led to fair-rent demonstrations and an upsurge in anti-landlord feeling, as some landlords took advantage of the situation, even evicting soldiers' families or widows. This led in Britain in December 1915 to the Rent and Mortgage Interest (War Restriction) Act which froze rents at July 1914 levels and was very much aimed at appeasing munitions workers. Holding down rents for families of mobilized men was also an issue taken up by socialists in France. In Germany, by spring 1918, the military were describing housing conditions in major industrial areas as 'calamitous'.[5] Food and fuel price rises were even more potent sources of wartime grievances in the urban industrial centres. Workers, who experienced long hours at work, were faced with huge queues, profiteering and the inequity of black market prices. This was often an especially heavy burden on married working women.

The huge labour demands of war economies brought many new recruits into industrial and white-collar work. For instance, in Britain the number of women employed in government establishments (dockyards, arsenals), industry, agriculture, transport, municipal services, the civil service, professions, finance and commerce and hospitals rose from 3,277,000 to 4,940,000 between July 1914 and November 1918, with an estimated 1,969,000 of these replacing males. There were very sizeable replacements in government dockyards, arsenals and national factories as well as in the metal trades; but, other than the combination of all these, the biggest replacement was in banking and finance. After one year of the war, Ministry of Munitions figures already showed big increases in women's employment in engineering (45 per cent over the 1911 census), leather (37 per cent) and electrical engineering (20 per cent), with high proportions on overtime in these (engineering 63 per cent, leather 55 per cent and electrical engineering 27 per cent). There were similar trends elsewhere. In Germany the percentage of women in the industrial labour force rose from 22 to 34 per cent between 1913 and 1918, with the greatest increases in armaments production.[6]

In these circumstances trade unionism spread to areas hitherto lightly unionized. In Britain, where trade union membership grew from 4.1 million to 6.5 million (in terms of density, up from 24.7 to 38.1 per cent), during the First World War in spite of the fall in the size of the civilian labour force, white-collar trade unionism grew from 0.5 million in 1914 to 0. 8 million in 1918, reaching 1.1 million in 1920. In several poorly organized trades, union densities shot up over the period of the war and the post-war boom: between 1911 and 1921 agriculture rose from 0.7 to 23.5 per cent, food and drink from 10.3 to 17.6, chemicals 9.6 to 23.6, leather 8.1 to 18.5, footwear 22.6 to 50.6, bricks and building 14.7 to 47.0, pottery 14.7 to 50.1, paper and board 5.8 to 50.2, gas 20.2 to 56.4, electricity 2.2 to 33.4 and insurance and banking 6.7 to 22.4.[7] In Germany trade union membership dropped in 1915 and 1916 before recovering and increasing so that in 1918 aggregate membership was 96 per cent higher than in 1914 (up from 1.8 to 3.5 million). The old bans on trade union membership in public-sector work were lifted and this, with the pressures of inflation, boosted trade unionism, including white-collar trade unionism. US trade union membership (according to the Bureau of Labor Statistics series) rose by 22 per cent between 1916 and 1918 (from 2.6 million to 3.2 million members). In France the Confédération Générale du Travail membership rose from 0.3 million in July 1914 to over 1.5 million in 1919, where again white-collar workers were a notable addition.[8]

The war years also saw marked trade union growth in neutral countries. In the cases of the Scandinavian countries trade union membership between 1914 and 1918 grew by 103, 60 and 120 per cent respectively in Denmark, Norway and Sweden. In Sweden the overall trade union density rose from 9.9 to 20.6 per cent, while that in mining and manufacturing rose from 19.0 to 37.7 per cent with that in commerce and distribution rising from 1.4 to 4.7 per cent.[9]

The role of the state was highly important in bringing about the expansion of trade unionism, as it needed organized labour's co-operation in securing higher output. In Germany, there was substantial resistance by employers to consulting trade unions or, indeed, their workforce in other ways. However, as General Wilhelm Groener, head of the Prussian War Office, put it, the war 'could not be won against the workers' and 'without the trade unions we cannot make the [Auxiliary Service Law of 2 December 1916] work'.[10] State co-operation with the trade unions legitimized membership as well as ensuring tangible gains from union membership. This was so in a liberal political system such as Britain, where trade union activism pre-1914 was liable to be rewarded by dismissal and boycotting by other local employers. In Britain the trade union leadership was involved in helping to secure higher production from at least the time of the Treasury conferences of March 1915. As state intervention and controls spread through the economy, there were extensions of collective bargaining to areas where trade unionism had been relatively weak, such as pottery. In the United States, while employers in war work tried to satisfy labour with non-union employee representation, the trade unions made advances in the more favourable conditions of increased state intervention under a Democrat administration.[11]

The expansion of trade union membership continued after the Armistice of 11 November 1918 through the post-war boom. By the end of the war there were ample pent-up demands and resentments. People expected to cash in politicians' wartime promises once the war had ended and the call of patriotic restraint was less powerful. In Britain, for instance (in an index with 1914 based at 100), the cost of living had risen to 180 in 1917 and 205 by 1918, while wages lagged behind at 135 and 175/80 respectively but, after substantial industrial action, by 1920 wages were at 260 to the cost of living at 252.[12] British trade union membership peaked (before the Second World War) in 1920 at 8.3 million, a density of 48.2 per cent. In Germany, with the democratic Weimar Republic, there was a favourable political and legal climate for trade unionism. Between 1918 and 1920 aggregate trade union membership went from 3.5 million to 9.4 million, a density of about 46 per cent. In the United States trade union membership rose by a third between 1918 and 1920, from 3.2 to 4.8 million, or in terms of density from 12.2 to 16.6 per cent. In Denmark, Norway and Sweden trade union membership rose by 12, 33 and 34 per cent respectively between 1918 and 1920. These Scandinavian countries saw marked rises in union density percentages over the war years: Denmark from 15.3 to 35.1 (with white-collar union density rising from 11.2 to 29.0), 1911–21; Norway from 7.6 to 20.4, 1910–20; and Sweden from 9.9 to 27.7, 1914–20.[13]

The growing strength of labour in the economy was reflected in more strikes, often with more successful outcomes, as the war went on. In the belligerent countries earlier patriotic restraint waned as there was increasing tiredness and greater doubts about war aims. The post-war boom gave workers

Table 9.1(a) *Numbers of strikes, 1914–21*

	1914	1915	1916	1917	1918	1919	1920	1921
Denmark	44	43	66	215	253	472	243	110
France	672	98	314	696	499	2026	1832	475
Germany	1223	141	240	562	532	3719	3807	4455
Italy	905	608	577	470	313	1871	2070	1134
Netherlands	271	269	377	344	325	649	481	299
Russia	3534	928	1288	707	–	–	–	–
Spain	212	169	237	306	463	895	1060	373
Sweden	115	80	227	475	708	440	486	347
UK	972	672	532	730	1165	1352	1607	763

Table 9.1(b) *Strikers, 1914–21 (thousands)*

	1914	1915	1916	1917	1918	1919	1920	1921
Denmark	3	2	13	10	9	36	22	48
France	162	9	41	294	176	1151	1317	402
Germany	238	48	423	1468	716	2761	2009	2036
Italy	217	180	138	175	159	1555	2314	724
Netherlands	17	17	20	32	44	62	66	48
Russia	1337	540	957	1528	–	–	–	–
Spain	76	35	160	86	136	199	264	99
Sweden	14	5	21	47	61	81	139	50
UK	447	448	276	872	1116	2591	1932	1801

Table 9.1(c) *Days lost through strikes, 1914–21 (thousands)*

	1914	1915	1916	1917	1918	1919	1920	1921
Denmark	–	–	241	211	182	878	690	1321
France	2187	55	236	1482	980	15478	23112	7027
Germany	2844	46	245	1862	1453	33083	16755	25874
Italy	–	–	838	849	912	22325	30569	8180
Netherlands	393	118	261	545	716	1057	2355	1282
Spain	1018	383	2415	1785	1819	4001	7262	2802
Sweden	620	83	475	1109	1436	2296	8943	2663
UK	9878	2953	2446	5647	5875	34969	26568	85872

Notes: The figures in (a) and (b) for Russia are for enterprises under factory inspection only. The Russian 1917 figures are only for 3 March–25 October 1917.

Sources: BR. Mitchell, *European Historical Statistics 1750–1975*, 2nd edn, London, Macmillan, 1981, pp. 181–6. The Russian figures in (a) and (b) are from Diane P. Koenker and William G. Rosenberg, *Strikes and Revolution in Russia, 1917*, Princeton, Princeton University Press, 1989, pp. 67 and 348.

chances to catch up on real wages and to make gains. In the United States, whereas between 1902 and 1915 probably something like 45 per cent of strikes had been lost, 35 per cent won and the remainder settled by compromises, in 1916–18 27.5 per cent were lost, 34.6 per cent were won and 37.8 per cent resolved by compromises. However, in the anti-red backlash after the war, 41.5 per cent of strikes were lost, 29.0 per cent won and 29.5 per cent resolved by compromises. The US strikes were mostly over wages and hours (the main issue in over 63 per cent), with union recognition being the next most cited cause of disputes (over 16 per cent).[14] It is notable in the strike statistics (see Tables 9.1a, b and c) that the broad trends are similar among many neutrals as well as among belligerents, with levels of strikes rising in the later part of the war and peaking in 1919–20.

In 1915–20 enhanced trade union strength contributed greatly to Labour's greater political strength. In turn, this reinforced trade unionism by helping to create conditions favourable to trade union expansion, a point most notably illustrated by the industrial relations legislation of the Weimar Republic.

THE WAR AND THE SOCIALIST AND LABOUR PARTIES

Governments' wartime needs for the economic, social and political support of their working-class populations resulted in labour politicians entering office in several countries. For the more militant or independent-minded socialists this was a controversial move, as was supporting war credits at the outbreak of the war. The war generally strengthened the political position of organized labour, but also accentuated and highlighted existing divisions and, in some cases, created new ones.

The outbreak of the war saw an end to most anti-war demonstrations and, after some heart-searching, also saw most Parliamentary socialists voting for war finance. The decision which had the widest ramifications within international socialism was that of the Germans. In Germany, the SPD supported war credits as a unified group, many in favour of doing so on the basis that it was a defensive war in which, in the east, Germany was resisting Tsarist Russia's forces and that it was a war already in progress (having begun with Austria-Hungary and Serbia). However, in so doing, they, and those who acted similarly in other Parliaments, undercut the aspirations of those in the Second International who believed that determined action by the labour movement could prevent a war breaking out or even one already in progress. The German SPD deputies were vigorously criticized by Allied socialists at the time. One contemporary author complained of their support for the German government, 'It was only possible to deceive them because they wished to be deceived'.[15]

However, very soon many of the Centre and Left of the SPD were uneasy about such support for the German government. In mid-September 1914 Rosa Luxemburg, Clara Zetkin, Karl Liebknecht and Franz Mehring made clear that they dissented from supporting the German war effort, even if 'Martial law presently makes it impossible for us to enlarge upon our point of view publicly'.[16] In time this was seen as a major stage in the split that occurred in December 1918 with the foundation of the German communist party (KPD). The roots of this division were, however, there before 1914 in ideological divisions within the SPD and exhibited in the more radical pre-1914 SPD branches. By December 1915 20 SPD deputies publicly opposed the vote of war credits in the Reichstag, criticizing Germany's annexationist policies which made an early peace improbable. Further opposition to war finance in March 1916 led to their expulsion and, in 1917, to the formation of the Independent Social Democratic Party (USPD). At the leadership level the divisions did not follow the pre-war radical Marxists versus revisionists lines, with leading figures from each, notably Karl Kautsky and Eduard Bernstein, belonging to the USPD. In terms of popular support the USPD did best in the old nineteenth-century heartlands of the SPD. The Luxemburg–Liebknecht group, who from early 1916 had secretly distributed revolutionary literature ('Spartacist Letters'), formed their own group, known as the Sparticists, which affiliated as an organization to the USPD.[17]

In France, the politicians of the Left supported the government against Germany. In so doing, Socialists drew on the language of the revolutionary tradition of the nation in arms. In his oration at the funeral of the assassinated Jean Jaurès on 4 August 1914, Leon Jouhaux, general secretary of the Confédération Générale du Travail (CGT), declared, 'Emperors of Germany and Austria-Hungary, Prussian squires and Austrian lords who, through hatred of democracy, desired war, we undertake to sound the death-knell of your reign'.[18] French trade unions were greatly weakened in 1914–15. Several unions took great care in the early part of the war to maintain contact with their members at the front, reading their letters at meetings and welcoming them to their meetings when they were on leave. While many of the middle class had fled Paris as the Germans advanced, the socialists organized communal meals and other services. Jean-Louis Robert has commented that 'the "sacred union" … was translated into networks of a rank-and-file socialist activity in defence of workers and socialists in their homes and localities'. Socialists not only entered the national government (with Albert Thomas proving effective in maximizing munitions output), but also participated in Paris's municipal government. However, this warm support for the war weakened or disintegrated in 1917, marked by an upsurge of industrial unrest, though it was resurrected to some extent during the German offensives from 21 March 1918.[19]

In Belgium Socialists also rallied to the national cause in the face of the invading German armies. Emile Vandervelde, President of the Second International 1900–19, entered the Belgian government as a Minister of State on 4 August 1914 before becoming Minister of Procurement in 1916. His most recent biographer has commented that in these dual roles he was 'personifying the potential contradictions between socialist internationalism and patriotic nationalism'. Vandervelde even attended the Paris Peace Conference both as a member of the government and as a representative of the Belgian Workers' Party. He served, alongside initially two other socialists, in the post-war governments, arguing, 'We must participate in the national reconstruction, because if it is done without us, it will be done against us'. On leaving office in December 1921, Vandervelde was the leader of the opposition and he and the socialists returned to office in the mid-1920s and mid-1930s.[20] Thus the Belgian socialists became a party of office with the First World War.

Britain was another country where Labour entered coalition governments. Unlike Belgium and France, there was no invasion as a justification for such co-operation, but nor was there immediate conscription. In the early part of the war the predominantly pro-war trade union leaders worked hard to avoid conscription either for the armed forces or for industry. Arthur Henderson, the leading trade unionist in the Parliamentary Labour Party, succeeded Ramsay MacDonald as its chairman on his resignation at the outset of the war, and became a member of the Asquith and Lloyd George coalition governments from May 1915 until his resignation in August 1917 over his efforts to support Kerensky and keep Russia in the war by agreeing to attend a proposed international socialist conference in Stockholm. Labour remained in the coalition government until the end of the war, but Henderson's departure assisted his efforts to reunite Labour around new post-war reconstruction and peace policies. Henderson and the Labour Party were strengthened as his resignation was followed by his energetic reorganization of the party. The British Labour Party, which before 1914 had been in electoral terms an auxiliary of the Liberal Party, became a contender for power. In the latter part of the war politicians and political commentators began saying it was not a matter of whether Labour would take office, but when. In January 1918 Lloyd George was recorded as predicting, 'He thinks it may come to a fight between him and Henderson, and that all parties, including Labour, will be split and reconstituted'.[21]

In all these European belligerent nations much of the socialist and labour movements were strengthened by representing working-class grievances during wartime, but doing so – at least in the earlier part of the war – in alliance with nationalism.[22] While in Germany the SPD only entered office in October 1918, a few weeks before the Armistice, the SPD also began its career as a party of government during the First World War.

LABOUR AND THE INTERNATIONAL ECONOMY

The First World War brought about such political instability and change that international investment and trade were shaken. The world was a much less safe place for capitalism, with Bolshevik Russia being an awful warning for investors. Elsewhere, often until 1921, sometimes later, there was a decided tilt in economic relations in favour of labour, including welfare provision as well as in industrial relations.

The loss of investments in Russia, following the Bolshevik Revolution of October 1917, was a substantial affront to capitalist ethics. A.J.P. Taylor, writing of German reparations, observed,

> The new attitude corresponded to the 'sanctity of contract' which is the fundamental element in bourgeois civilization. Kings and aristocrats do not pay their debts, and rarely keep their word. The capitalist system would collapse unless its practitioners honoured, without question, their most casual nod …[23]

While this may caricature the ethics of kings and aristocrats, it does state clearly the underlying presumption of international finance – that obligations will be honoured. In Russia foreign capital was half of all new investment in Russian industry and banking in 1909–13. In 1915 the cumulative total has been estimated to have been 2,205.9 million roubles (about £232.2 million at the pre-war exchange rate). The greatest foreign investor in Russia was France (687.9 million roubles), followed by Britain (535.4 million roubles), Germany (436.1 million roubles), Belgium (318.7 million roubles) and the USA (114.0 million roubles).[24] Thus, for the four major European investors the losses were very substantial.

The Allied blockade, which had been a major weapon in the war with Germany, was used after the Armistice to try to dislodge radical governments and to replace them with ones favourable to financial orthodoxy. On 17 May 1919 the Supreme Economic Council approved a British resolution,

> That it is desirable publicly to announce that the blockade of Hungary will be suspended as soon as a government is installed there which gives some assurance of settled conditions.

On 2 June 1919 the Supreme Economic Council agonized over Bolshevik Russia as well. They noted that reopening commercial relations with Russia 'would be going against the policy of the Entente' as it would be implicitly to recognize the Bolsheviks 'who are absolutely masters of the districts they occupy for the time being and who have destroyed all the commercial organization existing outside their regime'. It was also observed that

> The supply of foodstuffs and raw materials plays an extremely important part in the fight against Bolshevism: it was chiefly on account of revictualling that the Allies were forced to abandon Odessa, the population – lacking foodstuffs – having become hostile to the Allies. It is evident, therefore, that in feeding the populations under the Bolshevist regime, the Allies will lose one of their most formidable weapons against Bolshevism, especially if the populations fighting against Bolshevism are not adequately supplied with foodstuffs. ...
>
> There is also no doubt that the raising of the blockade of Bolshevist Russia would have an extremely grave moral effect on the populations and troops fighting against Bolshevism ...

However, the blockade of Bolshevik Russia was not a formal one. The chairman of the US War Trade Board warned against making a formal declaration, pointing out,

> As between Russia and the United States at least, a state of war does not exist. The declaration of a formal blockade would be the equivalent or preliminary to a declaration of war.[25]

While the Bolsheviks succeeded in defeating White and foreign interventionist forces, in Hungary Bela Kun's regime, after briefly reconquering Czechoslovakia (removed from Hungary by the Allies), collapsed before Romanian and Czechoslovakian forces. These examples of military intervention against revolutionary governments together provide one of many reasons why the German revolution of late 1918 did not 'follow Russia'. Military intervention before the signing of a peace treaty could be expected. The Allies required political stability and this expectation encompassed hopes of a return to economic orthodoxy.

However, the circumstances after the end of the First World War gave greater popular support for the broad, more moderate demands of the labour movement. Business people and financiers were faced with what was for a time an irresistible pressure for some redistribution of wealth not only in terms of pay but also in what was later called 'the social wage'. In most countries the morale of civilian populations had been kept up with promises that after the privations of the war there would be substantial social reconstruction. In Britain, Lloyd George launched his 1918 general election campaign with a speech with the theme-setting question and answer, 'What is our task? To make Britain a fit country for heroes to live in'.[26] While in the immediate aftermath of the Armistice revenge on Germany was more popular, soon social reform and action against profiteers became widespread demands. The returning soldiers and sailors also had their expectations. While those who were interested in joining veterans' associations might move politically to the right, in the period after the war most discharged servicemen expected their governments to provide more lavishly than they did.[27] They too became part of the post-war pressure for greater social welfare.

The most notable provision of welfare came in the Weimar Republic. The more moderate part of the SPD achieved many of their pre-1914 aspirations in the early years of Weimar, including a democratic republic, relatively very generous social welfare provision and considerable legal rights for labour in industrial relations. However, the increased housing provision, the expansion of welfare benefits and municipal services, accompanied by a larger civil service, required higher taxation. The substantial worker rights in a range of industrial legislation (which included trade union recognition, the Works Council Law, February 1920 and compulsory state arbitration) was increasingly contested from 1924 with the end of the high inflation period. Employers became determined to recover their flexibility in the face of intense international competition for markets in the sluggishly growing international economy of the 1920s. Equally they, as well as middle-class and rural taxpayers, were eager to roll back the welfare expenditure and were increasingly successful as economic recession saw welfare payments soar at a time when revenue was falling.[28] At the time, and later, orthodox economists argued that relatively high welfare benefits discouraged wage rates from falling, thus becoming a cause of unemployment and a lengthening of economic recessions.

There were similar, if less pronounced, developments among other former belligerent nations. In Belgium, at the end of 1918–21 Vandervelde and his colleagues could point to much of their programme being achieved, including universal male suffrage, the relaxation of laws limiting trade unions organizing, the 8-hour day, better welfare and measures protecting tenants.

In Britain, although Labour was out of office, the public expectation of welfare reform was imperative for two years, leading to increased housing provision and social welfare. There was also increased state intervention in industrial relations, with the setting-up of Whitley committees, the experiment with the National Industrial Conference and arbitration under the Industrial Courts Act, 1919.[29] As in Germany there was unease at the effects of state intervention. As early as late January 1919, Austen Chamberlain, the leading Conservative politician (and the then Chancellor of the Exchequer) complained that

> in recent years there has been an increasing reliance placed on the government as the ultimate arbiter in labour disputes, with the result that strikes were prolonged by the fact that neither side would say the last word as to what they were prepared to concede, as they expected the government to be called in.[30]

For a period at the end of the war and after it there was great anxiety on the part of Conservative politicians and the propertied classes generally as to what to expect from the working class. In Germany for a few weeks in

November and early December the middle classes were shaken by the defeat of the presumed invincible German army. By late December many had recovered their nerve sufficiently to support the mobilization of the *Freikorps* against the militant Left. In Britain, less dramatically, there was a move away from concession to financial orthodoxy. For instance, Austen Chamberlain, when a member of the War Cabinet without portfolio, was urging that with an armistice,

> Generally the principle to be borne in mind was that every legitimate effort should be made to prevent unemployment and its accompanying demoralisation. It was far better to run the risk of manufacturing commodities which would not be required ... than to have multitudes in receipt of unemployment benefit.[31]

Three months later, he was commenting,

> Our housing problem has got into such a condition that it is a source of danger to the stability of the state, and ... we have to deal with the problem in accordance with the programme which we took to the electors, on broad and generous lines, and go ahead with it as fast as we can, with due regard to carrying it out properly. I think that ought to be the first charge on the public resources which we have.[32]

By the summer he and many others felt such threats as there were to the political system had diminished, and he was championing orthodox finance which, among other things, involved reducing the housing programme.

The international recession of 1921–2 undercut organized labour in most countries (inflationary Germany being an exception for a further two years) and so relieved the pressure from this source on the international economy generally. Then international economic forces set real wages, through determining lower prices, at levels which removed most of the power of labour.[33] The weakening effect on militant labour was well illustrated in Germany in the early 1930s when a large majority of communist (KPD) members were unemployed, and calls to industrial action could not be effective, unlike in 1920 at the time of the Kapp putsch.[34] Ironically, capitalism weakened was replicated in labour also being weakened and its challenge to the capitalist system being undercut.

NOTES AND REFERENCES

1. For recent examples, see Helmut Gruber and Pamela Graves, *Women and Socialism, Socialism and Women: Europe Between the Two World Wars*, London, Berghahn Books, 1998, and Stefan Berger and Angel Smith, *Nationalism, Labour and Ethnicity, 1870–1939*, Manchester, Manchester University Press, 1999.
2. C.J. Wrigley, 'Introduction', pp. 2–5 in C.J. Wrigley (ed.), *Challenges* of *Labour: Central and Western Europe 1917–1920*, Routledge, 1993. A. Sked, *The Decline and Fall of the*

Habsburg Monarchy, London, Longman, 1989, pp. 261 and 278. M. Clark, *Modern Italy 1871–1982*, London, Longman, 1982, p. 186. P.E. Dewey, 'Military Recruiting and the British Labour Force During the First World War', *Historical Journal*, **27**, 1984, pp. 199–233. B.R. Mitchell, *European Historical Statistics*, 2nd edn, London, Macmillan, 1981, pp. 30–31. A.K. Wildman, *The End* of *the Russian Imperial Army*, Vol. 1, Princeton University Press, 1980, p. 95.

3. D.P. Koenker and W.G. Rosenberg, *Strikes and Revolution in Russia, 1917*, Princeton University Press, 1989, p. 30. S. Smith, *Red Petrograd*, Cambridge University Press, 1983, p. 10. R.B. McKean, *St Petersburg Between the Revolutions*, New Haven, Yale University Press, 1990, p. 328. J. Kocka, *Facing Total War: German Society 1914–1918*, Leamington Spa, Berg, 1984, pp. 18–19. A.W. Kirkaldy, *British Labour: Replacement and Conciliation 1914–1921*, London, Sir Isaac Pitman, 1921, pp. 1–3.
4. E.M. Morgan, *Studies in British Financial Policy, 1914–15*, London, Macmillan, 1952, pp. 91–4. James Hinton, *The First Shop Stewards' Movement*, London, Allen and Unwin, 1973. Keith Burgess, 'The Political Economy of British Engineering Workers During the First World War', and Friedholm Boll, 'Economic Cycles and Labor Conflicts in Germany During the First Quarter of the Twentieth Century', in L. Haimson and C. Tilly (eds), *Strikes, Wars, and Revolutions in an International Perspective*, Cambridge University Press, 1989, pp. 289–320 and 449–56. Dick Geary, 'Revolutionary Berlin 1917–20' and Hans Hautmann, 'Vienna: A City in the Years of Radical Change 1917–20', in Wrigley (ed.), *Challenges* of *Labour*, pp. 24–50 and 87–104.
5. Joseph Melling, *Rent Strikes*, Edinburgh, Polygon Books, 1983, pp. 59–103. John Horne, *Labour At War: France and Britain 1914–1918*, Oxford University Press, 1991, p. 142. Gerald Feldman, *The Great Disorder: Politics, Economics and Society in the German Inflation 1914–1924*, Oxford University Press, 1993, p. 83.
6. A.W. Kirkaldy (ed.), *British Labour: Replacement and Conciliation 1914–1921*, p. 2. C.F. Rey to Lloyd George, 15 July 1915; Lloyd George Papers, House of Lords Record Office D/11/4/1. C. Wrigley, 'The Impact of the First World War on the British Labour Movement', in M. Dockrill and D. French (eds), *Strategy and Intelligence: British Policy During the First World War*, London, Hambledon Press, 1996, pp. 139–59. J. Kocha, *Facing Total War: German Society 1914–1918*, Leamington Spa, Berg, 1984 (German original, 1973), p. 18.
7. G.S. Bain and R. Price, *Profiles* of *Union Growth*, Oxford, Blackwells, 1980, pp. 39–74.
8. Michael Schneider, *A Brief History* of *the German Trade Unions*, Bonn, Verlag J.H.W. Dietz Nacht, 1991, p. 384. Bain and Price, *Profiles of Union Growth*, p. 88. Home, *Labour At War*, pp. 10–14 and 176–7.
9. Bain and Price, *Profiles of Union Growth*, pp. 142–59.
10. Schneider, *Brief History* of *the German Trade Unions*, p. 117.
11. C.J. Wrigley, 'The First World War and State Intervention in Industrial Relations, 1914–1918', in C.J. Wrigley (ed.), *A History of British Industrial Relations 1914–1939*, Brighton, Harvester, 1986, pp. 23–70. Jeffrey Haydu, *Making American Industry Safe for Democracy*, Urbana, University of Illinois Press, 1997, pp. 87–91.
12. W.K. Hancock and M.M. Gowing, *British War Economy*, London, HMSO and Longmans, Green, 1949, p. 152.
13. Schneider, *Brief History of German Trade Unions*, pp. 384–5. Bain and Price, *Profiles of Union Growth*, pp. 88, 142, 151, 154 and 158.
14. P.K. Edwards, *Strikes in the United States 1881–1974*, Oxford, Blackwell, 1981, pp. 36–46.
15. P.G. La Chesnais, *The Socialist Party in the Reichstag and the Declaration of War*, London, Fisher Unwin, 1915, p. 103.
16. Peter Nettl, *Rosa Luxemburg*, abridged edition, Oxford University Press, 1969, pp. 371–3.
17. A.J. Berlau, *The German Social Democratic Party 1914–1921*, New York, Columbia University Press, 1949, pp. 146–7. Eric D. Weitz, *Creating German Communism, 1890–1990*, Princeton University Press, 1997, pp. 62–93.
18. Horne, *Labour At War*, pp. 43–5.
19. Jean-Louis Robert, 'Mobilizing Labour and Socialist Militants in Paris during the Great

War', in John Horne (ed.), *State, Society and Mobilization in Europe during the First World War*, Cambridge University Press, 1997, pp. 73–88. Roger Magraw, *A History of the French Working Class*, Vol. 2, Oxford, Blackwell, pp. 131–53. J.J. Becker, *The Great War and the French People*, Leamington Spa, Berg, 1985 (French edn, 1983).

20. Janet Polasky, *The Democratic Socialism of Emile Vandervelde*, Oxford, Berg, 1995, pp. 113–82.
21. Lord Riddell, *Lord Riddell's War Diary, 1914–1918*, London, Ivor Nicholson and Watson, 1933, p. 309 (entry for 27 January 1918).
22. Among a burgeoning literature on this theme see J.J. Schwarzmantel, *Socialism and the Idea of the Nation*, Hemel Hempstead, Harvester Wheatsheaf, 1991, and on Britain, Paul Ward, *Red Flag and Union Jack: Englishness, Patriotism and the British Left, 1881–1924*, Woodbridge, Boydell Press, 1998.
23. A.J.P. Taylor, *The Origins of the Second World War*, 2nd edn, Harmondsworth, Penguin, 1964, pp. 54–5 (1st edn, 1961).
24. LP. McKay, *Pioneers for Profit: Foreign Entrepreneurship and Russian Industrialization, 1885–1913*, University of Chicago Press, 1970, pp. 26–8. A. Milward and S.B. Saul, *The Development of the Economies of Continental Europe 1850–1914*, London, Allen and Unwin, 1971, pp. 390–394.
25. Printed in S.L. Bane and R.H. Lutz, *The Blockade of Germany after the Armistice 1918–1919*, Stanford University Press, 1942, pp. 473 and 500–504.
26. At Wolverhampton, 24 November 1918. P. Rowland, *Lloyd George*, London, Barrie and Jenkins, 1975, p. 467.
27. For valuable surveys of the complexities of ex-servicemen's attitudes see S.R. Ward (ed.), *The War Generation: Veterans of the First World War*, Port Washington, Kennikat Press, 1975, especially pp. 4–9.
28. On the details of the industrial relations legislation see Nathan Reich, *Labour Relations in Republican Germany: An Experiment in Industrial Democracy 1918–1933*, New York, Oxford University, 1938. On these Weimar measures see, for example, D.J.K. Peukert, *The Weimar Republic*, London, Allen Lane, 1991, pp. 31 and 109–46 (German edn, 1987).
29. Polasky, *Vandervelde*, pp. 165–71. K.O. Morgan, *Consensus and Disunity: The Lloyd George Coalition Government 1918–1922*, Oxford, Clarendon Press, 1979. Chris Wrigley, *Lloyd George and the Challenge of Labour*, Brighton, Harvester-Wheatsheaf, 1990.
30. War Cabinet minutes (521), 28 January 1919. Public Record Office (PRO), CAB 23-9-30.
31. War Cabinet minutes (491), 24 October 1918; PRO CAB 23-8-47.
32. Notes of a meeting, 25 February 1919; PRO CAB 24-75-370/2.
33. For a recent critical discussion of Keynes and the inter-war labour market see Mark Thomas, 'Institutional Rigidity in the British Labour Market: a Comparative Perspective', in S.N. Broadberry and N.F.R. Crafts, *Britain in the International Economy 1870–1939*, Cambridge University Press, 1992, pp. 271–315.
34. For a recent brief overview see Dick Geary, *European Labour Politics from 1900 to the Depression*, London, Macmillan, 1991, pp. 69–70. On the restructuring of conservative interests against the left, see Charles S. Meier, *Recasting Bourgeois Europe*, Princeton, NJ, 1975.

Index